Building Design Evaluation

TO MY WIFE AND FAMILY

Building Design Evaluation

Costs-in-use

P. A. STONE
M. Sc. (Econ.), Ph. D.

LONDON   NEW YORK
E. & F. N. Spon Ltd

First published 1967
by E. & F.N. Spon Ltd
11 New Fetter Lane, London EC4P 4EE
Second edition 1975
Third edition 1980
Published in the U.S.A.
by E. & F.N. Spon Ltd
in association with Methuen, Inc.
733 Third Avenue, New York, N.Y. 10017

© 1967, 1975, 1980 Peter Albert Stone

Typeset by Josée Utteridge-Faivre
Printed in Great Britain at
The University Printing House, Cambridge

ISBN 0 419 11720 2 (cased)
ISBN 0 419 11660 5 (paperback)

This title is available in both hardbound and paperback editions. The paperback edition is sold subject to the condition that it shall not, by way of trade or otherwise, be lent, re-sold, hired out, or otherwise circulated without the publisher's prior consent in any form of binding or cover other than that in which it is published and without a similar condition including this condition being imposed on the subsequent purchaser.

All rights reserved. No part of this book may be reprinted, or reproduced or utilized in any form or by any electronic, mechanical or other means, now known or hereafter invented, including photocopying and recording, or in any information storage and retrieval system, without permission in writing from the Publisher.

British Library Cataloguing in Publication Data

Stone, Peter Albert
   Building design evaluation. — 3rd ed.
   1. Building — Estimates
   2. Buildings — Cost effectiveness
   I. Title
   338.4'7'721   TH435   79-41571

ISBN 0-419-11720-2
ISBN 0-419-11660-5 Pbk

Contents

		page	
	Preface to the First Edition		xii
	Preface to the Third Edition		xiv
1.	Introduction		1
2.	Economics of Buildings		5
	Buildings for Producers and Consumers		5
	Optimizing Returns		5
	The Developer		6
	Example 2.1 The developer's balance sheet		7
	Commercial and Industrial Clients		9
	Clients as Consumers		9
	Financial and Resource Costs		10
	Building Costs as Rent		10
	Rates of Interest		11
	Interest and Inflation		11
	Interest and Taxation		12
	Life and the Annual Cost of a Building		12
	Initial and Running Costs		14
3.	Design Cost Consequences		15
	The Cost Consequences of Buildings		15
	Costs and Benefits of Building and Rebuilding		16
	The Choice of Sites and its Effect on Costs		17
	The Layout of Buildings and the Cost Consequences		18
	The Cost Consequences of Building Elements		21
	Walls		22
	Roof coverings		23
	Glazing		23
	The quantity and quality of light		25
4.	Tracing Design Consequences		26
	The Comparison of Alternative Solutions		26
	Comparative Durabilities		26
	Example 4.1 A simple comparison of alternatives with different lives		26

		page
	Comparative Durabilities (*continued*)	
	Example 4.2 A comparison with running costs	28
	Interpretation of Examples 4.1 and 4.2	28
	Example 4.3 A comparison with complicated running costs	30
	Example 4.4 A simplified comparison	33
	Other Running Costs	34
	Example 4.5 An annual comparison of service costs	35
	Example 4.6 A comparison involving operation costs	37
5.	**Building Elements and Design Development**	40
	Building Elements	40
	Suggested Elemental Analysis of a Framed Building	41
	Building Elements in the Comparison of Walls	43
	Building Elements in the Comparison of Roofs	44
	Design Development and the Form of Cost Analysis	45
	Example 5.1 The development of a wall design	46
	Example 5.2 The development of a roof design	47
	Design Variability and Optimum Designs	48
	The Number of Storeys and Costs-in-Use	49
	Example 5.3 The optimum number of storeys	50
6.	**Factors of Prediction**	52
	Basic Assumptions	52
	Future Prices	52
	Rates of Discount	57
	The Lives of Buildings	59
	The Life of Building Components	61
	The Levels of Taxation	62
	Example 6.1 The effect of taxation on the net costs of an industrial building	64
7.	**Problems in Costing**	66
	Types of Costs	66
	Construction Costs	66
	Disturbance Costs	69
	Fuel and Other Service Costs	70
	Operation Costs	72
	Indirect Costs	72
	Valuing Imponderables	74
8.	**Uncertainty and the Investment**	76
	The Uncertainty of Future Values	76
	Example 8.1 A preliminary test for the adequacy of a future fall in running costs	77

		page
	The Conditions for an Equality in Costs	78
	Example 8.2 A test for the adequacy of future falls in running costs	79
	Example 8.3 Estimating the condition for equal costs	79
	Example 8.4 The use of Decision diagram I	81
	The Uncertainty of Future Requirements	81
	Example 8.5 The costs of anticipating a future requirement	82
	Example 8.6 The use of Decision diagram II	85
9.	Prediction Errors and Interpretation	86
	Prediction Errors	86
	Sampling Errors	87
	Example 9.1 The errors in an absolute difference in design costs	87
	Example 9.2 The errors in a comparative difference in design costs	89
	Errors and Common Elements in the Items Costed	89
	Example 9.3 The effect of common elements in design comparisons	90
	Errors from Incorrect Assumptions	91
	Example 9.4 Effect of changes in assumed values on cost comparison	96
	Errors in Drawing Wider Inferences	97
10.	The Optimum Design and the Type of Client	99
	The Economic Design	99
	Type of Client and Costs to be Considered	99
	The developer	100
	The investor	101
	The occupier	101
	Private occupiers	102
	Public occupiers	102
	Local authorities	103
	Central government authorities	104
	Government agencies	104
	The community	104
	Taxation, Subsidies and other Government Interventions	104
	Building Sites	105
	Costs-in-Use and the Type of Client	106
11.	Design Evaluation in Practice	107
	Design and Design Evaluation	107
	New Building or Adaptation	107

		page
	Example 11.1 Reorganization within the existing space as compared with the provision of extra space on the same site	109
	Example 11.2 Reorganization on the existing site as compared with new development on a new site	110
	Geographical Location	111
	Site Comparisons	112
	Example 11.3 The comparison of two sites for office blocks of a similar size and function	112
	Space Requirements	113
	Building Shapes and Forms	114
	The Type of Structure	115
	Example 11.4 Suppose a single storey area of 30 metres square is to be roofed; it is economic to support the roof entirely from the perimeter of the building?	116
	Example 11.5 Another possible alternative would be to use a one-way post-tensioned concrete plate of the two-way system. These could be compared	117
	Example 11.6 A 'costs-in-use' comparison between a one-way post-tensioned concrete plate and a steel frame on a grid of 15 × 10 metres	118
	The Use of Glass	121
	Example 11.7 Suppose a decision is to be reached about wall glazing for a rectilinear space of 225 square metres with two external walls	121
	Example 11.8 Consideration of the cost effectiveness of glazing in a flat roof	123
	Example 11.9 Would costs-in-use be reduced by using double glazing in the roof?	125
	Heating Systems and Fuel	126
	Heating and Ventilating Systems	128
	Example 11.10 Suppose a commercial firm is considering the development of a new head office	129
	Lighting Levels and Systems	131
	Example 11.11 Suppose a decision is to be taken for the lighting system of an office with natural ventilation and use only during normal hours of work	132
	Finishes	134
	Equipment	135
12.	Planning Evaluation	137
	Housing Developments and Developers' and Users' Costs	138

	Contents		ix
	Example 12.1 Developers' costs and revenue	page	140
	Housing Developments and Community Costs		143
	Example 12.2 Tracing planning consequences to the community		146
	Housing Developments, Costs and Benefits		147
	Example 12.3 Costs and benefits of housing		148
	Housing and Overspill Development		148
	Commercial and Industrial Development		149
	Public Developments		150
	Town Development		151
13.	Renewals, Adaption and Other Uses of the Costs-in-Use Technique		154
	Future Costs and Benefits		154
	The Renewal of Equipment		154
	Example 13.1 The repair or replacement of a component		154
	Example 13.2 Replacement by an improved component		155
	Example 13.3 Replacement by a model that provides a different service		156
	Alterations		157
	Example 13.4 The value of an alteration		157
	Example 13.5 Using a break-even chart for testing alterations		158
	A Test of Comparability		160
	Example 13.6 Comparing an adaptation with a replacement		160
	Rebuilding and Modernization		161
	Example 13.7 Comparing rebuilding with the modernization of a commercial building		161
	The No-Action Test		162
	Example 13.8 A comparison between modernization and no action		162
	Maintenance Policies		162
	Example 13.9 A comparison of painting and washing cycles for a hospital ward		163
	Innovation of Building Components and Techniques		164
	Example 13.10 Ascertaining the competitive price of a new material		164
	Protection Against Hazards		165
	Insurance		167
	Codes of Practice and Statutory Standards		168
	Taxation		168

14. Decision Techniques Compared	page	169
Costs-In-Use		169
Cost-Effective Analysis		170
Discounted Cash Flow		170
Cost-Benefit Analysis		171
Threshold Analysis		175
National Project Comparisons		175
Appendix A		177
Compound Interest Functions		177
The Accumulation of a Fixed Sum		177
The Present Worth of a Single Payment Payable in the Future		178
Example A.1		181
The Present Worth of Regular Annual Payments		182
Example A.2		182
The Present Worth of Future Payments		185
Example A.3		187
The Annual Equivalent of an Initial Payment of Unity		191
Example A.4		191
Methods of Evaluating Streams of Payments		191
Adjustments for the Annual Time Pattern		192
The Use of Compound Interest Functions		193
Example A.5		193
Example A.6		194
Example A.7		195
Appendix B		196
Cost and Price Data		196
Costs and Prices		196
Changes in Price Levels		196
Regional Price Indices		198
Prices of Buildings and Works		198
Building Design Price Relatives		200
Prices of Building Elements		201
Maintenance Costs		202
Housing Maintenance Costs		202
Maintenance and Other Running Costs		202
Appendix C		205
Statistical Treatment of Durability and Maintenance Data		205
Data for Measuring Durability		205
Measuring Durability		205

	page	
The Life Table Method		206
Estimating costs from average lives		208
The actuarial method of estimating costs		211
Data for Measuring Maintenance Costs		212
Example C.1		215
Appendix D		215
Sampling and errors		215
Sampling		215
Example D.1		217
Statistical Errors		218
Propagation of Errors		218
Example D.2		219
Example D.3		220
Example D.4		220
Bibliography		221
Index		228

Preface to the First Edition

This book is concerned with the use of cost prediction techniques as tools of building design. The designer's problem is complex; perhaps more complex than many appreciate. Most design problems can be solved in a variety of ways. It is rare for one alternative to be an exact substitute for another: each solution tends to provide different benefits and to have a different cost. A design is judged not only by its appearance, by the way it functions or by its cost, but by all three, that is by the value it provides for the money spent. Value is difficult to assess; the relevant factors are numerous and complex. Rational choice is difficult. Appearance, comfort and convenience are inevitably subjective criteria on which each person places his own assessment. The way a building functions can be expressed in terms of the costs of renewing and repairing the fabric and fittings, of adapting to meet changing needs, of heating, lighting and servicing the building, and in terms of the cost consequences of the design of the building on the way it is used. These costs can be predicted and added to the amortized costs for constructing the building to give the costs-in-use.

Often the running costs of a building are three times as great as the first costs. Of course, the running costs are spread over the life of a building and it would be meaningless to add up their face values. The current and future costs need to be equated before the costs can be combined. Nevertheless, the running costs are usually at least as important as the first costs and it would be very mistaken to judge a design entirely in relation to its first costs without also considering its long-term costs. The technique described in this book is designed to meet the needs arising from design evaluation. It makes it possible to reduce the vast complex of factors on which judgement is necessary to a single figure of cost against which the truly imponderables of appearance, comfort and convenience can be set.

The technique described is only a rationalization of the way designers have always attempted to work. The problems of future uncertainty and the scarcity of information cannot be solved by the introduction of new techniques. The costs-in-use technique meets these difficulties by making the assumptions explicit instead of implicit. Thus, the effects of the assumptions can be assessed and the degree of uncertainty in the judgement expressed and evaluated. Few factors are completely unpredictable. Probable ranges can usually be determined and degrees of confidence estimated. This makes it possible to evaluate the assumptions and attach the greatest weight to those which are substantiated the most effectively. The use of the technique will bring an awareness of where knowledge is lacking and provide guidance to the type of information which needs to be collected and the type of research which is necessary.

The first three chapters of the book are mainly concerned with concepts and with building economics. In them explanations are provided of the various factors which determine the economy of a building, the way the features of a design generate various types of cost, the way cost consequences can be traced and the costs-in-use technique can be used to select the optimum design solution. The next seven chapters are concerned with the technique and its applications. The chapters deal with such topics as the relationship of building elements to the various cost consequences to which they give rise, the prediction of future work, costing, compound interest and the preparation of cost balance sheets. The next three chapters are concerned with the major applications of the technique described. Their use is explained in relation to building design, to the planning of urban development, to renewal and maintenance work and to the development of building components and the preparation of codes of practice. In the final chapter, the costs-in-use technique is compared with other related cost decision techniques. Three Appendices are provided, dealing respectively with compound interest functions and their uses, with the statistical treatment of durability and maintenance data, and with sampling and statistical errors.

I should like to express my gratitude to Mr C.T. Saunders, O.B.E., M.A., who, when he was the Director of the National Institute of Economic and Social Research, kindly agreed that I might accept the publisher's suggestion to prepare this book. Much of the development of the costs-in-use technique originated in the course of my studies of building economics at the Building Research Station. I should like to express my gratitude to Dr J.C. Weston, some time the Director of Building Research, for his encouragement in this work, and for allowing me to make use of material originally published while I was at the Building Research Station. Mr M.C. Fleming, B.A., Fellow in Building Economics at the Queen's University, Belfast, was kind enough to read the manuscript and made many useful suggestions from which I have profited. He is, of course, in no way responsible for any shortcomings which may remain.

November 1966   P. A. Stone

Preface to the Third Edition

The trends in costs of labour and materials, and the growing relative scarcity of some materials, particularly energy, pointed to in the preface to the second edition, have now become much more acute. These trends have increased the importance of a careful economic evaluation of designs, developments, alterations and rehabilitation, and maintenance. The evaluation techniques described in this book are now applied, under a variety of names, on a much wider scale in this country and abroad, especially in relation to the design of components affecting the use of energy. Far too few of the results of these studies are published and far too little research is undertaken to establish the relation between designs and the use of energy, other materials and labour, and costs.

The new surge in the cost of energy has once again drawn attention to the future scarcity of energy and the need for careful use. Energy costs are two or three times as great as maintenance costs and equivalent to a substantial proportion of structural costs. While energy savings can be made by alterations to the fabric and plant, far better value for money is obtained by building energy economy in at the beginning. As indicated in the book, practically every aspect of the design has an effect on energy consumption, not just the design of lighting heating and ventilation, but also the design of walls, roof, glazing and even of frame, shape and form of building and space utilization. The costs-in-use technique assists designers to find the best solutions for every aspect, both for the initial design and for conversion and maintenance.

The major problem found by those applying the costs-in-use techniques remains the shortage of suitable data on maintenance and other running costs. Significant progress is being made in collecting, analysing and publishing such data in a form suitable for use in design cost analysing but much remains to be done.

In preparing this edition the examples have been revised to reflect current costs. The discussion has been extended to take account of the changing economic situation, changes in technology and new work in the field. The tables of discount rates have been further extended to reflect higher rates, an additional appendix on building costs and prices has been added and the bibliography has been revised and extende to include the latest relevant literature.

July 1979   P. A. Stone

1
Introduction

Anyone spending their own money or advising others on the spending of money is concerned with obtaining good value for the money spent. No sensible person will knowingly accept an inferior article if a better can be obtained for the same money. Cheapness in itself is no virtue; it is well worth while to pay a little more, if as a result the gain in value exceeds the extra cost. The more complex the article the more difficult it is to decide whether one alternative offers better value for money than others, and the greater the need to seek the advice of a specialist consultant. Buildings are among the most complex products and laymen usually take specialist advice whether purchasing an existing building or having one designed or altered to meet their special needs.

Buildings possess a complex set of attributes, broadly those of appearance and function. Value for money depends on the trinity of appearance, function and cost. Appearance must always be largely subjective but function can usually be at least partly judged against various objective criteria. For example, the structure can be assessed in relation to its adequacy to support the building during its life without having an excessive material content or interfering with the use of the building. Materials can be judged in terms of their durability and freedom from the need for repairs and maintenance. Lighting and heating installations can be judged in terms of the adequacy of the internal environment to which they contribute. Judgement of the adequacy of the internal space and its arrangement can be related to the extent to which it facilitates the functions to be performed within the building.

The need for a careful assessment of a building design is all the more necessary today when there is such a large range of alternative building materials and techniques. While these have greatly increased the freedom of design, they have, by their very variety, increased the difficulty in finding the most economic solution. Of course, no completely mechanical decision criteria can be provided; in the last resort value is purely subjective and only limited expert assistance is possible. The obvious approach is to put all the measurable components on one side of the equation in the form of cost items, to be set against a value judgement on appearance, comfort and convenience.

Clearly a building design is always a compromise between the many facilities and amenities which the building is designed to provide. Buildings normally have a long life and hence provide their services over long periods. Similarly the costs of buildings do not cease with the costs of construction but continue throughout the life of the building in the form of maintenance and other running costs, the costs of adaptation to meet changing requirements and the costs of the inconveniences imposed by the building on the process and procedures carried on within it. Designers are well aware of the long-term implications of building designs and take account of them in reaching their design decisions.

The determination of the most efficient design cannot be an exact science. Hunch must always play a large part in reaching judgements. Some uncertainty is inevitable if only because judgements about a design can only be made against a background of an uncertain future. Nevertheless, in the field of building, as elsewhere, many techniques are available which can be used to reduce the uncertainty inevitable in most judgments and which can lead to an increase in the probability that the design will produce good value for money. In fact, an important aspect in the history of building, particularly in recent times, is the way in which greater economy has been obtained by techniques which reduce uncertainty in building design.

Once, large quantities of materials had to be used to try to ensure that the structure was strong enough to carry the loads require. Customary specifications were built up on experience and departure from them could be very hazardous. As a result buildings tended to be over-specified, costs were unnecessarily high and natural resources were used wastefully. Today the size and quality of materials can be calculated closely to meet the expected loads upon the structure. The properties of materials are far better understood and the amount and specification can be determined so as to provide for a given degree of performance, for example, in thermal insulation.

Similarly, techniques enable the desigher to calculate the volume and position of the system of fenestration to provide daylight of the strength required at the points at which it is needed. The sources, strength, colour ant quality of artificial lighting can similarly be calculated within a reasonable margin of error. Again, for example, the designer can calculate how much heat is required, the most suitable appliances and the most effective positions, and hence the size, type and quantity of fittings to provide the required heating service.

The ability to calculate the materials and equipment needed to provide a building with given attributes is matched by an ability to determine the attributes needed to provide users with the performance they require. Information on the way people use buildings and on the way processes and procedures are carried out in buildings enables the needs for space and equipment, and for other facilities and amenities to be figured closely. In this way the designer can determine with adequate precision how to satisfy the requirements the building is required to meet.

While the knowledge and techniques discussed above help the designer to meet the needs of the users and to provide a satisfactory building, they do not of themselves ensure that the design provides good value for money. To achieve this it is necessary to be able to estimate the costs of the various design possibilities so that the design alternatives can be compared in terms of cost and value. A considerable amount of information has been assembled on the prices of materials and equipment, and on the volumes and costs of the labour and organization necessary to assemble them into a building. Techniques have been developed which make it possible to estimate the costs of alternative ways of providing the same set of facilities. In this way guidance can be obtained as to the design which provides either the desired attributes at the lowest cost, or the best set of design features for a cost which can be afforded.

But as explained earlier, the cost of construction is only the first cost and is far less important than the subsequent costs associated with running the building and operating in it. Techniques which are only of value in minimizing construction costs hence fall far short of what is really required if the designer is to be in a position to provide buildings which offer the best value for money. For this purpose a technique is required to provide a way of evaluating both the way the building will function and its costs throughout its life. This is the purpose of the costs-in-use technique which is described in this book.

The costs-in-use technique is designed to facilitate the preparation of estimates of the cost consequences of building designs against which the inevitable subjective judgements of appearance, comfort and convenience can be set. The method is to trace the consequences of design alternatives in one feature of a building on the other features, and on the costs of construction, on the costs of running the building and on the costs of operating within it. Comparative tables are prepared setting out the costs and values arising from each design alternative. These facilitate the comparisons of design alternatives. Instead of weighing up and comparing different groups of attributes, many of which are measured in different units, if measured at all, it is only necessary to compare the values set on appearance, comfort and convenience on the one hand, against monetary figures which sum up the cost consequences of the designs.

The costs-in-use technique is equally applicable to design decisions for existing buildings as for new buildings, for evaluating existing buildings, for

4   Building design evaluation

the planning of groups of buildings and of urban development generally, for the development of new materials and components, and for preparing codes of practice and building standards. The use of the technique is explained in each of these fields.

2
Economics of Buildings

BUILDINGS FOR PRODUCERS AND CONSUMERS

The design which provides the most economic building depends to a large extent on the client and his situation. Clients may require buildings as a means of production or as a commodity to consume. In the former case the value of the building can be expressed in terms of the cash value of the contribution that the building makes to the production of the goods and services. In the latter case value can only be expressed in terms of the satisfactions which it provides to the users. In practice the owners and users of a building used as a means of production will give some weight to the satisfactions it gives them, while the owner-consumer will give some weight to its transfer value. For example, the industrialist will usually be prepared to spend at least a little extra to obtain a building which is pleasing to the eye and comfortable to work in over and above the value of these qualities in terms of prestige and staff contentment. The man who purchases a house in which to live will similarly pay some attention to the likely appeal of the design to others and hence to its sale price. Perhaps the client with the purest financial interest in a building is the developer building for sale or letting. He is concerned with the costs on the one hand and the sale price or revenue on the other. Since these depend on the attributes to which clients attach value, in the last resort he must consider client's tastes. Similarly the purest example of the consumer is the client who builds a monument or a folly, buildings which have a purely decorative and psychological function. But a client of either type will wish to obtain the best value for money.

OPTIMIZING RETURNS

In theory the greatest return on the total resources spent is obtained by viewing the whole of the resources at the same time and allocating their use to each project so as to obtain the same return for the last increment of expenditure allocated to each project. In practice, this is not usually possible; the allocation of resources has to be broken down into sector expenditures, the amounts to be spent in each sector being determined at one level and the expenditure on each project within the sectors being determined at a second level and so on through the stages. Thus, usually the amount to be spent on a particular building will have been determined before the detailed design is considered. In determining this sum consideration will normally be given to the standard and size of building which can be obtained for such expenditure. Normally the problem of the designer is narrowed to that of finding the most economic solution for a building to satisfy a broadly stated brief at a given cost level.

The most economic solution for a building, that is the solution that gives the best value for money, will be the one which has the minimum equivalent initial and periodic costs, costs-in-use, in relation to the values provided. It does not necessarily follow that the building providing the best value for money is the best choice, although normally this will be so. A situation could arise where the best solution for the building, considered in isolation, involves initial expenditure far greater than could be afforded from the total allocation of resources for the project. In such a case, the total returns might be greater with a less efficient design for the building than that obtained by maximizing the returns on the building itself. Thus, in practice, design economics may have to operate within the restriction imposed by a fixed upper limit to initial costs. The need to obtain the best value for money within this limitation still remains.

THE DEVELOPER

As mentioned above, the simplest case of building economics arises in the case of the developer who builds for sale or to hold as an investment. In either case both the value and the cost can be expressed entirely in money terms. Consider first the case of development for sale. The sale price is determined by the demand for the type of building to be erected in the position it is to occupy. The building will be purchased either by an owner-occupier or by an investor. In either case its market value will depend on the expected future flow of annual net revenues discounted at rates of interest appropriate in current conditions. The owner-occupier will consider the annual cost he can afford given the use of the building he proposes, while the investor will consider the rent he can expect now and in the future. While the evaluation of the rents will be likely to be similar, their capital value may differ as between would be owner-occupiers and different types of investors. The owner-occupier will discount at the rate of interest either he would pay for a mortgage loan, or at the rate of return he could obtain on his own capital. He will consider the net rate after allowance for tax. The rate of interest and investor will use for discounting will depend on the opportunities open to him. These rates will vary with the supply and demand of funds for investment,

Economics of buildings 7

with the state of his own portfolios of investments and his tax position, and with his expectations for rents and investment returns in the future. In some situations investors will let at rents lower than the equivalent costs of ownership to the building user.

The price of the land, the management of the development and the price of the building for construction are similarly fixed by market forces. The developer is concerned with the difference between the costs of the development and the price he can obtain for it. This depends on his skill in buying the factors of production, in determining the price the building will fetch and the brief that this requires, and on the skill of the designer in meeting the brief. The developer is not concerned with the values the building provides for their own sake but with the money price the purchaser will be prepared to pay for them. His direct transaction is a short-term one; he needs to take account of future costs only in so far as he anticipates that the client will take note of them. Hence if clients ignore running costs, durability and future changes in requirements, the developer can also ignore such factors and he can aim at minimizing initial costs in relation to the client's valuation of the immediate worth. If, however, as is more likely, there is an expectation that the client will consider such factors and make some estimate of future costs, the developer too must consider them. In fact, the developer may have to consider much the same set of factors whether he is developing for sale or for letting. Both client and developer will consider much the same set of factors; the difference will be not in kind but in the point of reference. The client will attempt to forecast the costs to himself, while the developer will forecast what he thinks the client will forecast.

Example 2.1 The developer's balance sheet
Suppose, for example, that a developer is proposing to build a block of offices either to hold as an investment himself or to sell as an investment. If it is to be let out in a number of separate units the landlord may provide most of the services, maintenance, heating and perhaps cleaning. The revenue can be estimated according to the market rates for the type of building, say £80 a square metre, and against this can be set the outgoings for the services, ground rent and rates, and an allowance for normal profit. The balance, when capitalized, forms the fund for financing the development (Table 2.1). The amount available for constructing the building can be obtained by deducting the other expenses of development. In the example considered the land might cost £1 100 000, fees, interest over the period of construction and bringing into fruition, expenses, contingencies and developer's profit, including an allowance for tax on it, £608 000; the amount for construction works would be £1 000 000: given 5000 square metres gross to construct,

8 *Building design evaluation*

this gives £200 a square metre. For this figure it is necessary to be able

TABLE 2.1 THE DEVELOPER'S BALANCE SHEET

	£	£
Revenue from office block 3000 sq. metres of lettable space at an inclusive rent of £80 per sq. metre		240 000
Costs for providing services, management and profit	60 000	
Balance to be capitalized as cost of building project	180 000	
	240 000	240 000
Capitalized value of £180 000 at mortgage rate of 6 per cent for 40 years		2 708 000
Cost of site	1 100 000	
Fees, expenses, profits and contingencies	608 000	
Balance for constructing building	1 000 000	
	2 708 000	2 708 000

to construct a building of the standard necessary to secure the assumed rent and with running expenses no higher than assumed in the estimate. If this does not prove possible the problem must be studied further until a set of conditions which are mutually satisfying is obtained. Such a balance of conditions might be found with a better class of building and a higher rent, or with a cheaper building and a lower rent.

It may not always be possible to find a satisfactory balance between revenue and expenditure. Such a situation would arise if the price of the site was too high in relation to the rents that were being offered in the market. At times rents are too low in relation to the rates of discount, prices of sites, and building costs, and development virtually ceases. In the long run either the demand for further space in general, or for space of contemporary design, pushes up the rents offered, or rates of discount, site prices or building prices fall and it once again becomes commercially worth while to develop new properties. Developers' profits will also change with market conditions.

It would generally be assumed that in the long run rents would rise in step with inflation, and so maintain the real value of the investments.

COMMERCIAL AND INDUSTRIAL CLIENTS

It is not as simple for the commercial or industrial client to draw up a balance sheet as for the developer since the revenue for the building is in this case embodied in the revenue from the goods or services produced. The building that houses the process cannot be looked at in isolation; it is a part of the costs of production. The need is not to minimize the costs of the building in isolation but to minimize the total costs of production in relation to revenue. An increase in costs is worth while if as a result the revenue is increased sufficiently to raise the return on the capital employed. There is usually more than one way of producing the output required and the various factors of production trend to interact. For example, a better standard of lighting, while more expensive, may enable the proportion of rejected products to be reduced. The value of a prestige building in creating the goodwill of customers and staff may make it possible to reduce costs in other directions more than sufficient to offset the extra costs of constructing and running the building. A change in the planned layout of the building may make it possible to cut production costs by more than the costs of constructing the building. Thus commercial and industrial clients have to examine their building requirements within the context of the business to be carried on within it: the building is just another factor of production. The revenue to be attributed to the building and set against its costs needs to be estimated from the production accounts. The absence of a profit motive does not affect the principle. The need to measure the effect of the building design on the costs of producing goods and services is just as relevant to non-profit-making concerns, such as public corporations and social service organizations, as it is to business firms. Hence the need to predict the effect of the building design, not only on the costs of constructing and running the buildings but also on the costs of the processes and proceedings to be carried on in the building. Methods of making such predictions will be discussed later.

CLIENTS AS CONSUMERS

Consumers value buildings not for the revenue they provide but for the satisfaction obtained in terms of comfort, convenience, prestige and delight. While satisfactions of this type cannot easily be given a money value, they can still be compared with costs. Comparisons between alternatives can be made in terms of comparative satisfactions against costs. Decisions can be based on the value of additional satisfactions as against additional expenditure. Such valuations are inevitably personal and subjective. The designer can help the layman by analysing the factors to be considered and by suggesting buildings that can be used as a point of reference. Help can be obtained from analyses of the costs over the life of the building of alternative methods of obtaining similar satisfactions.

In the long run the client is concerned with spending his resources so as to obtain the greatest sum of satisfactions and hence is concerned with comparing satisfactions and costs over his entire field of activities. Clients are often collective rather than individual, consisting of families, societies, communities and nations. Assessing their collective satisfactions raises new problems but the principles of value for money remain unchanged.

FINANCIAL AND RESOURCE COSTS

The optimum solution depends on the circumstances of the client, particularly on his personal scale of values, method of operation and financial situation. This last factor depends not only on the capital available but also on the incidence of expenditure and the incidence of taxation. Costs to the building user are the costs which the user has to bear himself. These are called internal costs. Many of the costs created by the design of a building and the way it is used are borne by other individuals and by the community at large rather than by the user. For example, the smoke from a low chimney may cause as much or more damage and expense to users of neighbouring buildings as to the user of the building from which the nuisance arises. An ugly, unpleasant building will reduce the satisfactions of occupiers around it and tend to reduce the value of their properties. Thus some of the costs created by a building and some of the benefits will spill over to the users of other buildings and to the community at large. These are called external costs. The financial costs to the user will be different from the resources costs to the community at large and the decisions taken by individual users will be different from the decisions that would be taken by the community. Differences in cost and hence in decisions also arise from the effect of taxation, and from the effect of subsidies. The effect of company taxation in Britain is to encourage companies to spend too little on the construction of buildings and too much on running them as compared to the best levels for the community. These matters will be discussed more fully later.

BUILDING COSTS AS RENT

The starting point of the proposition to develop the office block was the expected rent of the building. A large proportion of industrial and commercial firms in fact rent rather than purchase their buildings because purchasing would increase their need for fixed capital to a serious extent.

Many firms could not operate if they had to raise sufficient capital to finance the purchase of a building as well as to operate their business. Even if firms have the capital, they can often use it more profitably in their business than by investing it in their buildings. Often firms seek to increase their working capital by mortgaging their buildings, or by selling them to a property company and leasing them back. Whether a building is rented or owned, or whether the capital is owned or borrowed the effective cost is an annual one. It is the rent or the cost of amortizing the capital borrowed, or the loss of interest and the cost of replacing capital used in purchasing the building. Of course, to the annual equivalent of the capital cost must be added the running costs.

RATES OF INTEREST

Thus usually the annual equivalent of the initial cost of the building is of more importance than the initial cost itself. The annual cost depends on the rate of interest and on the economic life of the building as well as on the costs of development. The higher the rate of interest and the shorter the life, the greater the annual cost. For example, for a building with a sixty-year life, an increase in the rate of interest from 5 to 7 per cent has the same effect on the annual amount payable as an increase in the capital cost of about 38 per cent (Table 2.2). The shorter the life the smaller the proportional effect of a change in the rate of interest. Over a twenty-year life span, a change in the rate of interest from 5 to 7 per cent is only equivalent to a rise in the capital cost of about 20 per cent. However, in most societies the effect of the rate of interest is modified by inflation and by taxation.

INTEREST AND INFLATION

In the long run the value of money tends to fall. Inflation has been general in most countries continuously over the last two decades. In Britain, over most of this period, prices in general were rising 3 to 4 per cent a year. In the last few years, the rate of inflation has increased not only in Great Britain but generally in the western world; rates of 8 to 10 per cent and even higher have been widely experienced. For example, in Great Britain, house-building prices doubled over the five years (from 1973). Thus mortgage debts have been paid in money, the real value of which has been falling each year. The real cost to the borrower has been 4 per cent or more less than he contracted to pay. If £100 was borrowed for a year at 9 per cent, the £109 of capital and interest payable at the end of the year would be worth only 103 per cent of the money borrowed given inflation of 6 per cent; the real rate of interest

TABLE 2.2 ANNUAL REPAYMENTS AND CAPITAL COST

Capital cost	Annual repayments over sixty years (£'s)							
	Rate of interest							
	3%	4%	5%	6%	7%	8%	9%	10%
800	29	35	42	50	58	65	72	80
900	33	40	48	56	64	73	81	90
1 000	36	44	53	62	71	81	91	100
1 100	40	49	58	68	78	89	100	110
1 200	43	53	64	74	85	97	109	121
	Annual repayments over twenty years (£'s)							
800	54	59	64	70	76	81	88	94
900	60	66	72	78	85	92	99	106
1 000	67	74	80	87	94	102	110	117
1 200	74	81	88	96	104	112	121	129
1 200	81	88	96	105	113	122	131	141

paid and received would be only 3 per cent.

Rents are often fixed for long periods so that their real cost may fall considerably during periods of inflation.

INTEREST AND TAXATION

In Britain and in many other countries tax is deductible from interest paid on money borrowed to finance property development or improvement. Since individuals and firms purchasing buildings are usually tax payers, the net rate of interest is often considerably less than the nominal rate. For example, a rate of 15 per cent with tax at 50p in the £ is reduced to a net rate of 7·5 per cent. Thus at that rate of taxation, tax payers, whether using their own capital and sacrificing interest, or borrowing, only pay interest at 50 per cent of the nominal rate. The rent for a business property is similarly subject to a tax rebate.

Mortgage rates have often been so low in relation to inflation and rates of tax relief that the true rate of interest has been negative.

LIFE AND THE ANNUAL COST OF A BUILDING

As shown earlier (Table 2.2) the rate of interest has less effect on the annual equivalent cost for a short-life than for a long-life building. The length of life,

TABLE 2.3 ANNUAL EQUIVALENT OF £1 OF INITIAL COSTS

	Rate of interest			
Life in years	3%	5%	7%	10%
	pence	pence	pence	pence
10	11.7	13.0	14.2	16.3
15	8.4	9.6	11.0	13.2
20	6.7	8.0	9.4	11.7
30	5.1	6.5	8.1	10.6
40	4.3	5.8	7.5	10.2
50	3.9	5.5	7.2	10.1
60	3.6	5.3	7.1	10.0
70	3.4	5.2	7.1	10.0
100	3.2	5.0	7.0	10.0

however, can have a considerable effect on the annual equivalent cost. As the life which can be taken for the building increases the annual equivalent cost falls. The rate of fall declines as the life increases until a point is reached at which the annual equivalent cost becomes relatively stable. With a rate of interest of 3 per cent relative stability is reached with a life of about seventy years; the corresponding period is about fifty years when the interest rate is 7 per cent and 40 years when the rate is 10 per cent. (Table 2.3). The capitalization value of the residual net rent (Example 2.1) would have been reduced from £2 708 000 to £2 065 000 had the period of capitalization been twenty instead of forty years. Had the other costs remained the same, the amount available to construct the building would have been reduced to less than £72 a square metre; clearly insufficient to construct a building of the type required.

Thus at the rates of interest normally paid for money borrowed on the security of buildings the annual cost is about double for a short-life building that which it would be for a long-life building. The lower the rate of interest the greater the difference in annual equivalent costs. Generally there is little saving in costs of construction for a short-life building as compared with a long-life building, although other things being equal there may be a small saving in maintenance costs. Shortening the lives of buildings tends to reduce their value without reducing their cost. Until methods of construction are found which will provide short-life buildings, with a life perhaps of ten to fifteen years, at perhaps half the cost of a building with a long life, few people or communities will be able to afford a rapid turnover of their buildings. This is difficult to achieve because usually half the initial costs arise for

14 *Building design evaluation*

fittings, finishings, equipment and site works which are necessary in much the same form whether the building is permanent or temporary.

INITIAL AND RUNNING COSTS

The annual equivalents of the initial costs (Tables 2.2 and 3) provide a guide to the relationship between initial and running costs. For example, the annual equivalent for a long-life building of an initial cost of a £ at an interest rate of 5 per cent is about 5 pence. Five pence is equivalent to the mortgage repayment which would be made to a building society for every £ borrowed. On these terms it would be worth while to accept annual payments of anything less than 5 pence to save a £ of initial costs, or anything less than a £ of initial costs to save 5 pence a year in running costs. For example, if it cost £3 000 a year to man a manually operated lift, or a boiler installation, it would pay to spend anything up to £60 000 in addition on capital equipment to obtain an automatic lift or stoker. Thus under the condition of a long-life building and with net interest at 5 per cent, the ratio between annual and initial costs of 20:1 can be taken as the break-even point. Anything less than 20 units is worth spending to save one unit of annual costs and anything less than a unit to save 20 units of initial costs.

The break-even ratios decline with the life of the building. For a short-life building the break-even ratio is about 10:1 (fifteen years) and about 8:1 (ten years). As would be expected, the shorter the life the less it is worth spending in order to reduce running costs. The converse is that the shorter the life the greater the running costs relative to initial costs which it is worth to bear. For example, whereas it was worth spending £60 000 to eliminate the need for an operator in a long-life building, it would only be worth spending up to about £23 000 if the life of the building was limited to ten years.

Increases in the rate of interest tend to have the same type of effect as a reduction in the expected life. The higher the rate of interest the more needs to be saved in running costs for each £ of initial costs which are spent. For example, whereas for a building with an expected life of 100 years it would pay to spend £1 to save running costs of 3·2 pence per year when the net interest is 3 per cent, it would be necessary to save 5 pence per year if the net interest were 5 per cent, and 7 pence if net interest were 7 per cent (Table 2.3).

Thus the shorter the life and the higher the rate of interest the more it is worth while to limit immediate costs and to postpone expenditure to the future.

3
Design Cost Consequences

THE COST CONSEQUENCES OF BUILDINGS

Over the life of a building the running costs are usually considerably greater than the costs of construction. However, as already explained, sums of money payable at different dates cannot sensibly be compared at their face value. In order to compare such sums they are first converted to their equivalents either in terms of their present worth, or in terms of their annual equivalent costs. The ratios between different types of costs are the same whichever method is used, but the ratios vary considerably with the rate of discount. In terms of their equivalents, running costs are usually less than the initial costs of a building, the proportions varying with the type of building. (Table 3.1). The proportions of running costs tends to be lower the higher the initial cost of the building and the fewer the hours per year for which the building is used. The most expensive type of building is probably a hospital, for which, in spite of its being in continuous use, the running cost proportion is the lowest. The percentages naturally vary with the design and use of the building. The agreement between the percentages for the house and the factory is incidental.

TABLE 3.1 ESTIMATED COSTS-IN-USE FOR TYPICAL BUILDINGS*

Percentages

Type of costs	Offices	High flats	Houses	Factories	Hospitals	Schools
Initial	53	61	56	56	65	60
Maintenance	14	13	16	16	19	19
Fuel and attendance for heating and lighting	33	26	28	28	16	21

* Net rate of discount 5 per cent.

The initial and running costs of building are by no means the whole of the costs which are affected by design decisions. The design also tends to affect the way a building is used and hence the costs of operating within it. The way such cost consequences arise depends on the building and the form of use.

COSTS AND BENEFITS OF BUILDING AND REBUILDING

The desire to build usually arises in one of three ways, from a need for additional space, for space in a more efficient form, or for space in a new area. The need for additional space may be satisfied by the extension of an existing building or by building more space somewhere else. The need for more efficient space might be met by new building or by adaptation. Where the need is for space in a new area there is the choice between building to meet the individual requirements or acquiring and adapting an existing building.

The cost consequences of having a building designed and built to meet individual needs can be quite complex. Bespoke building inevitably takes some time to be designed and erected, whereas a speculative built one, or a second-hand one can be occupied almost at once. While a bespoke building should meet the client's needs better than one already built, this does not always follow, partly because of the problems of communication between client and designer — the layman often finds it easier to appreciate the way an existing building will function than the plan of one to be built — and partly because needs often change rapidly, and however well a new building may have been designed to meet current needs, it may adapt to new conditions no better than an existing building. Again it may be no easier to find a suitable situated site than it is to find a suitably situated building.

Thus in choosing between a bespoke and an existing or ready-made building a balance will be struck between the costs of commissioning the design and construction of a new building and the costs of purchasing and adapting an existing one. Allowance will need to be made for the effect of delay on the business or service to be housed and for the effect of the difference in plan and situation on the costs of the operations to be performed in the building.

Extra space can often be obtained by changing the arrangement of space already available. The costs of any necessary adaptation, of the disturbance to production during reorganization, of the sale of the existing building which is foregone and of any shortfall in efficiency in the process for which the building is used consequent on using a building designed for some other purpose, can be set against the alternative costs of acquiring other land and buildings, of erecting new buildings or of adapting buildings to be occupied for the first time and differences in relative efficiency arising from a different location.

Design cost consequences

The cost consequences of change are set against current costs. The costs to be considered are those which will arise in the future. No consideration is necessary of money already spent in constructing or purchasing a building, or on its adaptation and running, since such expenditure is irrecoverable. This is equally true whether the cost has been met or is still outstanding as unpaid accounts or as loans. Bygones are for ever bygones; the economics of any proposition are judged in terms of future costs. Clearly 'no action' is always one of the possible alternatives and so the cost consequences of the various possible changes considered are set against each other and against the costs of carrying on without change.

Changes in the design and layout of a building complex are perhaps more likely to affect communications and transport costs than direct production or process costs, and are more likely to affect labour costs than the amount of materials. Direct production or process costs, whether these are, for example, for machine production, attending a hospital patient or teaching are largely determined by the nature of the machinery, the labour and the process itself. The effect of the building upon their costs is generally through the way the layout affects the number of units which can be housed. The indirect costs, the time taken to move goods and personnel from one production point to another and thence out of the building depend very much on the shape and layout of the building. The relationships between the various work spaces affect the size of the stocks and perhaps the degree of wastage from breakages and other causes, as well as the number of staff required.

THE CHOICE OF SITES AND ITS EFFECT ON COSTS

Sites can vary widely in quality as well as in size. The quality of the land itself, its load bearing capacity, slope and drainage will affect the costs of construction through the foundations, site preparation and the provision of site works such as road, hard-standing and drainage. If site conditions are unsatisfactory it may not be possible to use the site for intensive building. Supplies of power, water and access to adequate main drainage are usually of importance; for some purposes rail and water communications are also of value. Again, for many purposes it is not sufficient to have access to public roads, the value of the access depends on the ease with which vehicles can enter and leave. The distance in kilometres and time from suppliers and customers is, of course, also of considerable importance. For commercial sites the flow of potential customers past the site is of importance. Factors such as these effect not only the costs of construction and the running costs, but also the costs of operating in the building and the business potential of the site. Clearly, the consequences of such factors need to be reflected in the cost comparisons for alternative sites. Those factors which are inherent in the site itself are reflected in the site value which acquires the residual value of the development.

THE LAYOUT OF BUILDINGS AND THE COST CONSEQUENCES

A large number of factors need to be considered in determining the most suitable layout of buildings and the final arrangement can only be a compromise between the best solutions to meet the different needs. First, the space provided should be sufficiently large to allow the activity to be organized in the best way. There is a need for adequate ceiling height and an adequate internal environment. Secondly, the spaces for each activity should be related so as to minimize the space devoted to circulation and the time and cost of communications between the various spaces. Thirdly, the buildings on the site should be disposed so as to obtain the best relationship with regard to access to the site and with public services, and so as to provide adequate outdoor space in the best position and a pleasing composition of buildings.

While the factors to be considered are well understood, finding the best compromise is always difficult. In the long run the best solution can only be determined by comparing the equivalent costs and benefits of all the alternatives. Clearly, it is not possible to evaluate every alternative. A stage by stage approach is the best method in practice. The starting point is a preliminary examination of the range of alternatives in order to determine which are the most promising lines of development. At this stage use can be made of previous cost evaluations of building designs as a guide to the type of result that might be obtained.

In the past, and usually today, the layout and shape of buildings has been largely dominated by the attempt to provide a satisfactory internal environment largely by natural lighting and ventilation.

Daylight will only penetrate, at an adequate strength, comparatively short distances into a building. Greater penetration can be obtained by raising the height of the glazing, which often necessitates greater ceiling heights and introduces problems of glare. In single-storey buildings and in top storeys daylighting can be provided by the use of roof lights. Where roof lights cannot be provided deep rooms can only be lit by artificial means. The strength of natural lighting, even on cloudy days, is normally much greater than the strength of light necessary for ordinary tasks and it is now customary to raise the level of artificial lighting to combat glare from the windows and to combat a sense of gloom away from them. Often, even in internal rooms, the levels of lighting provided are much greater than is necessary for the tasks to be performed; again the reason is usually to brighten the room so that the absence of natural light does not engender a feeling of gloom. Thus, in one way or another the costs of lighting are increased considerably in deep buildings where roof lights are not feasible.

Ventilation also becomes more difficult in deep rooms since natural ventilation through openable windows ceases to be satisfactory. The combination of forced and natural ventilation in itself creates difficulties and often it proves easier to have sealed windows and to rely on forced ventilation.

The effect of building spaces deeper than can be lit and ventilated naturally is to raise the capital and running costs of lighting and possibly ventilation, usually to a considerable degree. To some extent these additional costs are off-set by savings in the costs of constructing and maintaining walls and in heating. The extent to which such savings would off-set the extra costs for lighting depends on the price of electricity. Clearly, the balance will vary with the price levels for the different factors and with the climate. The nearer the equator the greater the angle of the sun and the greater intensity of light. Cloud also affects the depth into the building natural light can penetrate. In hot dry climates it may be an advantage to have sealed windows to keep out the hot air and to stop the loss of artificially provided cooled air. The price of electricity will clearly be an important factor in determining the most economic solution.

Noise is also an important environment factor, particularly in the centre of cities. Openable windows, even when closed, still admit a considerable amount of noise. Traffic noise is a major source of disturbance in the home. The Road Research Laboratory estimates that 20 per cent of the urban population lives in roads with noise levels judged to be undesirably high, a figure which could easily rise to 30 per cent if the noise output of individual vehicles is not reduced. Usually in city centres tolerable noise levels can only be obtained by using sealed double glazing; this necessitates the use of forced ventilation, possibly air-conditioning. This usually adds considerably to the costs of construction and to the cost of operating the building. In so fas as sealed double glazing and forced ventilation are necessary, the additional costs of deep buildings may be less than normal buildings. The extra costs of providing an artificial environment and the high cost of land in city centres may result in out-of-town sites becoming more worth while for some types of users.

Planning regulations affect the costs of construction and operating buildings. The current planning regulations, which in this country tend to encourage the deep office buildings of a tower on podium form, with large areas lit and ventilated artificially, were designed to ensure that sufficient light fell on the face of surrounding buildings to afford adequate natural lighting. Another consequence of this form of building is that it allows traffic and other noises to penetrate all round the buildings. If city blocks were developed as continuous buildings, as they were in the recent past and used to line the traffic routes, they would shield the areas behind from a large part of the noise. The areas lying within the protection of the buildings along the traffic streets would then be reasonably quiet. While sealed double glazing would be necessary along the street fronts, normal openable windows could be used for the rear rooms and for buildings within the precincts, thus avoiding the need for forced ventilation throughout the building and its costs.

A more intensive use of sites can be obtained by using a greater number of storeys. In Britain, prices per square metre tend to rise substantially as the number of storeys is increased. This is not universally true in all countries. It would appear that the deeper the building the less the rise in price per metre with an increase in the number of storeys. As long as the depth is limited to the distance to which adequate natural light can penetrate, the buildings cannot be more than about 9 metres deep. This is about the depth of housing and school buildings. Under these conditions prices per square metre tend to rise substantially as the number of storeys is increased. In Britain, housing is around 50 per cent more expensive in tall multi-storey blocks than in two-storey blocks. Running costs tend to increase in about the same proportion. Initial costs rise because of the need to use frames and to provide lifts and a greater proportion of circulation space. Running costs rise because of the additional services necessary in multi-storey blocks.

The rise in price per square metre for large industrial buildings tends to vary with the intended use. For buildings suitable for light industry construction prices per square metre tend to rise slowly as the number of storeys is increased. Where it is necessary to use heavy structures prices per square metre tend to be less for two storeys than for one-storey buildings, but to rise in relation to the number of storeys, although less than in proportion. The way prices change will depend on such factors as floor loadings, the load-bearing capacity of the soil, the concentration of services and the extent and nature of internal communications. Prices per square metre of useful floor area tend to rise more rapidly with the number of storeys where a large number of lifts and elevators become necessary, and where floor loadings necessitate large columns. The rises in price are partly a result of reductions in useful floor space and partly in the cost of extra building work and plant. Running costs will tend to rise as the area lit by roof lights is reduced. Running costs per square metre will also tend to rise where extra plant needs to be operated to provide internal communications.

The layout of a building cannot be decided without taking into consideration the operations to be carried on within it. Shape and layout may affect both the labour and the material costs of the operations to be performed. Often the effect on the costs of operating within the building are more important than the effect on the costs of constructing and operating the building.

The first consideration is the area of useful space. The costs of constructing, maintaining, heating, lighting and servicing space have to be borne whether the space is useful or not. The scale of use of the spaces may be considerably reduced if the dimensions are just too small to accommodate an additional unit of operation. Thus the effective space cost per hospital bed, per machine, per desk or per sales counter may be greatly increased if the shape and dimensions are not matched to the units to be housed in the spaces. On the other hand, too much attention to designing the space to meet current needs lead to diseconomies later. Buildings with generous space standards tend to be far more flexible in use than buildings with tight space standards.

The dimensions of a space can have a profound effect on the way operations are performed. Operations may have to be divided if there is not sufficient space to accommodate a continuous chain of machines or related work spaces. Handling by overhead gantries is not possible if the height is very limited. The differences in operation costs may in some cases be sufficient to make it worth while to spend large sums on converting or rebuilding to suit particular methods of operation.

The way spaces are linked is also of great importance. Often if spaces used for related operations can be brought together, staff can be shared, and both stocks and the consumption of materials can be reduced. Close proximity also reduces the time and costs of internal communications. The use of several floors may be worth while, even if this results in higher costs for constructing and running the building, if as a result operation costs are reduced by a large amount. For some industrial processes for which gravity feed is satisfactory (e.g. milling), tall, narrow multi-storey buildings may be the most economic. The use of large areas, which need to be provided with artificial environments, will be worth while only if the high costs of maintaining them are more than offset by the savings from having large, compact, closely related spaces.

THE COST CONSEQUENCES OF BUILDING ELEMENTS

The cost consequences of the design of each building element can be examined in a similar way to the cost consequences of the layout of a building. For most building elements there is a complex inter-relationship between its design and its initial, maintenance and other running costs, and often between its design and the costs of carrying out the functions of the building. The design of the building elements also interact between themselves. The sum of the optimum design of the building elements may not produce the optimum building design. The remainder of this chapter is concerned with a more detailed consideration of the design-cost aspects of some of the more important building elements.

Walls

Walls serve a number of purposes. Where there is no frame they form a part of the structure as well as insulating spaces from each other and from the environment outside the building. In non-framed buildings they carry the floor and roof loads as well as acting as insulants and contributing to the aesthetics of the building. In framed buildings the form of wall structure is often the same as is used in non-framed buildings but no use is made of the load-bearing capacity of the walling materials. Frames are used in situations either where load-bearing walls lack the capacity to carry the loads, or where frames can do it more efficiently.

The range of materials suitable for walls is very wide as is their range of properties and costs. Appearance depends on texture, not just of the material when it is new but throughout its life. Materials, such as bricks, which generally are very durable and which weather well, usually require little maintenance or cleaning, except in very dirty atmospheres. Their running costs are thus very low and in areas suitable for their production they tend to provide walling which is cheap both to erect and to maintain. Usually brick provides adequate insulation against rain, snow and wind, against hot sunshine and extreme cold, noise and fire. Its insulation properties can be fairly easily increased by treating the internal face and by cavity construction. Concrete can be designed to possess many of the properties of brick at a similar range of price. Generally, concrete does not weather as well and frequently maintenance and cleaning costs are higher than for brick.

Masonry construction of any type is generally heavy and bulky. Its weight adds to the costs of foundations and structure, and its bulk, and that of the frame which supports it, tends to reduce the amount of useful floor space. In buildings, in which useful floor space is very valuable as in city office blocks, the reduction in the thickness of walls and columns may be important. The construction and removal of masonry for the purpose of alterations interferes with the functions carried on in the building. Masonry does not provide either a method of enclosure which is easily adapted or within which services can be easily housed. Hence the tendency to favour the use of easily demountable dry, light-weight and non-bulky substitute materials. Often, however, these are more expensive than masonry and generally do not provide equally effective thermal insulation.

While there is a large range of materials suitable for wall claddings for framed buildings, few of them possess as good a set of properties as masonry materials.

With the exception of timber, in timber-producing countries, most of the dry cladding materials are expensive in relation to the properties they possess. Frequently they lack the durability of the masonry materials, weather badly and need frequent cleaning and painting. However, many of them take up far less space and are much lighter than masonry. While it is difficult to ensure the same degree of fire resistance and the same degree of insulation against noise, backing materials can be easily added to give adequate thermal insulation. Cladding composed of light-weight dry materials and partition walls built up in this way can easily be moved to facilitate the formation of different spaces, and for inserting and altering service connections. However, often the final costs after restoration are no less than with masonry materials. It is difficult to generalize; the costs-in-use of each design needs to be examined individually. Often the final justification for the choice of a particular material depends upon putting a very high evaluation on its appearance.

Roof coverings

There are a wide variety of roof coverings, although the field of choice depends on the shape and pitch of the roof. While the developed area of a roof depends on the pitch, the flat roof giving the minimum developed area, the costs-in-use do not necessarily increase with the pitch. Pitched roofs are usually easier to build and maintain in a weather-tight condition than are flat roofs. Materials suitable for pitched roofs are often cheaper than those for flat roofs. On the other hand, while pitched roofs are often cheaper to support than flat roofs, they have a larger exposed area to clad and through which heat can be lost and often they result in a larger volume within the building to be heated. Some roofing materials are so expensive that only a very high evaluation of their appearance can justify their use.

Glazing

Glazing is usually more expensive to install, maintain and to clean than the wall cladding it replaces. Moreover, heat losses through glass are greater than through most other cladding materials. Economically the use of glass has to be justified in terms of the off-setting saving in lighting costs and in its aesthetic and amenity value.

The value of glass in admitting light varies with its position and with the use of the building in which the glass is used. The light admitted by glass, at or near the floor is of little value, since most of it falls on the floor instead of penetration into the room at bench or table level. The further the glazing is raised above the floor, the further the light will penetrate and the longer will be the period during which it will be unnecessary to use artificial light. Thus, the value of the glazing will be raised in relation to its cost. Unfortunately, the greater the height of the glazing the more likely it is that problems of glare will arise. Glass in roofs usually admits more light than glass in walls, but the quality and value of the light depends on the way the glass is distributed in the roof. The heat losses also depend on where the glass is situated. Heat losses per unit area of glass are greater through horizontal glass than through vertical glass and greater through glass facing some aspects than others. Glass admits heat from the sun as well as losing heat to the atmosphere. In cold weather solar gain may be of economic value, if the heating system is sufficiently flexible to allow advantage to be taken of it. In some situations it will add to the comfort of the building but its incidence is, of course, unreliable. In hot weather solar gain may be a nuisance and necessitate more cooling and greater costs.

The balance of gains and losses in the final costs-in-use comparison will depend on the use of the building. If the process produces an excess of heat, losses of heat may not matter and gains may need to be removed. If the heating system is flexible solar gains may be an advantage. Sometimes the change in heating loads that would result from changes in the amount and distribution of glazing may be sufficient to enable a smaller size of heating plant to be installed.

In a regularly used building heating loads are only affected marginally by the hours of use, since in order to provide adequate heating during the hours of operation, the temperature must be maintained during much of the unoccupied period. Lighting costs for fuel, and lamp use are more or less directly proportional to the hours during which the lighting is used. An increase in the area of glazing tends to reduce costs but only during the hours of daylighting during which the building is used. Hence, the greater the hours of use during the hours of daylighting, the greater the saving in lighting costs which tend to result from the extra glazing.

Double glazing makes a considerable reduction to the heat losses but is expensive to install and results in some reduction in the light penetration. Clearly, the greater the difference between internal and external temperatures and the longer the hours the building is used, the greater the likelihood that double glazing will be economically worth while. In a country such as Britain, double glazing, even when used in the most favourable economic circumstances, tends to result in only marginal economic advantages. Most other forms of thermal insulation give better economic results.

The quantity and quality of light

While a minimum light intensity is necessary, varying with the operation, for practical purposes there is little limitation on the maximum level of light under which operations can be performed. Under a clear sky in summer the intensity of light is often fifty to a hundred times greater than the level of intensity necessary to carry out various common operations, for example, reading, writing and various machine tasks. While some forms of lighting cause discomfort, by and large, differences in the intensity and quality of lighting above the minimum standard have little affect on the standard of performance of the operators except for certain tasks where, for example, colour recognition is of particular importance. On the other hand, the higher the intensity of artificial light, the greater tend to be the costs of installation and operation. Similarly some forms of lighting are economically less efficient than others. The economic justification for the use of higher intensity and more expensive forms of lighting must be based on comfort and other psychological advantages.

4
Tracing Design Consequences

THE COMPARISON OF ALTERNATIVE SOLUTIONS

The design of a building involves innumerable decisions, each of which consists of choosing between a range of possible solutions to a given design problem. While the alternatives may consist of totally different ways of solving the problem, they may consist of no more than a choice between different dimensions for the same form of construction. The choice might, for example, lie between a roof of timber and felt, and one of steel and asbestos cement sheeting, or between roofs with different angles of pitch.

The easiest way to demonstrate the method of approach to such comparisons is to consider a number of examples. In the following sections examples have been chosen to demonstrate the various types of problems which arise. The technical problems which arise in estimating the comparative costs will be considered in later chapters.

COMPARATIVE DURABILITIES

A common feature in all costs-in-use problems is the factor of time. Buildings are durable, most last many years, but often the components need to be replaced several times over the life of the building, and repairs and maintenance need to be carried out regularly. Comparison therefore implies, not just comparison between present costs, but comparisons between streams of payments occurring at different moments in time. As explained earlier, since the sums of money are payable at different times they cannot be added until they have been converted to their equivalent worths. The calculation of equivalent worths and the use of compound interest functions is explained fully in Appendix A, to which the reader should now refer.

Example 4.1 A simple comparison of alternatives with different lives
Suppose a choice is to be made between asbestos cement and vitreous enamel ware rainwater goods. Suppose that the latter is 50 per cent more expensive to purchase and fix than the former, but that it lasts sixty years; twice as long as the asbestos cement goods. Suppose further that dismantling existing

rainwater goods and erecting replacements costs 10 per cent more than the original cost. The following flow of payments are thus to be considered:

Asbestos cement	£1000	£1100	£1100	£1100
	0	30	60	90 years

Vitreous enamel	£1500		£1650	
	0		60 years	

Clearly it is necessary to decide for how long the building is required in order to know for how long the renewal cycles will continue. For the purpose of this example two lives will be considered; sixty years and 120 years. For the former life, given the assumptions, it would be necessary to renew the asbestos cement goods once, but it would not be necessary to renew the vitreous enamel ware; for a life of 120 years it would be necessary to renew the asbestos cement goods three times and the vitreous enamel ware once. Obviously ther is no need to renew at the end of the life of the building. The

TABLE 4.1 COMPARATIVE COSTS-IN-USE OF ASBESTOS CEMENT GOODS AND VITREOUS ENAMEL WARE*

Materials	Life of building 60 years			Life of building 120 years	
	Initial costs	Renewal costs	Total C.i.U.	Renewal costs	Total C.i.U.
Asbestos cement	£1000	£1100(0·231) v^{30} = £254	£1254	£1100(0·231 + v^{30} v^{60} v^{90} 0·054 + 0·012) = £327	£1327
Vitreous enamel	£1500	—	£1500	£1650(0·054) v^{60} = £89	£1589

* See Table A.1 for the compound-interest functions.

problem is to find the equivalent worths of these flows of payments. For the purpose of the example the equivalent worths will be expressed in terms of present worths, that is in terms of the discounted values. A net rate of interest of 5 per cent will be used. The rate to be used would, of course, depend on the type of client making the decision and the rate of interest and tax applicable

28 *Building design evaluation*

to him. The decision would, of course, also be affected by the incidence of grants and subsidies. These points will be discussed later.

It will be seen that, other things being equal, the asbestos cement goods provide the cheaper solution (Table 4.1). In the example the life assumed for the building has little effect on the comparative advantage of the asbestos cement goods, since much the same cycle would be repeated. The additional costs arising from a longer cycle would be small since the longer the period of discount the less the present worths of the items.

Example 4.2 A comparison with running costs
A third choice for rainwater goods might be cast iron. It will be supposed that cast-iron goods would cost, to purchase and fix, about 20 per cent more than asbestos cement goods, but that they would last about sixty years if painted regularly every five years. It will be assumed that painting would cost about £200. The payments to be considered are:

Cast iron	£1400	£200	£200	£200	£200	£200	£200	£200	£200	£200	£200
	0	5	10	15	20	25	30	35	40	45	50	55

If the life of the building is taken as 60 years, the rainwater goods would need to be supplied and fixed only once, painted when fixed and repainted at the end of each five years, until and including the fifty-fifth year after erection; clearly no repainting would be necessary at the end of the sixtieth year when the life of the building is assumed to be at an end.

TABLE 4.2 COSTS-IN-USE OF CAST-IRON RAINWATER GOODS*

Initial costs		£ 1400
Renewal costs	$v^5 \qquad v^{55}$ £200(0·784 + ... + 0·068) = £200(3·372)	674
Total costs		£ 2074

* See Table A.3 for the compound-interest functions.

Clearly the cast iron would be more expensive than either of the other two solutions.

INTERPRETATION OF EXAMPLES 4.1 AND 4.2

The interpretations of costs-in-use comparisons will be dealt with fully in a later chapter, but some idea of the interpretation of the comparisons is useful at this stage. Consider first the results for a building of a life of sixty years. The appearance of these three alternatives are different. Asbestos cement goods are not usually thought to have as satisfactory an appearance as the other two products. It might be thought that the appearance of the vitreous enamel ware was well worth the extra £246. Some might think that asbestos cement goods would have as acceptable an appearance if they were painted but painting, even if it cost no more than painting cast iron, would add £874 (£674 + £200 for initial painting) and would bring the cost to £2128 higher than the cost of painted cast iron. The appearance of the vitreous enamel ware might be as acceptable as the cast iron, but since the cast iron has to be regularly painted, an option to change the colour is available every five years. On the other hand, a cost of £574 might be thought a high price to pay for this advantage. The equivalent of the first repainting is £200 (0·784), about £157; thus, if the vitreous enamel ware were accepted and, even if its decorative appearance was changed after ten years and it was subsequently painted every five years, it would still be cheaper (£2017) than the cast-iron solution. The three materials stand up rather differently to impact damage. Asbestos cement goods are very brittle and sections might be damaged and need replacement. If on average the asbestos cement goods had to be replaced at twenty and forty years, instead of thirty years, the equivalent cost would be

£1000 + £1100 (v^{20} + v^{10}) (0·377 + 0·142) = £1571 and it would be more expensive than the vitreous enamel ware. The other two products would stand more impact damage, although damage to the surface might need touching up.

All estimates and predictions are inevitably subject to error and it is necessary to decide whether the errors are so large that they invalidate the conclusions drawn from them. It will be noticed that between 70 and 100 per cent of the costs-in-use relate to initial costs. The prices of the components are ascertainable and fixing costs can usually be estimated within fairly narrow limits. Errors might be made in assessing the life of the building, the lives of the materials and the future costs of their renewal and painting. Changes in the life of the building will tend to affect the costs of the alternatives in much the same way. The lives of the materials must change radically to make cost differences large enough to change the order of the alternatives in relation to their costs-in-use. As will be shown later, general inflationary price changes do not need to be considered and again differential price changes would need to be large to affect the order in terms of the costs-in-use. For example, if it were accepted that the errors in estimating the initial costs were not more than 5 per cent then the difference in the costs-in-use of vitreous enamel ware and painted cast-iron ware resulting from prediction errors

could be as much as £429 without leading to an incorrect interpretation
(£2074 −0·05 £1400 −1·5 £1500). A difference as large as this would accommodate a percentage error in predicting the cost of painting of over 60 per cent. On this basis the vitreous enamel ware would still have the lower costs-in-use, even if it had to be painted in the fifteen year and every five years thereafter £200 (1·976). Thus the prediction errors would need to be very considerable to reverse the order of the alternatives in terms of costs-in-use.

$v^{15} \ldots v^{55}$

It will be appreciated that the problem of prediction errors is not introduced by the use of the costs-in-use analysis. Prediction errors are implicit in any decision between one alternative and another. If no analysis is made on the grounds that prediction is too uncertain, the implicit argument is that the actual costs are so uncertain, that either a random choice (by the toss of a coin) or reliance on the selector's intuitive choice is more likely to select the most economic alternative than a selection based on cost analysis. Either would be bold claim, especially in relation to some of the more complex choices to examined later.

In the cases of the examples already discussed the choice would lie between the asbestos cement goods and the vitreous enamel ware. On the assumptions accepted the cast iron goods would be so much more expensive than vitreous enamel ware that the latter would be likely to be cheaper. The risks of impact damage would differ between the other solutions. The asbestos cement goods would be more vulnerable than the vitreous enamel ware. If appearances were of no importance the asbestos cement goods would give the best value for money except where there was a large risk of impact damage. If appearance were important the vitreous enamel ware might be thought to offer better value for money.

Example 4.3 A comparison with complicated running costs
Often, of course, the interactions between the alternatives and other components of the building result in complicated cost differences. The choice between solid fuel heating and under-the-floor electrical heating in a block of flats provides an interesting illustration. One example must suffice. It will be supposed that full heating is to be provided in the living room and hall, elsewhere in the flats electric points will be provided for portable electric fires and a point will be provided for an electric cooker in the kitchen. Water heating will be either by means of a back-boiler behind the solid fuel fire with an immersion heater for the summer, or entirely by an immersion heater where under-the-floor electric heating is provided. A panel fire will be provided in the living room for occasional heating in the summar.

The cost comparison can conveniently be made by comparing the extra costs of the two systems against those for a flat which was heated by portable electric fires and with no provision for heating water. If a solid fuel fire is fitted there would be extra costs for the grate, hearth and surrounds, radiator and pipework, for the chimney breast complete with plastering and decoration, and for a fuel store. The cost of this work for supplying and fixing might be taken as £400. If under-the-floor electrical heating is provided the corresponding extra costs would be for the heating cables, thermostat, panel fire, an extra inch of screed over the whole dwelling area and a compensating extra inch on the storey height. The total costs might be taken as £280. The hot water cylinder, cold water cistern and immersion heater would be common to both systems but if solid fuel was used for heating the water an expansion tank, a back-boiler and extra pipes would also be needed. These might cost about £120. Thus in terms of capital costs the solid fuel system might cost about £520 extra as against about £280 extra for the electrical heating system.

The maintenance of the two systems would also have some common features. The extras for the solid fuel system as compared with the electrical system would be annual flue cleaning, about £4, boiler descaling and replacement of grate and side bricks, which might need to be carried out about every ten years at a cost of about £60, and the replacement of the back-boiler, together with attention to the pipes and tanks, needed about every twenty years and which would cost about £100. The corresponding extras for the under-the-floor system would include replacing the thermostat, about £25 every ten years, replacing the panel fire, about £40 every fifteen years, and the renewal of the heating cables which together with the repair of probable intermediate breaks might cost about £320 every thirty years. These costs include for the incidental builder's work and making good. For example, the costs for the renewal of the heating cables includes for breaking and removing the floor, the replacement of the screed, a new floor finish and additional costs of redecoration.

The maintenance costs can be capitalized as before and added to the capital costs (Table 4.3).

In calculating the figures given in Table 4.3 it has been assumed that the life of the building would be sixty years, and that the appropriate net rate of interest would be 5 per cent. It will be noticed that no renewal is required in the last year of life.

The cost for installing and maintaining the solid fuel system is over 70 per cent more than for the under-the-floor system. It is unlikely that prediction errors would be as large as this. The major difference lies in the costs of installation, the costs of which can be estimated with the greatest amount of certainty. Given a difference in installation costs of over 80 per cent

TABLE 4.3 COMPARISON OF SOLID FUEL AND UNDER-FLOOR-ELECTRICAL HEATING*

System of heating	Costs	Frequency	Factor	Present worth
Solid fuel	£520·0	Initial	1·0	£520·0
	£ 4·0	Yearly	$v^1 + v^2 \ldots + v^{59}$ 18·88	£ 75·0
	£ 60·0	10 years	$v^{10} + v^{20} \ldots v^{50}$ 1·45	£ 87·0
	£100·0	20 years	$v^{20} + v^{10}$ 0·52	£ 57·0
	Total			£734·5
Electrical	£280·0	Initial	1·0	£280·0
	£ 25·0	10 years	$v^{10} + v^{20} \ldots + v^{50}$ 1·45	£ 36·3
	£ 40·0	15 years	$v^{15} + v^{30} + v^{45}$ 0·82	£ 32·8
	£370·0	30 years	v^{30} 0·23	£ 73·6
	Total			£422·7

* See Tables A.1 and A.3 for compound-interest functions.

and installation costs at least twice the equivalent worth of maintenance, very large errors could occur in the latter without much affecting the cost relationships.

It is interesting to consider whether a change in the planned life of the building would have an important change on the comparative costs. Suppose the planned life was seventy years; the solid fuel system would then incur another 10 annual charges of £4 and charges of £160 in the sixtieth year. The under-the-floor system would incur a charge of £385 in the sixtieth year. Of course, the periods of renewal are not in practice as rigid as the assumptions suggest. It might be possible to keep the systems in operation for another 10 years without much extra expense beyond that incurred for a sixty-year life. However, even if the extra payments were incurred, their discount values would be small, about £10 and £20 respectively. The addition of such sums would make little difference to the comparison.

Example 4.4 A simplified comparison
The under-the-floor electrical system costed above was of the type for which the cables would be embedded in the screed. If the screed were laid with ducts and access panels were provided, the cables could be repaired and replaced without damaging the floor. The initial costs would be higher but the maintenance costs would be lower. Since the costs of the water heating system, the thermostat and the panel fire would not be affected, a comparison of the costs of an embedded against a withdrawable system can be made entirely in terms of the floor heating units. The installation costs of the items affected would be about £128 and £260 respectively, while the renewal and breakage

TABLE 4.4 COMPARISON OF EMBEDDED AND WITHDRAWABLE SYSTEMS*

Type of system	Costs	Frequency	Factor	Present worth
Embedded	£128.0	Initial	1.0	£128.0
	£320.0	30 years	v^{30} 0.23	£ 73.6
		Total		£201.6
Withdrawable	£260.0	Initial	1.0	£260.0
	£100.0	30 years	v^{30} 0.25	£ 23.0
		Total		£283.0

* See Table A.1 for the compound-interest functions.

repairs would cost about £320 and £100 respectively. The comparison could be made in the usual way (Table 4.4).

On these figures, other things being equal, the embedded system is obviously the cheaper, although its face cost is greater. The saving in the capitalized worth of the renewal costs would not offset the substantially higher costs of installation. It would be simple to work out the conditions under which the withdrawal system would be worth using. Clearly it would only be sufficiently cheaper either if the initial costs could be substantially reduced, or if the incidence of repairs and renewals of the cables was much greater than the figures assumed in the above examples.

OTHER RUNNING COSTS

The choice between solid fuel and electrical heating cannot be made in terms of initial and maintenance costs alone; allowance must also be made for the running costs, for instance, fuel and meter charges, cleanning costs and the costs of fuel handling. Such costs will vary with the actual user as well as with the heating system and with the building. The costs to be considered would depend on the nature of the comparisons to be made. If the purpose of the comparisons was to determine the relative economies of different systems of heating the comparisons would be made in terms of identical heating loads and the loads used for the comparison would be chosen to avoid giving marginal advantages to one of the fuels to be compared. However, one form of heating may have advantages over others for a particular pattern of use and this would be taken into account when comparisons were made from the point of use of a given user or type of user. For instance, electricity and electric fires tend to be economic as compared with solid fuel or oil heating systems where short-term but instantaneous heat is required. Some users are prepared to accept a lower standard of heating from some systems than from others. For instance, households who pay a fixed sum for their heating tend to demand high temperatures and almost unlimited hot water 24 hours a day, whereas those whose heating is charged by the unit tend to be satisfied with partial heating for a few hours a day and will often accept lower temperatures. The heating systems which give the best results for the money spent will vary with the demands to be satisfied.

The comparison given in Table 4.3 could be extended to include the fuel and servicing costs. Additions would need to be made to the solid fuel system for the coal or coke consumed each year and in the case of the under-the-floor system for the electricity used. The problems of projecting changes in fuel costs will be considered later. The systems under comparison are clearly for dwellings where servicing labour would be unusual. If, however, one of the systems were central heating the costs of the boiler room staff would need to be included and allowance would need to be made for the costs of removing the ash. Rooms with direct solid fuel heating are likely to become dirtier than thos with electric heating and allowance would be necessary for extra cleaning and decoration costs. While costing services purchased from the market is straighforward, it is more difficult to cost householders' labour in an objective way. It is difficult to know what valuation householders place on domestic jobs, or how much they would be prepared to pay to avoid such jobs. The following example suggests one way of dealing with this problem.

Example 4.5 An annual comparison of service costs

There is a widespread choice of methods of handling domestic refuse in blocks of flats; four typical methods will be considered. The first method is to provide individual dustbins, one for each flat, the bins being placed in the courtyard. The second method is to provide communal bins. A third method is to incorporate chutes in the blocks. These would be sited over removable bins and disposal points provided on each floor of the blocks. A fourth method is to incorporate a water-borne system of disposal with pipes linking special openings in the kitchen sinks with a collecting tank and possibly drying and burning facilities. The initial and maintenance costs of these systems will naturally vary, as will service charges. An investor erecting flats for letting and providing maintenance and portering would consider the initial and servicing costs. A local authority would consider also the costs of collecting and disposing of the refuse. It is cheaper to handle a few large bins than many small ones and it is cheaper to handle and dispose of the clinker from the incinerator of a waterborne system than to handle and dispose of untreated refuse from bins.

In a comparison of this kind in which regular servicing is important it is often more convenient to compare the annual equivalent costs than the present worths (Appendix A). The annual equivalent costs are calculated in the usual way from the predicted costs (Appendix A). The results of the analysis are set out below (Table 4.5). The costs shown are reasonably typical for these types of system.

It will be seen that the systems analysed are successively more expensive. The differences in the predicted annual equivalent costs to the owners of the flats are too large to be the result of prediction errors and represent real differences. Owners would be unlikely to accept one of the more expensive systems unless either they could expect to be able to pass the extra costs to the tenants in the form of rents or save the equivalent in some other way, perhaps in letting costs. It is, therefore, necessary to consider the values which tenants might place upon the system.

It is difficult to see why a tenant should prefer to use a collective dustbin rather than an individual one. There are, however, advantages in the use of a duct or refuse chute since this saves a trip down to the courtyard with every parcel of refuse. The time and effort needed to walk from the flat to the yard would be saved and a trip outside would be avoided. Since the bin would normally be enclosed, the chut system would be less unsightly although it would be likely to add to the noise. The difference in cost between individual bins and a chute system to the owner would be equivalent to about 19 pence a week: tenants might be prepared to pay this amount for the conveniences obtained. With a water-borne system it is possible to

TABLE 4.5 ANNUAL EQUIVALENT COSTS FOR REFUSE DISPOSAL FROM FLATS (£'s)

Type of costs	Individual dustbins	Collective dustbins	Ducts and bins	Water-borne disposal
Permanent installation	–	2·2	7·6	30·0
Renewable installation	2·4	3·0	2·8	Unknown
Maintenance and service	–	1·8	1·8	20·0
Total equivalent annual costs to owner of flats	2·4	7·0	12·2	50·0 +
Local Authority refuse service collection costs	9·0 / 3·0	6·0 / 3·0	6·0) / 3·0)	1·6
Total costs	14·4	16·0	21·2	51·6 +

dispose of most daily refuse through a trap in the kitchen sink and most trips from the flat to an external point of disposal would be aoided. The difference in cost would be over 90 pence a week, a figure which might be thought excessive for the advantages obtained. How much more than 90 pence is unknown, but if this figure is considered excessive it is immaterial that the full costs are not available.

If the collection and disposal costs are added the difference between individual and collective bins is reduced to about 3 p a week. The difference between the costs of ducts and the water-borne system would be at least 60 pence, even after allowance for the saving in collection and disposal costs. Sometimes it is argued that water-borne systems will have long-term advantages because of future difficulties in obtaining operatives for refuse disposal work or obtaining them only at a relatively much higher price than today. The importance of this argument can be assessed from cost analysis of the type described here. The costs of refuse collection and disposal would need to rise at least fivefold in relation to the other costs before the costs of the water-borne system and the chute system broke even. This is on the assumption that the renewal costs of the water-borne system would be zero; this would seem to be unlikely.

Example 4.6 A comparison involving operation costs
In the example above it was demonstrated that it is sometimes necessary to examine the effect of the building design, or the design of its components on subsequent servicing operations. Sometimes the building and the operations to be carried out within it are so much of a unity that it is necessary to analyse the costs of the two together. One such example, which will serve to illustrate this type of problem, is a storage building required to handle baled material. It will be assumed that the bales are heavy and bulky, and that mechanical handling is essential. The choice of handling system will be assumed to lie between a fork-lift truck and a gantry crane. The fork-lift truck has a limited reach and because of this, and because of the need to manoeuvre, would require a large floor area. The gantry crane would impose no limitation on height (although the strength of the storage units might), would not require ground space for manoeuvring, but would require a strengthened frame. Thus a building suitable for fork-lift truck operation would be long and low, while that for gantry operation would be shorter but taller.

It is convenient to regard the buildings as a part of the storage and handling unit. Since the buildings would differ in shape and loadings and since the handling equipment would also differ, nearly every element of the building would differ in some way and would need to be costed. The storage units would be, however, the same in type and quantity, although assembled in a different form.

The costs which matter to the client would be the net costs after allowance had been made for the effect of taxation. Under current tax regulations in Great Britain, tax allowances are available for industrial premises and for industrial plant both in respect of capital costs and running costs. In some circumstances grants are also available. The levels of taxes and grants vary from time to time and from one part of the country to another. Some allowance has been made for these at average current levels. The methods of introducing these into costs-in-use estimates will be discussed later.

It will be seen that the overhead gantry crane solution has the lower predicted costs-in-use (Table 4.6). The estimated saving is about £4600, a difference of about 6 per cent. Prediction errors of 3 per cent could easily occur; if these were in opposed directions the prediction errors could be as large as the difference in the estimates. Often it is possible to set the limits to the prediction errors more closely than this. The example under discussion provides an excellent illustration. It will be noticed that the nature of the materials and the operation to be carried out for most of the building elements would be similar in the two solutions. For example, the wall cladding would be of the same form in both designs and would differ in

TABLE 4.6 CAPITALIZED COSTS-IN-USE OF TWO STORAGE SYSTEMS* (£'s)

	Fork-lift truck		Overhead gantry crane	
Building element	Initial costs	Capitalized running costs	Initial costs	Capitalized running costs
Stanchion bases	800	–	960	–
Foundations and floors	5 800	2 000	4 800	800
Structural frame	8 800	–	7 600	–
Roof	13 600	3 000	7 600	1 600
Walls	7 000	4 000	8 000	3 000
Drainage	880	80	680	80
Lighting	4 400	5 680	2 800	3 400
Heating	4 400	10 000	3 840	8 600
Handling equipment	2 280	7 200	14 400	7 120
Total	47 960	31 960	50 680	24 600

* Costs are net of tax.

quantity but not in quality. The only element that would be completely different in the two designs would be the handling mechanism. Hence it would be unlikely that prediction errors would be opposed and more likely that they would be proportional. Therefore, it would be likely that the comparative difference in costs would be larger than the prediction errors. Even a 10 per cent error in the costs of the handling equipment would be likely to be too small in its overall effect to upset this conclusion.

However, while the overheat handling system appears to be the cheaper solution there are still certain differences between the designs which have not been fully reflected in the costs and to which consideration should be given. The major differences relate to land and to flexibility. The cost of land could, of course, readily have been included in the costs-in-use analysis but the saving of a small area of industrial land would normally be small compared with the other costs and often would not be a consideration since the building would be erected on part of a much larger site. In some circumstances the site might already be congested and the difference in land required might be worth more than its cost. The fork-lift truck system offers more flexibility than the overhead gantry solution. The fork-lift truck could be used to operate outside the storage building and in other parts of any complex of buildings. Moreover, extra trucks could be purchased if the amount of handling merited this step. While the gantry crane could be built to operate outside the storage building, this would increase the costs of construction, heating and operation. Separate trucks would be necessary for horizontal transport to other parts of the building complex. The lower but longer building used with the fork-lift truck solution would generally be more useful for other purposes than the taller building with less floor space. Where it is possible to foresee some changes of use for the building an allowance can be made in the costs-in-use analysis. Even where no forecast of change is possible it is still not difficult to make some estimate of the value of the building should it no longer be required for its designed use. For example, the extra costs-in-use of the longer building expressed as the costs per square metre of additional floor space would only be about £8. This would be inexpensive even if half the life of the building had expired before its use was changed. The probable values of the various other features can readily be assessed and used as a guide to the choice of the handling system.

5
Building Elements and Design Development

BUILDING ELEMENTS

It has been stressed that the first step in comparing the costs-in-use of design alternatives is to examine the designs in physical terms and to determine which of the building elements are common to the design alternatives. Common design elements are then eliminated from the cost studies. The comparison of the design alternatives is made in terms of relatives rather than absolutes, because prediction errors are usually relative rather than absolute. Clearly, building elements, which have the same costs because the operations arising from them are the same, do not contribute to comparative prediction errors. However, the addition of common cost elements to the total costs reduces the apparent relative difference between the costs of the design alternatives and conceals significant cost differences. The elimination of common elements reduces the amount of costing necessary. It is, however, important to ensure that all the elements which are affected by the differences in design are fully considered. The first step is to examine the range of design solutions to be considered and to divide the designs into their building elements. The elements are the largest groups of components which are common to the designs to be compared. Each element is a complete unit and forms part of a functional group, of which there are several for each design. Each element is taken to include the connections to the element which precede it in the course of construction. It is thus simple to substitute one form of a particular element for another. If the area or shape of a building is also under investigation, it is useful to make a distinction between internal and external elements. It is often sufficiently accurate to adjust internal elements on the basis of area and external elements on the basis of a linear measure. A comparison between this method and detailed costing for some studies of frames indicated errors in the frame costs of less than 2 per cent.

The substructure and superstructure of a frame building can conveniently be divided into foundations, frame, floors, walls, roof and vertical access. It is not possible to lay down any one set of elements: the division into elements will depend on the type of building, on the form of cost data available and on the way the analysis is to be used. The headings listed below are thought to provide a useful starting point but the analyst may prefer to follow his normal practice.

Where the normal types of Bill rates are available there will be no difficulty in costing each element separately. Working from an elemental bill would be even easier. Operational costing is claimed to be more accurate. This form of costing can readily be applied to cost analysis of this form. The materials for each element can readily be estimated separately but the costs of labour can often only realistically be estimated for a group of elements, the group forming a single building operation. The frame of a building will often form a single building operation, but the walls will usually be divided between several trades and form several operations.

SUGGESTED ELEMENTAL ANALYSIS OF A FRAMED BUILDING

	Building element
Substructure	Foundations for
	Internal columns
	External columns
	Walls
Superstructure	Ground-floor slab
	Frame
	Internal columns
	External columns
	Internal beams
	External beams
	Internal roof trusses
	External roof trusses
	Intermediate floors
	Secondary beams
	Structure and finish
	Lining and finish
	Walls
	External cladding support
	Internal cladding support
	External cladding and finish
	Internal cladding and finish
	Insulation
	Glazing
	Doors
	Vertical access
	Lift well
	Stair well enclosure walls
	Stair flights
	Landings

42 *Building design evaluation*

	Building element
Superstructure	Roof
	Support for covering
	Covering and finish
	Lining and support
	Internal finish
	Insulation
	Drainage
	Soffit, facing boards, etc.

The elements for the substructure would normally each include the excavation, concreting and any brickwork, reinforcement or piling. The ground-floor slab would similarly normally include for removing top soil, concreting and reinforcement. The elements of the frame would normally include for all the materials and work involved, including the connections to the foundations and the protection of the frame members; for a steel frame painting would be included. In a similar way the connections between the intermediate floors and the frame would be included with the floors. Again, the external walls would be treated as an addition to the frame, so that the work related to connecting the walls to the frame would be included with the wall elements. The elements for vertical access and for the roof would be treated in a similar way. Clearly it is only necessary to add or subtract the appropriate sets of building elements to obtain a suitable set of elements for some other type of building. For a non-framed building the groups of elements associated with the frame would be eliminated but it would generally be necessary to include a set of elements for load-bearing internal walls. Additional groups could be added for nonload-bearing partitions, for heating, ventilating, lighting, internal transport, plumbing and other engineering functions and for floor and other finishes. The form of elemental analysis can be adapted to any type of building.

This form of elemental analysis provides a convenient basis of analysis whether the comparison is between radically different types of building or forms of construction, or between a range of solutions for particular elements. Comparisons of the latter type are nearly always necessary, for however radical the major choice of design, it is still necessary to find the best solution for each element.

As pointed out earlier the first stage is to examine the alternative designs to be considered from the point of view of the constructional and operational processes. Elements which are common are then eliminated. Similarly for a comparison of the alternative designs for any particular functional group of a building, groups of elements which do not interact with the group to be considered can be eliminated from the design comparison. For example, the type of roof will not be affected by decisions on wall claddings, floor finishes or the provision of sanitary ware. Normally for a framed building comparisons of roof designs will only involve the consideration of foundations, frame and roof elements. Often the range of roofs which can be employed with a similar frame will be quite wide and only differences in the roof elements would need to be analysed. Many of the roof elements will be comparable over the range of designs to be examined and a cost analysis would only be necessary for three or four elements.

Where a design office is designing many buildings of a comparable type, or is developing an optimum design system for buildings to be handled by system building or prefabrication, there is considerable convenience and economy in devising a universal set of elements. This facilitates the use of costings from one design to another. The convenience of such an elemental system is equally valuable whether costs-in-use or only first costs are to be studied.

BUILDING ELEMENTS IN THE COMPARISON OF WALLS

The choice of wall claddings may interact with the foundations and with the frame of the building. Normally a sub-frame will be needed to support the cladding and the internal lining of the walls for a framed building. The choice of external cladding can often be made independent of the choice of internal lining; insulation can usually be added to bring the wall up the required thermal value. The choice of wall cladding will be restricted by the previous choice of frame and foundations. The weight category of the cladding would need to be determined at the time the frame and foundations were decided. There would, of course, be more choice in the case of a single-storey building since the weight of the cladding would be more likely to affect the foundations than the frame. In these circumstances the cladding elements to be considered would be:

External cladding,
External cladding support,
Structural protection,
Internal cladding support,
Internal cladding,
Internal finish.

In general it will be necessary to consider maintenance and heating costs as well as initial costs.

Normally the thermal insulation would be provided by the cladding materials themselves and additional thermal insulation would be provided in conjunction with the internal lining. Where necessary, however, an additional element could be added for insulation. In some cases there may be an interaction between window and door elements and the cladding elements. Where this possibility exists, window and door elements would need to be introduced. For instance, lintels would need to be provided over openings in brick or block walls. The cost of providing these would tend to result in such walls providing comparatively less favourable solutions where the wall has openings than where it is free from them.

BUILDING ELEMENTS IN THE COMPARISON OF ROOFS

The choice of roof may interact with the frame of the building and with the foundations since some types of roof are heavier and need more support than others. If the choice of roof is to be unrestricted, in the first place the analysis would need to include all the elements of foundations, frame and roof. Usually, however, the choice is far more restricted than this. Beyond a certain point the greater the column spacings the greater the frame costs tend to be. Column spaces will not usually be greater than is necessary for the functions of the building. The frame chosen will often be satisfactory for a range of roof designs and hence the choice of the roof design will not interact with the other building components.

For example, there are a number of types of flat roof which could equally well be used with a simple steel framed building. Suppose the choice were between a number of unglazed flat roofs. The choice might be between an asbestos cement cavity deck, a metal deck, and a boarded roof; all of which would normally be broadly comparable in weight, would have the same surface area, similar drainage and similar external soffit and facings treatment. The elements to be considered would therefore be:

Support for covering,
Covering and finish,
Lining and support,
Internal finish,
Insulation.

If the insulation can be adjusted so as to bring the roofs to be compared to a common U-value, no allowance would be needed for differences in heating costs.

If the comparison were limited to an asbestos cement cavity deck as compared with a metal deck, only two elements would probably need to be considered:

Support for covering,
Insulation,

since the same covering and finish and the same lining and support and finish could equally well be used with either type of roof. Only initial costs would need to be estimated since maintenance costs would not normally arise either for the support for the covering or for the insulation. If, however, one of these were to be compared with the boarded roof, the five items listed earlier would all need to be considered, since each item would differ from one design to another. Moreover, it would be necessary to consider both initial and maintenance costs, and heating costs.

Since there is a large range of suitable types and thicknesses of insulation material, it will normally be possible to bring each type of roof to about the same U-value. The difference in heating costs will, therefore, normally be marginal and it will normally be sufficient to cost the effect of the differences in U-values on the costs of heating by allowing for heating at an average cost per therm. However, where the heat loads consequential on designs differ substantially, the choice of one design rather than another may affect the sizing of the boiler and lead to substantial savings in the initial and running costs of the heating system.

DESIGN DEVELOPMENT AND THE FORM OF COST ANALYSIS

The purpose of the design evaluation technique is not simply to enable one design to be compared against another but to try to find the optimum solution. The form of cost analysis can be arranged to facilitate the development of the optimum design. For this purpose it is unnecessary and often misleading to consider the absolute costs; it is the relative costs which matter. Since man and his activities must normally have some protection against the elements, some solution must be found. The solution which provides the best value for money may be only marginally different from the solutions which were first examined. It might lie in a smaller building, in some slight modification of the building currently used or in some temporary structure. The method of presenting the cost relationships needs to be designed to bring out the underlying factors, so that the analyser can see how to develop the design so as to improve its value for money relationship.

It is not possible to lay down any form of standard accounts for costs-in-use analysis. The development of the most suitable form of account is part of the analytical technique itself. Any attempt to lay down a standard form would be self-defeating. A form of account which would be general enough to be widely applicable would be unwieldy and would tend to lead to unnecessary costing. There would be a danger that the procedure would be used mechanically, without thought as to the nature of the cost relationships and, as a result, the possibilities of developing more efficient hybrid designs might be missed.

The use of formulae, instead of accounts, would not be an advantage. The necessary degree of generalization would lead to excessive work and there would be a considerable danger of their use in a mechanical way. The solution by formulae would completely conceal the cost relationships and render it difficult, if not impossible, to discern the lines of further development of the design. Moreover, it would be difficult to determine where the prediction errors lay. It would be necessary to work with a large margin for prediction errors and, as a result, the chance of missing significant differences in costs would be increased.

The method of using the cost prediction technique as a guide to the development of design solutions can best be understood by the use of examples.

Example 5.1 The development of a wall design
Two of a number of comparative designs for the walls of a single-storey factory building are demonstrably superior to the others. Of the two, the cavity brickwork wall is over 10 per cent more expensive than a wall built up from asbestos cement sheets lined with insulating plasterboard. The brick walling is less likely to be damaged by accidental impact or by vandalism than the alternative. Many people would prefer its appearance to that of the asbestos cement sheets. The unit costs of the work to the foundations and for a therm of heat are similar for the two designs. Hence, the prediction errors are not likely to be as large as 10 per cent. There is little doubt that the brick wall design would be the more expensive of the two (Table 5.1).

It will be noticed that the difference between the costs of the walls of brickwork and asbestos cement sheets is largely accounted for by the costs of the lintel. Since the lintel is only necessary to carry brickwork over openings, it is not required in walls which neither have openings nor clerestory windows. For such designs the brickwork solution will be little more expensive than the asbestos cement sheet solution. The use of lintels could also be avoided if lightweight cladding were used in place of the brickwork over any openings. In this position it would be unlikely to be damaged by impact or by vandalism. This would provide a new solution with most of the advantages of brickwork and at only a small additional cost (Table 5.1). Special attention would be given to the sizing of the heating plant. A small change in the heating load, such as might arise from

TABLE 5.1 THE CAPITALIZED COSTS OF WALLING (£'s)

Building element	Cavity brickwork	Asbestos cement	New design
Foundations	2 800	1 000	2 800
External cladding	9 800	3 200	6 800
External cladding support	–	3 800	1 800
Internal cladding support	–	400	200
Internal cladding	–	1 400	480
Lintels	2 900	–	–
Heating	10 800	13 400	11 800
Total	26 300	23 200	23 880

a change in the U-value of the cladding, might result in a change in the size of the heating plant and as a consequence change the balance of the costs of the design alternatives.

Example 5.2 The development of a roof design
Corrugated asbestos cement sheets and roofing felt over boards, both common types of coverings for equal pitched roofs, proved to be the best of a number of alternatives. In making a comparison between them it was found that there was no interaction between the roof coverings and the other elements of the building. The differences in weight between the forms of covering were so small that the frame and foundations were suitable for each of the coverings examined. The design of the two best roofs only differed by five elements. These are set out below (Table 5.2).

While the difference in the capitalized costs-in-use was only about 7 per cent as between the asbestos cement roof and the felted roof, the unit for some of the elements were common to both designs, for example, for the insulation and for a therm of heat. The lining was similar in both designs. An allowance for the effect of these common cost elements about doubles the percentage difference in capitalized costs-in-use. While some allowance must be made for the possibility of errors in calculating heat losses, there can be little doubt that the asbestos cement sheet design was more costly than the felted design.

An examination of the cost analysis indicated that the major sources of difference lay in the costs of the cover support, and lining and support. The cover support for the felted roof was much more costly than that for the asbestos cement sheet roof because of the need for an additional material, the boarding, to support the felt. The costs of the felted roof could be reduced if a cheap substitute could be found for the boards. On the other

TABLE 5.2 THE CAPITALIZED COSTS OF ROOFS (£'s)

Building element	Corrugated asbestos sheets	Felt on boards	Modified asbestos cement sheets
Finish and covering	8 900	9 100	8 900
Cover support	7 800	13 500	4 800
Additional insulation	1 900	400	1 900
Lining and support	13 200	3 600	3 600
Heating	28 500	29 600	28 500
Total	60 300	56 200	47 700

hand, the costs of the lining and support were much greater for the asbestos cement sheet roof than for the felted roof. The cause of the difference lies in the cost of the channelling used to support the plasterboard lining, necessary for the asbestos cement sheet roof, but not for the felted roof. It is usual to use timber purlins in the boarded and felted roof so that the boarding can be nailed direct to the timber purlins. The plasterboard lining could also be nailed to the timber purlins, eliminating the need for channelling. However, it is unusual to introduce an additional type of material in the construction unless it is really necessary, since normally this would lead to the use of an additional type of labour and tend to increase costs. For an unlined roof, steel purlins are the obvious solution. Timber purlins could be used in the asbestos cement sheet roof. Their use would result in some saving in the costs of the cover support and a large saving in the costs of the lining and support (Table 5.2). While the modified design for the asbestos cement sheet roof would be substantially less costly than the earlier design, it would retain most of the important properties of the earlier design. As a result, the roof based on asbestos cement sheets would be markedly less costly than the roof design based on felt on boards.

DESIGN VARIABILITY AND OPTIMUM DESIGNS

Design alternatives do not always present themselves as a choice between different forms of construction. Frequently it is possible to vary the designs by gradually changing the dimensions of certain materials or of the building itself. The width of cavities and the thickness of some types of insulation can be varied by small amounts. There is often a choice of plan ratios and of the position and areas of heating and glazing. In such cases the object is to find the shape of the curve which describes the relationship between the design parameter and the costs. The method is to hold all the design parameters constant except the one to be studied and to vary this over the range of interest. The costs can then be plotted against the values of the parameter and the points on the graph joined to find the shape of the curve and hence the value of the parameter at which costs are at a minimum. The minimum number of values of the parameter which must be analysed is three. Additional points can then be evaluated at points where the curve changes its slope. With a little experience the choice of significant values of the parameter under examination presents little difficulty.

While generally there is an optimum value for each parameter, this is not always so. Sometimes, because of a change in the value of a parameter, it is worth while to change the form of construction and sometimes the new form is increasingly economic as the value of the parameter is increased. Thus it is sometimes woth while pursuing an apparent unprofitable line of development in the hope of a break-through. This type of situation sometimes arises in considering the number of storeys to which a building should be constructed. This situation is worth further consideration.

THE NUMBER OF STOREYS AND COSTS-IN-USE

There is often a choice in the number of storeys to which construction can be carried. The same floor area can be provided on one, two or several floors. The costs-in-use will vary both with the costs of providing the building itself and with the costs of running and operating in it. Clearly, the greater the number of storeys, the smaller the area of site which will be necessary. On costly land this is usually the main reason for building high. Generally the greater the number of storeys, the greater the work to the foundations and to the frame, the larger the area of the walls but the lower the area of roof. At one time, reductions in roof area were of particular value, not only as a way of reducing the area to be constructed and maintained but also because of the comparative greater heat losses per square foot from the roof than from the walls. It is now so simple and cheap to insulate the roof that comparative heat losses are now not usually very important. The more storeys a building has the greater the area of suspended floor. This can add considerably to the costs as compared with solid floor especially where the floor loads are large. Vertical access also tends to be more expensive than horizontal access and to take up more floor space. For the reasons, costs per unit both for construction and for maintenance are often greater for tall than low buildings. The costs of operating within buildings is often related to the number of storeys. The optimum number of storeys depends on the type of building, on its form of construction and on its use.

Example 5.3 The optimum number of storeys

A large factory building was required. The land was not very expensive, about £100 000 per hectare. Production in this case without any appreciable change in production costs, could be carried on in a multi-storey building. If the building was developed several storeys high, part of the site could be sold or retained for possible expansion later. The greater the number of storeys the less would be the value of the land used for the erection of the building, but the higher the costs of construction work for foundations, superstructure and lifts, the higher the costs of maintenance and lift operation, and from three floors upwards, the higher the cost of the heating. Since the building would generally be a very deep one, the lighting would need to be provided artificially and its cost would not be greatly or consistently affected by the number of floors.

The costs of the foundations were found to rise in steps. The strip foundations were replaced by a raft when the design for three storeys was reached: costs per unit of floor area were then found to fall as the number of storeys were increased (Table 5.3). The pattern repeated itself when raft construction gave way to piled foundations for a design for six storeys. Other costs, except

TABLE 5.3 THE COMPARATIVE COSTS-IN-USE OF A FACTORY BUILDING (£000's)

Number of storeys	1	2	3	4	5	6	8
Land	100	52	36	28	20	16	12
Foundations	20	28	76	64	60	144	124
Superstructure	420	440	452	472	500	520	548
Maintenance	44	48	52	56	60	64	72
Heating	124	96	96	180	104	108	116
Vertical circulation	–	28	36	48	64	84	144
Total	708	692	748	768	808	936	1016

for lighting, tended to rise with the number of storeys, at least in the long run. It will be seen that the two-storey design had the minimum costs. Of course, no allowance has been made in the figure for the costs of lighting, partitions and other elements, the costs of which were not affected by the number of storeys. It will be noticed that the difference in the costs-in-use between one- and two-storey buildings was, in this case, not very large. Slight reductions, for example, in the costs of land or heating, or rises in the costs of the structure or lifts would reduce or negative the saving. Moreover, a single-storey building could be of a substantially lighter construction and be fitted with roof lights over the entire area and probably as a result would have had much lower costs-in-use. Future operations on several floors might have become more expensive than on a single floor. In other cases the costs might differ, particularly costs of land and vertical circulation. Much of the space about buildings is frequently used for parking and it might be cheaper to provide multi-storey parking than multi-storey production areas.

6
Factors of Prediction

BASIC ASSUMPTIONS

In order to calculate the estimated costs-in-use certain assumptions have to be made; assumptions relating not only to the designs being evaluated but also to the economic conditions under which the buildings will subsequently be operated. The assumptions to be considered include future prices, rates of discount, lives of buildings and their component parts and levels of taxation.

FUTURE PRICES

Prices change in two ways, in relation to the value of the currency and to conditions for their supply and demand.

Prices increase as the value of units of currency fall. The currency of most countries has become devalued to a considerable extent, at least over the last two decades. During such an inflationary period, units of currency lose some of their purchasing power and all prices rise. In so far as prices change for this reason they change in the same ratio and their relationship is not disturbed. The real costs, that is the costs measured in terms of resources, or measured in terms of each other do not change, since the only change in the situation is the change in the purchasing power of the currency. Thus, real costs to the community are not affected by inflation; it requires as much, but no more labour, management time, plant time and materials to complete an operation after a period during which inflation has been occurring as before.

In fact, of course, building work and goods and services of all types are purchased for cash, not by bartering other goods and services. Clearly, during a period of inflation the money costs for a given operation will rise. But more money, and in the same proportions, will be received and paid out by the building client. As far as price changes are a result of inflation, all transactions are affected equally. The money costs change but the real costs, that is, the volume of labour and materials, are not affected. Hence it would be incorrect to adjust future costs because of possible inflationary price changes.

Confusion often arises because it is assumed that unspent resources are stored in money terms. This would only be true if unspent resources were converted into cash and the money itself stored in a box. When resources are saved, as for example when it is decided to accept a cheaper immediate solution and to spend more on repairs and renewals, the money saved is not put in a box but put to some remunerative alternative use. If this were not done the rate of discount would be zero. An income is obtained from the alternative use which is eventually realized and turned into money at its current value. Money saved by postponing building construction or servicing is either put into business activities, or invested for others to put into business or other productive activities. The goods and services so produced are sold at current prices. For example, business profits are shared between the owners of the equity capital in proportion to their holdings and are only expressed in terms of the face value of the capital. The rates of interest paid on savings represent a risk premium, as well as an element of pure interest. The risk premium is required to cover inflationary losses as well as losses from defaults. If the real value of the return obtained from loans was eroded by inflation, the risk premium would be too low as compared with those earned by equities, the amount of money coming forth for loans would tend to fall and the price − the rate of interest − would tend to rise. Government agencies spend tax revenue as well as borrowing; if there was a fall in the amounts spent, less tax might be collected at that time. An inflationary rise in prices of building work would be matched by a rise in the money value of the tax payers' income, and hence in the Government's tax income. Thus, for the purposes of costs-in-use analysis purely inflationary rises in prices are ignored.

Relative price changes are however, of importance and cannot be ignored. There is a tendency in the long run for the real prices of manufactured goods to fall relative to that of the wages paid to labour (Figures 6.1, 6.2 and 6.3). This is because the productivity of labour in manufacturing tends to increase faster than in construction. In the short run, as for the period since 1973, prices can move very much out of line, especially when governements distort price increases by interferring with market operations, for example, through wage policies, currency markets, price controls and monopoly pricing of raw materials available from only a few countries. In the same way the productivity of labour in new building work, tends to increase faster than in maintenance work; in fact, there is little evidence of any increase in the productivity of maintenance work. In the recent past the real prices for new construction work have probably declined by about a twentieth while those of maintenance work have increased by a fifth. The expectation for the future is that the prices of renewal and maintenance work will rise relative to those for new construction work and rise proportionally more the greater the element of labour to materials.

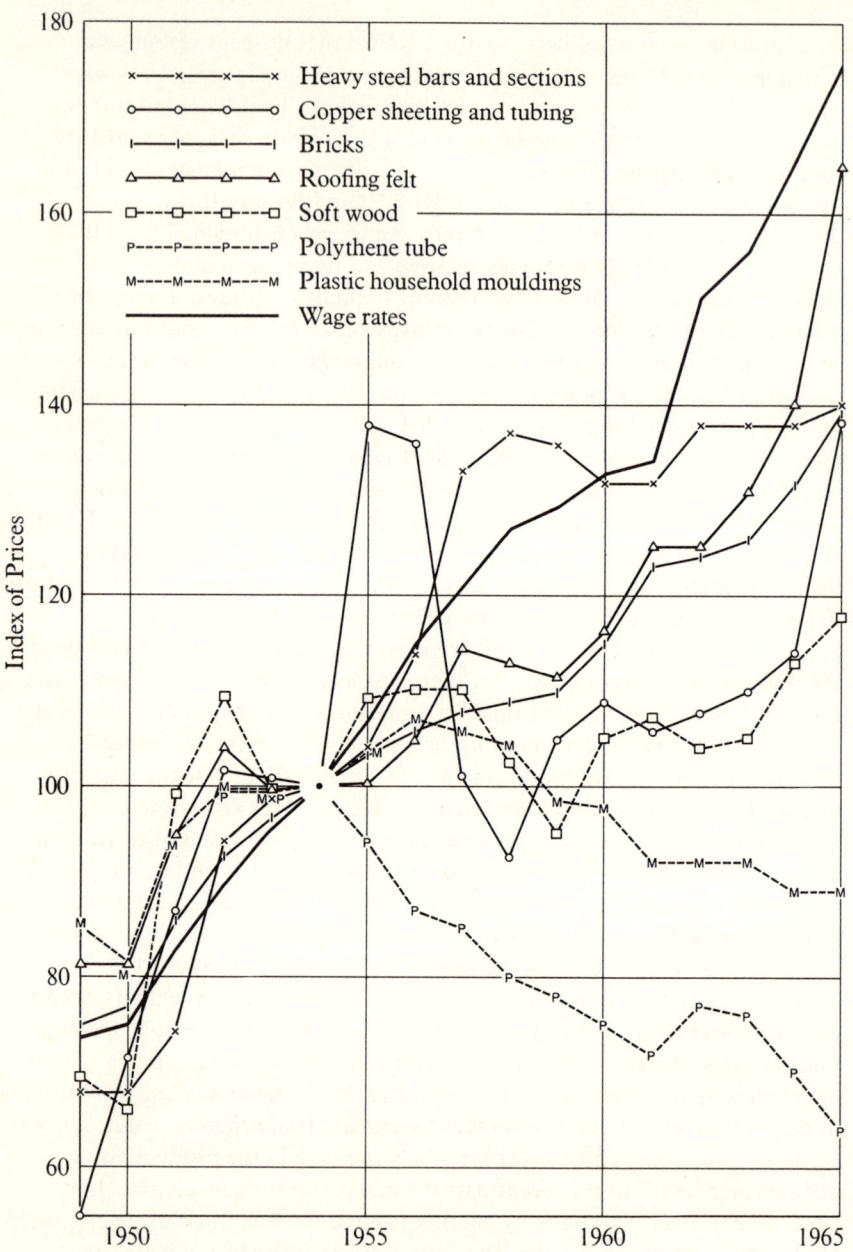

Figure 6.1 The movement of prices of selected materials and labour.

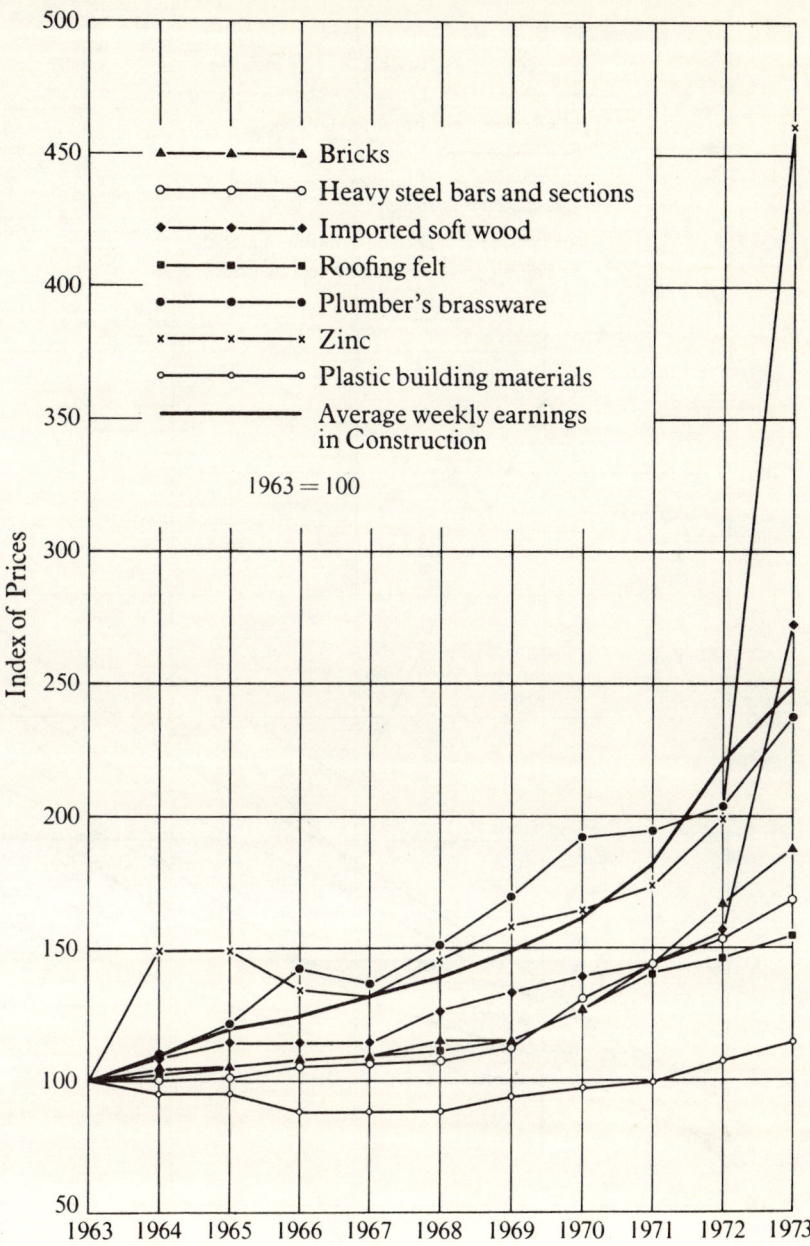

Figure 6.2 Movement of prices of selected materials and labour over the decade 1963 to 1973.

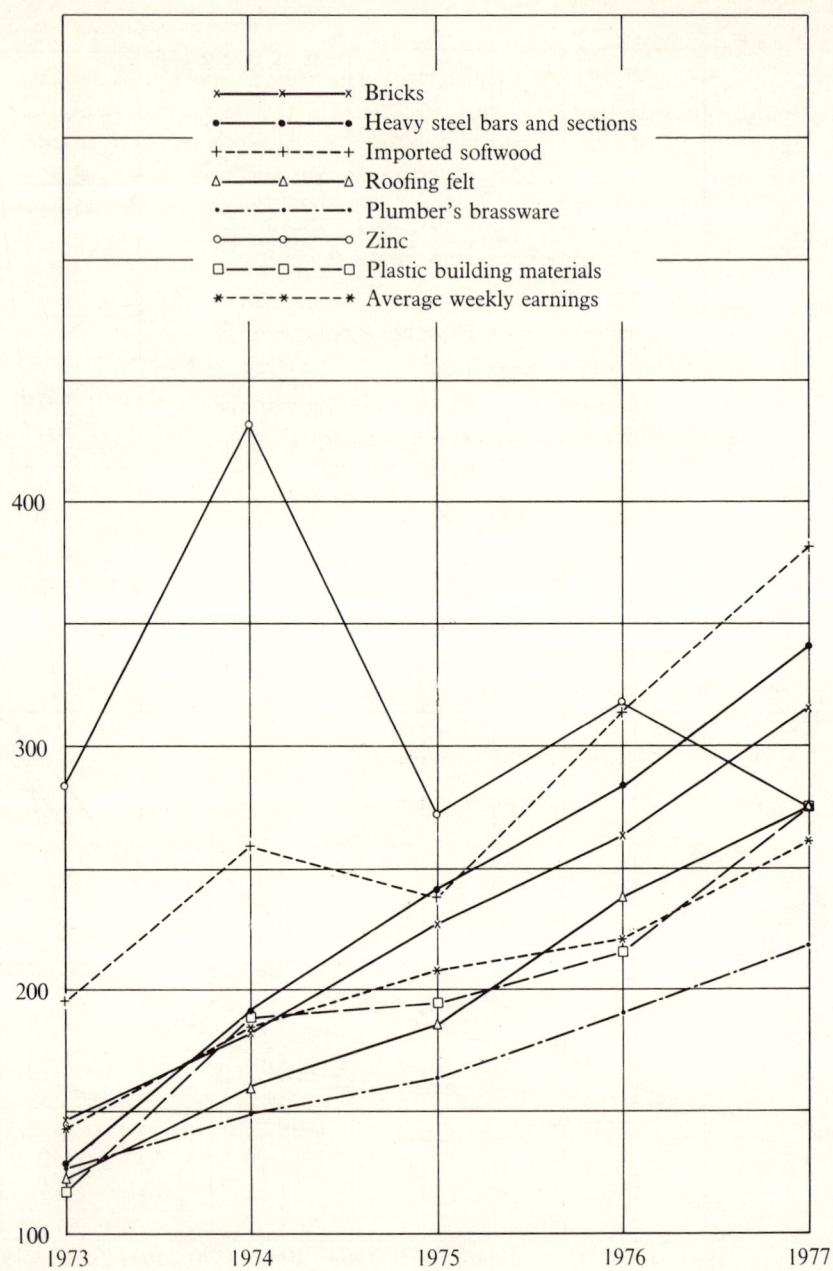

Figure 6.3 Movement of prices of selected materials and labour from 1973 to 1977.

The prices of materials change in relation to each other, partly because of differences in improvements in productivity and partly because of changes in their supply. Often there is little scope for innovation or for economies of scale in the manufacture of traditional materials and price increases in the raw materials and in labour are passed on in full. The prices of such materials as bricks, structural steel and roofing felt have generally followed the movement in the prices of labour and raw materials (Figure 6.1). In contrast the prices of such materials as plastic household mouldings and polythene tube, largely established in the last two decades, have fallen sharply. The prices of imported materials, for example, soft wood and especially copper, fluctuate violently, partly as a result of the effect of exchange rates, and partly as a result of changes in their supply, sometimes itself a result of political action. For similar reasons the price of fuels change in relation to each other and it is difficult to forecast future price movements. Fossil fuels are gradually being used-up but new supplies are still being discovered. Such new sources of supply and substitutes are often much more expensive than the original, so that fuel prices are likely to rise relatively to most other materials. Techniques for dealing with the uncertainty of future prices will be considered later, but it will be appreciated that the prices of measured work change less in relation to each other than the prices of materials.

RATES OF DISCOUNT

Building developers either borrow money to finance the building or sacrifice an alternative use for their own money. The real rate of discount which is implied is either the market rate for money borrowed on the security of buildings, or the average return which could be obtained from money invested in the developer's business. The average return is, of course, a great deal lower than the predicted return often required for the acceptance of a proposed business investment. It is important not to confuse the period over which the prediction is made with the life of the asset, or the average rate of return on the assets invested in the business with the predicted return thought necessary to justify an individual project. A clearer method is to use the true rate of interest and either the actual life, or the life over which foreseeable predictions can be made, together with an allowance for the residual value. The cost of the building on this basis can be compared with the return expected from the building: any surplus can be expressed as a profit and compared with profits likely from alternative uses of the money. This approach is particularly useful for buildings, such as houses, shops, offices and normal factory buildings, which satisfy the requirements of most users of that type of building and hence which can normally be sold or leased. It is important to use the true rate of interest since the rate affects the decision taken. The lower the rate of interest, the lower the cost of servicing the capital and the more worth while to spend now to reduce costs in the future. A low rate of interest encourages high-class construction. In contrast, high rates of interest encourage minimum standards of construction since the resulting higher running and operating costs are heavily discounted.

It is sometimes argued that public bodies, such as government departments and hospital authorities, do not borrow to obtain money to construct their buildings but meet the costs from payments derived from taxation. However, while the central government does raise money from taxation, it also borrows and most countries have a very substantial national debt. In the final resort, therefore, the money needed for construction is either borrowed on the market or obtained by reducing the repayment of national debt.

Except in a national sense the community cannot be a net borrower since one part of the community borrows from another part. However, resources used for one purpose are not also available for other purposes. The cost of resources used for buildings is hence the return which could have been obtained from them had they been used in some other way. Hence the future is still discounted even when design evaluations are made for the community, that is for the public at large.

The actual rate of discount to use in design cost evaluations will depend on such factors as the client's average internal rate of return, his credit-worthiness, the expected future rates of return and the expected rate of inflation. The appropriate rate of discount will vary with the building owner. Owners borrowing from the market, directly or indirectly will pay the pure rate of interest, together with a premium to cover currency inflation and the risks of default. The risk premium will be small for buildings suitable for many owners and likely to be marketable. Where the market rate is above the internal rate the owner will usually use his own capital if sufficient is available and will cost at the average internal rate of return. Public authorities will normally be able to borrow at little more than the pure rate of interest plus an allowance for inflation. This rate is usually appropriate for costing for community purposes. Rates fluctuate; when they are high capital needs will be met by temporary borrowing until rates again fall to their normal long-term level. Thus the long-term rate of interest is usually appropriate for costing. For costing for public buildings and for the community this has in the past averaged at about 5 per cent. In recent years this rate has been at a higher level partly because of the continuing inflation and partly because of the need to attract and hold funds from overseas to reduce the demand for sterling and hold its value. If inflation is expected to continue this rate will be higher in future. The higher the expected rate of inflation the higher the rate of discount. For other types of users risk premiums may add 2 to 3 per cent to this rate. But if money is borrowed or lent, as distinct from being invested in business or community activities, the real net amount payable at the end of the loan period will be reduced by the incidence of inflation. The effect is to reduce the net rate earned on the loan by the percentage by which money is losing value. The net real rate of interest with inflation at x per cent a year is x per cent less than the money rate of interest.* This is the rate before the premium to cover inflationary losses of value is added. The position is more complicated where taxation needs to be considered.

THE LIVES OF BUILDING

The cost predictions for the various components under consideration are made within the pattern set by the predicted life of the building itself. This period should be realistic and should normally be the period over which the building is expected to earn an income, for it is only during this period that the costs can be recovered. If the period of prediction for the building is limited to the period of expected occupation by the first owner, allowance should be made for the residual value. Buildings usually have a substantial life of the order of forty to eighty years. Their actual physical life (the period before physical obsolescence sets in) could often be much greater, but frequently they are demolished before the end of their physical life in order to make way for a more profitable use of the site (financial obsolescence), or because it is found to be cheaper to clear and re-build rather than to adapt the building to meet a change in the requirements (functional obsolescence). The period over which the building is financed, or over which tax allowance can be obtained is, of course, quite irrelevant as a basis of cost prediction.

The annual equivalent of the initial cost of a building is not very sensitive to changes in the period of life unless the period considered is a short one. The higher the rate of discount the less the effect of the period of life. Thus errors of five or ten years in the predicted life will not make very much difference to the predicted equivalent costs when the life is fifty to sixty years or more. The shorter the life, the greater the effect of errors in determining it (Table 6.1). The errors in predicted costs, and hence in design decisions, are likely to be greater when the life of the building is taken as substantially

* Strictly in order to compensate for the loss of value where the rate of inflation is p, $(1 + i)$ should be multiplied by $(1 + p)$. Similarly, the real return is reduced by $(1 + p)$ where the rate of inflation is p. Unless the rates of inflation and interest are high, the error from simply adding or deducting the rate of inflation is small.

TABLE 6.1 PERCENTAGE ERRORS IN EQUIVALENT COSTS FROM OVER- OR UNDERESTIMATING LIVES*

	Equivalent costs		Percentage error from incorrectly assumed life	
Assumed life	Capitalized	Annual	Actual life 40 years	Actual life 60 years
20	12.5	0.080	+38	+52
30	15.4	0.065	+12	+23
40	17.2	0.058	0	+10
50	18.3	0.055	−1	+4
60	18.9	0.053	−9	0
70	19.3	0.052	−11	−2
80	19.6	0.051	−13	−3

* Rate of discount is 5 per cent.

shorter than conditions warrant than when the life is taken as longer than justified (Table 6.1).

Conservatism in fixing the predicted life does not reduce risks, but actually increases the risks of error in predicting the costs-in-use. Hence conservatism increases the probability of reaching wrong decisions. One of the most common reasons for predicting lives on a very conservative basis is in order to make some allowance for financial or functional obsolescence. To do this by shortening the predicted life is crude and misleading. For example, functional obsolescence in building usually leads to conversion rather than to demolition. The latter solution is usually only adopted in the case of financial obsolescence, for example, on very expensive sites where the value of the land is high compared with the value of the building, or where a large increase in site value can be obtained by redevelopment. Thus the redevelopment usually results in additional profits. The costs of conversion are merely a special type of cost within the life of the building. If the incidence of functional obsolescence is known at the time of the design, an allowance can be made and a decision can be taken on the extent to which adaptability should be built into the construction. This will be considered later.

Most buildings will have a normal expectation of life of about sixty years. As illustrated, the exact period to be taken for a normal life is not very important since the interest factors are not very sensitive to changes in the period at that length of life (Table 6.1). If the owner cannot predict the use of the building over such a long period, the period of predicted use can be taken but in that case an allowance is necessary for the resale value of the building. Portable buildings have rather shorter lives and may be erected in situations in which their use will be for a shorter period than their normal lives, possibly because the site will be needed for a permanent building. Again, in such cases allowance is necessary for the resale value.

THE LIFE OF BUILDING COMPONENTS

Whereas the natural physical life of a building is usually reduced by functional or financial obsolescence, the natural physical life of most building components is reduced either because it is cheaper to replace than to repair them, or by the life of the building itself. Plant, of course, also becomes functionally obsolete in the sense that a new form of plant becomes available which is either cheaper to purchase and operate, or which gives a service sufficiently greater than the existing one to lower the unit cost of its output. The natural physical life of building components is, of course, dependent on adequate maintenance.

Theoretically, the lives of materials and components should be determined on the basis of observed probabilities of failure but such data are rarely available. Often, the only information is in respect of the number which fail with no record of the number which do not fail or of the number at risk and it is difficult to avoid overestimating the rate of failure and hence underestimating the lives of the materials and components (Appendix C).

The usual convention is to attribute the life of the main element to the life of the component as a whole and to treat the renewal of the minor parts of a component as maintenance. Clearly, the life of a component or a material depends on the way it is maintained; more or less maintenance may extend or diminish the life. The use of a particular life for costs-in-use hence carries with it the appropriate programme of maintenance. In the absence of the observed costs for such a programme the costs can be estimated by visualizing the programme necessary to maintain the building component in order for the predicted life. For convenience, repairs and maintenance can be divided into renewals, that is, the replacement of particular minor components at particular intervals of time, and general maintenance and cleaning. The latter will also normally follow a broad regular cyclical pattern. The results of costing the programme can be checked against such maintenance cost data as may be available. For most types of buildings maintenance costs per unit of floor area average at about 1·5 per cent of first costs at constant prices. Up to a point they vary with age and also with planned life. Often maintenance provides an opportunity to fit more modern and higher standard components and this may raise costs by about a third.

While the normal life of many materials and components is generally recognized, this is by no means universally true. Moreover, frequently the comparison of costs required is between traditional and new materials. Possibly the best procedure is to list as many materials and components as possible which have generally recognized lives. The materials and components can be tabulated by the length of life; the lives of other materials and components can then be estimated by comparing the material whose life is to be assessed against the lives of known materials. The materials and components could be listed into groups with lives of one, two, three, five, ten, fifteen, twenty, thirty, forty and sixty years. The steps in years of life can be made progessively larger because the effect of an additional year of life on the discounted value becomes less and less as the life increases. The use of a list of this type simplifies the testing of the lives of items against other relevant items.

THE LEVELS OF TAXATION

The effect of taxation, grants and subsidies on the cost of buildings varies with the user, the type of building and the location. Taxation, subsidies and grants are transfer payments from the point of view of the community since they represent payments made by one part of the community to another and, therefore, do not affect the true costs, that is, the resources which are used. In Great Britain, government departments, government agencies and charitable bodies are not generally subject to taxation and do not usually receive grants or subsidies which are related to expenditure or decisions about buildings. Local authorities do not usually pay tax on general local authority services but they may be subject to tax on trading services. Often, however, local authorities receive subsidies and grants which are related to decisions about buildings. In Great Britain, housing subsidies have in the past been in part related to the number of storeys. Private persons do not enjoy tax allowances in respect of buildings, although, of course, interest paid by them for most purposes concerned with property is deductible from their taxable income. Annual expenditure on buildings used for business purposes is a business expense, so that account is taken of all payments for maintenance, cleaning and other services in calculating taxable profits. Industrial, hotel, agricultural and some transport and public utility undertakings also obtain allowances in respect of the capital costs of buildings and for their plant. These allowances take the form partly of initial allowances and partly of annual allowances, the capital cost being spread over the statutory life of the building or plant. The statutory life of buildings is generally shorter than the physical life, but a range of shorter periods are used for various types of plant. For example, initial allowances of 50 per cent are available on industrial building and 20 per cent of hotel building, with annual writing down allowances of 4 per cent.

Single allowances of 100 per cent are allowed on expenditure to meet fire safety regulations, for thermal insulation in industrial buildings and safety certificate work for a sports stadium. Additional allowances and cash benefits are also available; their amount and form tend to vary from year to year, and in some cases from one region of the country to another. It is of little practical value to list the tax regulations now in force since they vary substantially from time to time and with the situation. Tax regulations introduce another type of uncertainty for which allowance needs to be made. Interest paid by business for any purpose is also, of course, treated as a business expense. The allowances and benefits and the rates at which tax is levied, vary not only from time to time but also from one country to another.

The arrangements made by the building user to finance his building do not usually in themselves affect the design costs. However, some types of user are able to obtain finance more cheaply than others and some users effectively pay a lower net rate of interest than others because they are subject to a higher rate of tax. The financial arrangements made for buildings are often only a small part of the total investment arrangements. The overall effect on interest rates may be small and, in such cases, it may be better to treat such arrangements as financial transactions rather than as borrowing related directly to the building. Often it will pay to borrow the capital to construct a building even though the owner has the funds available. This possibility arises either because the owner's funds are invested under some form of contract made at an earlier date when interest rates were higher, or because he is prepared to invest his own money in a form which carries higher risks than money borrowed for financing his buildings. In this way, he may be able to earn an additional risk premium. But this type of arrangement can be thought of as using the building as security. Such arrangements are not related to the building design and should not influence it.

The rate of tax paid varies from user to user and from time to time. At one extreme are building users who are not subject to tax, or whose incomes are too low to be liable to tax, and at the other extreme are the wealthy tax payers who pay the greater proportion of their incomes in tax. Tax rebates on interest paid or on business or depreciation allowances are calculated at the rate of tax paid. Allowance is necessary for expected changes in both the level and form of taxation. If no tax is incurred clearly no rebate can be obtained. Thus the proportion which net interest bears to gross varies considerably from one class of tax payer to another. Hence the rate at which building users exchange capital for running costs varies considerably. Other things being equal, the higher the effective rate at which tax is paid, the lower the net rate of interest and the more it is worth spending initially to save running costs.

The effective rate of taxation is influenced by the treatment of initial and running costs for tax purposes. Even in the case of industrial buildings the net equivalent effect of tax allowances is generally greater for items of running costs than for items of initial costs. Since no tax allowances are available in respect of the initial costs of commercial buildings, other than hotels is frequently pays to rent rather than to own the buildings required.

Consideration must also be given to Vat. While this broadly covers most goods and services, there are exceptions. For example, new construction is generally not subject to this tax, while repair and maintenance work usually is. Again special arrangements are made for most public authorities.

Tax regulations have been changed so frequently in recent years and vary so much from country to country that there is little value in setting out their provisions in detail or in proving tables for calculating tax savings. It is advisable to consult the tax expert for the owner or user of the building in each case. It is, however, worth considering some typical arrangements as an example of the necessary calculations.

Generally for industrial buildings the capital costs could be set against profits over the tax life of the building. Sometimes there has been an investment allowance, say 15 per cent, and initial allowance, say 25 per cent, and an annual allowance, say 4 per cent. The allowance for the first year would be taken as the sum of the investment allowance, the initial allowance and the annual allowance. On the figures given, this would be 44 per cent of the initial costs. The annual allowance thereafter would be 4 per cent; since the initial and annual costs would generally not be allowed to exceed 100 per cent, annual allowances of 4 per cent would be available for seventeen years after the first year, with a final allowance of 3 per cent in the nineteenth year. In the case of industrial buildings which were defined as plant, allowances equalling 130 per cent of the initial costs have sometimes been given. In districts defined as Assisted Areas, the investment allowances have been even more generous, 20–22 per cent and have been given as cash grants.

It will be appreciated that there would be lags in time between the earning of profits and the assessment and payment of tax. This would vary with the type of tax. For instance, it would have been longer in the case of surtax than in the case of income tax; currently this distinction has been removed. An example will illustrate the method of calculating the equivalent worth of tax allowances in the circumstances described.

Example 6.1 The effect of taxation on the net costs of an industrial building
Given allowances at the rates set out above, a tax lag of eighteen months and

an effective rate of tax of 40 per cent, find the equivalent effect of tax allowances on the initial and running costs of an industrial building.

For the Initial Costs the successive tax allowances would be:

54 per cent for the first year,
4 per cent for the second to twelfth years, and
2 per cent for thirteenth year.

Hence the discounted value of each £ of initial costs would be:

£40/100 . $v^{3/2}$ [54/100 + 4/100 ($v^1 + v^2 + \ldots + v^{11}$) + 2/100$v^{12}$]
= £40/100 (0·904) [54/100 + 4/100 (1·499) + 2/100 (0·444)]
= £0·4 (0·904) (0·84884)
= £0·322

Hence the discounted value of the allowances for tax purposes on the initial costs would be £0·322 for each £ of initial costs if the discount rate had been taken as 7 per cent net.

For running costs the tax allowances would be the amount spent each year. The discounted value would be

£40/100 . $v^{3/2}$ ($v^1 + v^2 + \ldots + v^n$) (annual expenditure)

where the life of the building is n years. The annual expenditure equivalent to an initial expenditure of unity would be:

$1/a_n$

Hence with a rate of discount of 7 per cent the capitalized value would be

£ 0·4 ($v^{3/2}$) . a_n . $1/a_n$
= £0·4 (0·904)
= £0·3616.

The real value of the tax allowances on the running expenses in this case would be about 12 per cent more than on those for initial expenses.

7
Problems in Costing

TYPES OF COSTS

While any type of cost planning involves estimating construction costs, the estimating of maintenance costs is less familiar. Maintenance work is usually carried out in small items of work and most items of overheads tend to be greater than for construction work. To the building user the costs of building work are only part of the costs of maintenace; the disturbance costs are often greater. These are the costs which arise from the temporary loss of usable space and from the inefficiencies which arise from working under disturbed conditions. Many other types of costs arise in servicing buildings in addition to maintenance costs. These include the costs of fuel and other consumable stores used in heating, lighting and cleaning, the labour used for maintenance, operating and cleaning, insurances and other management costs. The costs of operating within buildings arise in many ways. Usually in evaluating building designs only certain types of operation costs need to be studied. Yet other types of costs arise in considering the relationship between buildings and urban settlements, and buildings and the public at large. Some of the cost consequences of designs cannot be costed directly but only through the costs of restoring amenities lost as a consequence of accepting one design rather than another. Finally some consequences cannot be costed because their effects are personal and affect satisfactions rather than the resources required. The value of such satisfactions can often only be measured in comparative terms.

CONSTRUCTION COSTS

The traditional method of estimating building costs is to take off the quantities of each item and to apply unit rates taken from Bills of Quantities. There are a number of difficulties in using this method, [Appendix B].

Unit prices are not necessarily very representative of the prices at which the work would be carried out in the case of the designs under analysis. Contractors do not compete on unit prices but for jobs as a whole. The unit prices are relevant to the contractor only as a means of pricing work for interim payments and for pricing variations. As long as the unit prices are sensible and total to the contract price when grossed up with the numbers of units of work and the preliminaries, they will normally be accepted as a part of the contract. Usually contractors do not cost their jobs on the basis of unit rates but in terms of the materials, labour, plant and other overheads which they expect to incur. It is generally accepted that the most accurate basis of costing is to base it on the programme of operations needed to carry out the job as a whole. The contractor generally has neither the basis nor the incentive to provide realistic unit prices. Moreover, it is in his interests to put in unit prices which have the effect of bringing forward the rate at which payment is made and which minimize the prices of items likely to be reduced or omitted and maximize the prices of items likely to be increased.

There is no uniform practice in the treatment of the preliminaries to cover the preparatory and general work. The proportion of the price of this work which is reflected in the unit rates varies considerably from contract to contract. This element of the price can be spread proportionally over the unit rates. While this procedure is likely to result in too much being charged to some types of work, there is no other obvious course in the absence of detailed information on the build-up of the preliminaries.

Usually the designer does not prepare detailed plans of the specialist work. The designs for the specialist work are not usually available at the time the Bills of Quantities are prepared even when the work is carried out by specialist consultants. Frequently the designs for the specialist work are prepared by the specialist contractors. In neither case are unit rates usually available. The position in Scotland, where Bills are usually prepared for specialist work, is better.

It is not surprising to find that unit rates are very variable. Studies have shown that the coefficients of variation for the unit prices for similar units of work range from about 10 to 50 per cent; the range of prices would be about six times as great as this. Thus the price given for a unit of a particular item of work might be 100 per cent larger or smaller than the average of rates for that item of work. Clearly, little reliance can be placed on the unit prices from individual Bills. It is necessary to average the prices from a large number of Bills. In the past, prices have changed rapidly over time and it is difficult to obtain sufficient Bills which relate to the same date to provide an adequate sample. Usually the prices will need to be inflated to current levels before the average is found. The price indices available for repricing are themselves rather unreliable.

An even more fundamental objection has been raised against the use of Bill rates. While the material content of a Bill item is reasonably constant, the labour content depends on the way the operation is to be carried out and the way it relates to the other operations to be performed. It is claimed that the labour contents of operations are far less variable than those of items because the operations are based on the natural unit of work. The contractor normally plans his work in operations and records the time taken on this basis. He thus has the material needed to programme the job and cost the operations to be performed. This information is not available to designers unless they either consult the contractor during the design stage, which is difficult if the job is to be put out to tender, or change to Operational Bills.

Pricing by operations is more objective than pricing by items of work since the pricing relates directly to the work to be carried out and to the conditions under which it will be performed. The building elements used for costs-in-use analysis usually correspond closely with building operations. Operational pricing is related to the scale of work and to the other operations involved.

The design evaluation will often relate to groups of buildings rather than to the detailed construction of an individual building. A substantial amount of price data is now published for individual buildings. Data for developments are less easy to obtain. Building price data is not always representative because less data are published for standard buildings than for buildings of particular architectural interest. The variation in the prices of complete buildings is often greater than for units of measured work. This is partly because buildings vary greatly in their specification and partly because the price quoted often includes for work unrelated to the building itself. Prices also vary regionally. The extent and reasons for regional differences in price are at present very imperfectly understood. The evidence is contradictory and it is not known to what extent the observed regional differences are a result of permanent differences in site conditions and specification, or temporary differences in the levels of productivity and market conditions.

Books such as Spon's Architects' and Builders' Price Book and journals containing building price data, measured work rates and the prices of building and civil engineering rates are listed in the Bibliography.

A price information subscription service is provided by the Surveyor Collaborative for members by the Royal Institution of Chartered Surveyors.

Some useful price relatives are given in Appendix B. A strict definition of maintenance costs, limits the term to the work necessary to preserve a building or works, with its finishes and fittings, in its initial state, so that it continues to provide the same facilities and amenities as it did when it was first erected. In this sense maintenance implies the renewal of the building components, their repair and sevicing, decoration and cleaning. Building components are usually taken to include the fabric and finishings, the fittings permanently attached to the building (those which can only be detached by the use of a tool) and the mechanical and plumbing services. Strictly, renewal implies replacement by an identical item. Naturally items

Problems in costing 69

are replaced by the most suitable available. Any additional cost thus arising, or arising because an item is replaced before it is worn out, is not strictly a maintenance cost but a cost arising from improvements.

As explained in Chapter 6, the life of a component is related to the standard of maintenance: the predicted life implying an appropriate programme of maintenance. In costing the necessary programme of maintenance, allowance is made for the scale of the work both in itself and in relation to other work to be done at the same time. Maintenance work will inevitably be expensive as compared with comparable initial construction work. This is partly because of the reduced scale of the work, partly because of the greater difficulties arising from the need to strip out old work, from working in confined spaces and from making good and partly from the need which frequently arises to work overtime in the evenings, at night and at weekends. The costs of maintenance programmes can be checked against published and other data available for maintenance. Definitions vary and some maintenance figures include costs incurred for improvements.

While the maintenance costs of a building are large in themselves, they are made up of numerous small items and these are rarely recorded separately. Many attempts have been made to collect maintenance costs in a comprehensive form but with only limited success (Appendix B). The detail which would be of value for costs-in-use studies is rarely worth the trouble of recording to the building user. Nevertheless, the results available provide at least some guide to the levels of costs to be expected. Methods of analysing maintenance costs are discussed (Appendix C).

A substantial proportion of maintenance to dwellings is undertaken by householders, particularly by owner-occupiers. In monetary terms this can considerably reduce labour costs — real costs will depend on how the householder values his time (he may enjoy the work and value it negatively). Clearly, however, maintenance costs will be substantially affected.

DISTURBANCE COSTS

The disturbance costs can be estimated by setting out the changes in operations necessary while maintenance work is carried out.

In the productive sector of the economy the effect of disturbance will usually take the form either of a loss of output or additional expenses to ensure the same output. The cost of the lost output can be estimated by comparing the difference in expenses between normal and reduced output with the difference in revenue. The comparison would normally be limited to the production unit affected by the maintenance work, although allowance might need to be made for general overheads. Output might be maintained by working overtime prior to the maintenance work being commenced or by overtime during the period of maintenance. A reserve of space might be kept to allow for the loss of space during maintenance work. Additional expenditure incurred in this way and expenditure incurred for covering plant and other effects, would be charged as disturbance costs.

While in the consumption sector of the economy there are no losses of production, there are losses of amenity which can be costed even if they are not made good. There are also costs which arise from the need to move and protect furniture, fittings and other effects. The loss of amenity can be quantitied on the basis of the imputed rent of the space lost. The imputed rent would include for the depreciation of the building at replacement costs, interest on the capital (net of tax), maintenance and service costs, rates and insurances. It is often convenient to calculate the rent for the building as a whole and then to proportion is to the space lost as a result of the maintenance work. The expenses incurred in moving and protecting effects would also be included in the disturbance costs.

FUEL AND OTHER SERVICE COSTS

Heating costs can be estimated by computing the heating losses in therms and evaluating them in terms of the average price per therm. A perfectly sealed and insulated building would retain the heat once the temperature had been raised to the required level. Heat is lost partly through the fabric, partly from ventilation, partly from fortuitous heat losses from opening doors and other vents, and from the movement of heated solids, liquids and gases out of the building. The main sources of heat gain are space heating, process heat, heat generated by the lighting, the heat given off by the bodies of the people using the building, heat from materials entering the building and heat from solar gain. An estimate of the heat balance can be made from the constants which have been calculated from experimental studies.

Not all the heat gains are useful. How far incidental heat gains are of value depends on the flexibility of the heating systems. In buildings such as foundries and plastic press shops the total incidental heat gains are usually greater than the need for space heating and forced ventilation is often necessary to remove the excess heat. Heating systems cannot usually match the scale and speed with which the levels of solar gain change and much of the heat gained from the sun usually has to be removed through ventilation. Generally the heat gains derived from persons occupying the building can be utilized for heating purposes.

The first step in calculating the volume of space heating to be provided is to determine the extent to which the internal temperatures are to be raised over the external temperatures. This will depend on the use of the building and local climatic conditions — records of the latter are available locally. Usually a minimum temperature is required during stated periods during the day and week, for given months in the year. The temperatures at other times, unless a minimum is set because of needs arising from the materials or plant used, is usually the minimum compatible with the provision of the required levels of heating during periods of occupation at minimum costs. The hourly heat loads can then be calculated, allowances being made for heat gains. In this way, the information is built up for sizing the heating appliances and for estimating the total space heating requirements. The fuel requirements can be obtained by converting the heat loads into units of fuel by applying constants for their thermal content and for the efficiencies with which different appliances convert fuel to heat.

The air to be moved by forced ventilation and the requirements for conditioning it can be calculated by a similar process and the units of fuel required can be subsequently estimated.

The design of buildings will mainly affect the heating load through the fabric losses. These depend mainly on the area and exposure of the wall and roof claddings and their thermal insulation properties. The design may also affect the ventilation losses. Changes in the total heat losses will affect the fuel consumption and sometimes also the sizing of the heating system. Minor changes in design will normally affect the former but not the latter.

Fuel costs vary from one region to another and local tariffs often vary with the type of user and the periods of use. The type of heating system and fuels which results in the lowest costs will depend to some extent on these local conditions.

Lighting requirements again vary with the user, the way the building is to be used and with the locality, as well as with the design of the building. While electricity is now more or less the universal fuel for lighting, costs both for installation and for running vary very much with the form of the system and with its design.

Because of the way in which tariffs operate, it is important to consider the demand for all purposes together, for such fuels as gas and particularly for electricity. Information on fuel and other service costs and for maintenance is given in the references quoted in the Bibliography. Costs for maintenance and operating can be estimated by programming the operations as suggested earlier.

The costing of other building services can be estimated in the usual way by first examining the pattern of use. It is far more realistic to cost in terms of man-days and man-weeks than in man-hours, since in practice it is often not feasible to dovetail several duties together. Often no economy in labour is obtained from reductions in operation times because it is not possible for the operatives concerned to carry out any additional operations.

While sometimes cleaning duties can be combined with other duties, often cleaning can only be carried out while the building is otherwise not in use. Cleaning and servicing are often contracted out and cost estimates can be based on contractors' rates.

Estimated costs can be compared with the costs incurred by building users (Appendix B).

OPERATION COSTS

The need to estimate operation costs does not arise in costs-in-use studies as often as the need to estimate other types of costs. However, sometimes the plan and design of a building dominates the way an operation is carried out and hence its costs. The type of operations most affected in this way are handling and transport but supervision and management can also be affected. In such cases it is necessary to programme the whole operation in relation to the designs to be compared and cost out the programmes. Usually, such an excercise will need to be carried out in conjunction with a production engineer.

INDIRECT COSTS

Not all the cost consequences of design differences can be costed directly. Some of the effects of design differences are indirect and their effect on costs are rather uncertain. Factors of appearance and comfort are of this type. Their effect in the commercial and industrial sectors may be reflected in prestige and staff morale, through additional good-will towards the firm or organization and through contentment and its effect on output, quality of work, safety and labour turnover. The way in which appearance and comfort operates and affects good-will and contentment is very imperfectly understood and it is difficult to estimate the likely cost consequences.

While the costs of design features which improve the appearance and comfort can be estimated in the normal way, indirect means are often necessary for assessing their effect on operation costs.

Prestige will presumably be reflected in terms of a greater ease in raising capital, in obtaining credit and in securing business. Generally it will only be people who call at the building who are likely to be much impressed by its design features. Passers-by- will only be exposed to the exterior appearances; unless the building's exterior features are very striking, few will notice them. It is probably unlikely that a building's appearance will have much impact on the investors or potential customers unless they actually visit the building. Clearly, it is difficult to estimate the value of the effects of prestige treatment. One possible approach is to relate the costs of prestige treatment to the costs of raising capital and credit, sales and other aspects of the activities of the building users, and to consider whether savings in these costs are likely to be large enough to offset the additional costs of the prestige treatment. An alternative test is to relate the additional costs of the prestige treatment to advertising costs and to consider whether better results could be ontained if the extra expenditure were spent on advertising.

The possible value of improved staff morale can be approached in a similar way. Estimates can be made of the effect on operation costs per unit of increases in output and quality, and falls in the rate of accidents, rejections and labour turnover. It is then possible to estimate what changes in these directions would be necessary to balance the extra costs of raising the prestige and comfort of the building. Again it is desirable to consider the costs of achieving similar changes in operation costs per unit by other means.

Building design affects not only the costs and benefits enjoyed by those who own and use the buildings, but also the costs and benefits enjoyed by the public at large, that is the community interest. A change in the use of a site or a change in the building on it will affect the appearance of the neighbourhood, the daylight, sunlight and view enjoyed from neighbouring buildings and from the streets and open spaces, possibly the level of noise, dirt and air pollution and the density of traffic in the neighbourhood. Town planning is concerned with good neighbourliness and with whether the community on balance gains or losses from changes in land use. The direct gain in goods, services and and amenity to the building user, and the social costs and benefits need to be considered together. To some extent losses of social benefit are limited by the application of planning regulations, for example, those relating to the bulk of building and its height, and their effect on the quality of light and the traffic the site generates.

Appearance, of course, is largely subjective and a value cannot be placed directly on its worth. One approach is to estimate the cost of offsetting the losses resulting from a building of a poor appearance. For example, unsightly buildings can be concealed behind screen walls or plantings of trees and shrubs. The cost of this can be compared with the value of the amenity otherwise lost. Similarly, while it is difficult to measure the loss of amenity resulting from an increase in the level of noise, unless it results in space becoming usable, it is possible to estimate what the costs would be of protective measures to counter the increase in noise level. The cheapest protective measure is often to treat the noise at its source by the use of absorbent material or noise-proof barriers. It is difficult to protect people in the street and in other open places except by treatment at source. People in buildings can be protected by the use of sound insulation in walls and roof. Windows create a more difficult problem; a substantial reduction in noise level can only be obtained by the use of deep, sealed double galzing, the use of which creates the need for forced ventilation.

The effect of traffic can be measured through its effects on traffic movement, on access to buildings by vehicles and pedestrians, on accidents, on noise, vibration and on air pollution. The cost of traffic congestion can be measured in terms of delay and the value of time lost by vehicles, drivers and passengers, and by pedestrians. The effects on access to buildings can similarly be measured in terms of delay and its consequences. Despite the suffering and losses for which accidents are responsible, their incidence on short lengths of road are usually statistically too small to be measured reliably except over long periods of time. Nevertheless, the cost of even a single accident in terms of damage to vehicles and their users, and delay to other vehicles is considerable. While the cost of delay, the cost of restoring property, medical expenses and losses in terms of national income as a result of injuries and deaths can be evaluated, it is not possible to evaluate the human suffering. Often an alternative approach can be used. This consists of examining what needs to be done to offset the effects of a given change in land use on traffic and its consequences. The cost can be measured in terms of the costs of additional road widening, bridge and underpass construction, and traffic engineering.

Another possible approach to the evaluation of benefits lost as a result of changes in land use is through changes in the value of property affected. This method has a number of limitations. The two most important are that changes of prices of affected property do not reflect the loss of benefits to people who use the area other than as owners of buildings and that it is difficult to isolate the effect of changes in land use on the prices of buildings from effects arising from other causes.

VALUING IMPONDERABLES

By definition an imponderable is something which cannot be valued, at least in a quantitive way. However, implicit imponderables are valued whenever decisions are taken. While it may not be possible to put an objective quantitive value upon them, in the final analysis the person taking the decision between alternative designs cannot avoid putting his own value on aspects of the benefits left outside the formal costs-in-use analysis. The objective of design evaluation is to quantify as many of the consequences of the design as possible. As new techniques are developed fewer and fewer aspects of

Problems in costing 75

buildings and developments will be left as imponderables.

Where it proves completely impossible to value every aspect of a building or a development, even indirectly, there still remains the possibility of devising systems of marking which can be set against the balance of costs and costed benefits. The attributes can be set out in homogeneous groups and marks can be awarded according to how well the total requirement is met. Similarly, observers can be asked to assess the relative importance to be given to different types of attribute, so that a final assessment can be obtained on a percentage scale. Confidence in such a system would depend on the extent to which there was a consensus of opinion among a group of observers of the marks to be awarded. Such a system could be used to measure the likely reactions of users to buildings and developments. Since it is unlikely that users would be able to assess the satisfactions to be obtained from designs from the plans themselves, the assessment of plans would need to be made by experts trained in assessing the way planned buildings and developments would be likely to work. But it would be necessary to calibrate the markings of the experts against those of users. Users' opinions could not usefully be collected until they had gained considerable experience with the buildings or developments in question. Little experience of such systems of marking has so far been obtained.

8
Uncertainty and the Investment

THE UNCERTAINTY OF FUTURE VALUES

Since design cost problems are concerned with the costs of servicing and operating in the future, there is an inevitable degree of uncertainty about the values appropriate to many of the factors. The values appropriate to some factors are much more uncertain than for others. In some cases it may not be possible to find any basis for estimating future values; even so, a decision has still to be reached. The best procedure is to equate the costs-in-use of the design solutions to be compared so that it is possible to establish the value of the least predictable parameter or parameters for which the costs would be equal. If, for example, a new process for the manufacture of a component was in the course of development, the future supply price might be the least predictable element. Clearly, the new price would need to be less than the old as otherwise the process under development would not be adopted. The decision between the design solutions would depend on whether the fall in price required for the costs to be equal was greater or less than appeared probable. In other cases, the least predictable parameter might be the life of a new material. The life necessary for the costs to break even could be calculated and the decision based on the probability of this life being exceeded.

Sometimes it is worth while to accept a design solution more expensive than an available alternative solution because it is expected that the running costs will fall sufficiently in future to out-balance possibly higher initial costs and the higher running costs during the first years. The advantage of choosing the currently more expensive alternative depends on the running costs falling fast enough and far enough for its costs-in-use to be lower than those of the currently less expensive alternative over its life. This type of situation is only likely to arise when the running costs are large compared with the equivalent initial costs.

The choice between heating systems often involves problems of this type. For instance, generally the costs-in-use of directly used fuels such as solid fuel and oil heating systems are lower, on present cost levels, for continuous heating than for heating systems based on produced fuels such as electricity. But developments of nuclear power and other techniques for electricity generation give some promise of lower comparative costs in the future.

The uncertainty lies in whether such changes would result in a sufficient and early enough fall in prices of these fuels to offset the higher costs likely to be incurred during the earlier years of operating the heating system. The future price of fuels is very uncertain. It is necessary to consider not only changes in technology but also changes in accessible supplies, political and industrial relations. Futures are very difficult to predict.

Situations of this type can be found in other fields as well as in heating. For example, the growth in the use of a new system may result in large economies in the production of spares, cleaning materials and consumable stores. The effect may be to reduce the future operating costs of the alternative solution below that of the currently cheaper system. A similar situation could also arise if the costs of operating the currently cheaper solution were expected to rise relatively to the costs of operating the alternative solution.

Since the situation would arise because the annual equivalent costs of the alternative solution were greater than those of the traditional solution at the time of installation, costs could never break even over the life of the component or the building unless the annual equivalent cost ratio of the alternative to the traditional solution fell to less than unity. Hence if it were improbable that the ratio would fall to less than unity, the traditional solution would be the more economic. Therefore, the first step would be to examine the probability that this could happen. Since the costs of construction would have been met, any saving would be confined to the element of operation the cost of which was expected to fall relatively to the traditional solution. As a result the percentage fall in the cost of the variable element would need to be larger than the percentage fall in the total annual equivalent cost ratio.

Example 8.1 A preliminary test for the adequacy of a future fall in running costs
Suppose that the annual equivalent costs for the traditional design solution were made up as follows.

Construction	£300
Repairs and renewals	50
Fuel	150
Total	£500

and that the costs for the alternative design solution were:

Construction	£200
Repairs and renewals	100
Fuel	450
Total	£750

Building design evaluation

The initial ratio of the annual equivalent costs of the alternative solution to the traditional solution would be:

$$R_i = 750/500 = 1\cdot 5$$

A final ratio of unity, $R_f = 1$, other things being equal, would imply a total annual equivalent cost of £500, leaving £200 for fuel. This would imply a reduction in the price of fuel of

$$100\,(450 - 200)/450$$

that is, 55 per cent. This would be a substantial but not an impossible rate of improvement, since in the present test the fall could be over the life of the building or component whichever is appropriate.

If, in the circumstances of the case being examined, a study of the supply costs and probable changes in the methods of production suggest a fall in real prices of something greater than this ratio a more detailed examination of the comparative costs of the design solutions would be justified.

THE CONDITIONS FOR AN EQUALITY IN COSTS

The annual equivalent costs of the alternative to the traditional design solution have a value R_i. If the annual equivalent costs of the traditional solution are taken as unity, the corresponding costs for the alternative solution are initially R_i. They fall to R_f in t years in accordance with a given rate of reduction.

The capitalized costs of the traditional solution are:

$$\sum_{r=1}^{r=n} v^r$$

where n is the life of the building or the component and v is the rate of discount.

If the ratio remained constant for t years and then fell to R_f, the capitalized costs of the alternative solution would be:

$$\sum_{r=1}^{r=t} v^r.R_i + \sum_{r=t+1}^{r=n} v^r.R_f.$$

If the ratio fell linearly from the beginning to a value of R_f in t years the capitalized costs of the alternative solution would be:

$$\sum_{r=1}^{r=t} v^r [R_i - (R_i - R_f)(r-1)/(t-1)] + \sum_{r=t+1}^{r=n} v^r . R_f$$

The capitalized costs for an alternative solution where the value of R_i falls to R_f in t years according to some other law could be written down in the same way.

The values of R_f and t, for which the capitalized costs of the traditional and alternative solutions would be equal over the life of the building or the system, can be worked out. The choice between the two systems is then made on the basis of the likelihood of the ratio and the time necessary for equality being attained. Thus the point in the calculation at which uncertainty is the greatest is exposed and the decision is based directly on the evaluation of the uncertainty.

Example 8.2 A test for the adequacy of future falls in running costs
Suppose R_i is 1·5, that it is expected to remain constant for ten years, and then drop to $R_f = 0.8$ and that $n = 60$. Is this a sufficient set of conditions for the capitalized costs of the traditional and alternative design solutions to break even? Interest will be assumed to be at 5 per cent net.

The capitalized cost of the traditional solution would be:

$$\sum_{r=1}^{r=60} v^r = 18.9.$$

The capitalized cost of the alternative solution would be:

$$\sum_{r=1}^{r=10} v^r . (1.5) + \sum_{r=11}^{r=60} v^r . (0.8) = (1.5)(7.7) + (0.8)(11.2) = 20.5.$$

Clearly the costs of the alternative solution do not fall fast enough to make it cheaper than the traditional solution.

Example 8.3 Estimating the condition for equal costs
It might be asked how far the relative price would need to fall in ten years' time for the alternative solution to be cheaper over the life of the building. Again it will be assumed that R_i is 1·5, n is 60 and the rate of interest 5 per cent net. Equating the capitalized costs of the systems, we have:

$$\sum_{r=1}^{r=60} v^r = \sum_{r=1}^{r=10} (1 \cdot 5) \cdot v^r + \sum_{r=11}^{r=60} (11 \cdot 2) R_f$$

$$18 \cdot 9 = 11 \cdot 55 + (11 \cdot 2) R_f$$

$$R_f = 0 \cdot 66.$$

Thus, the ratio would need to fall from 1·5 to 0·66 at the eleventh year for the two solutions to be equal in cost over their lives and a little more if the alternative solutions was to be the cheaper.

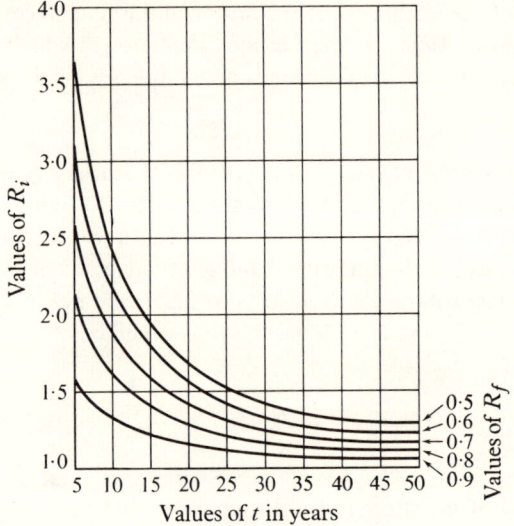

Figure 8.1 Decision diagram I. Values of R_i, R_f and t which satisfy the equation

$$\sum_{r=1}^{r=n} v^r = \sum_{r=1}^{r=t} v^r [R_i - (R_i - R_f)(r-1)/(t-1)] + \sum_{r=t+1}^{r=n} v^r \cdot R_f$$

where R_t falls linearly to R_f, $n = 50$ and the rate of discount is 5 per cent.

Since the saving can only possible be made in the running costs, the reduction in those would need to be greater than that implied by the fall in the ratios. Suppose that the costs were as given in Example 8.1. An R_f of

0·66 would imply a total annual equivalent cost of £(0·66). 500, that is £330. If the saving had to be provided by the fuel cost alone, a fuel cost of £30 would be implied, a reduction of 93 per cent, which would normally be most unlikely. Of course, the real cost of the traditional fuel might be expected to have risen; this would reduce the scale on which the real cost of the alternative fuel would need to decline.

In cases where the ratio falls gradually in value over a long period the arithmetic becomes rather tedious. Since in its general form this relationship applies to a large range of problems it is often worth while to calculate a range of values and express the results graphically. Figures have been calculated for a range of values of R_i, R_f and t, given that n is 50, that the ratio falls linearly with time and the rate of interest is 5 per cent net (Figure 8.1). Thus, given the value of R_i it is possible to read off the values of R_f and t which are necessary for the capitalized costs to break even.

Example 8.4 The use of Decision diagram I
Given a building with a life of fifty years, an initial ratio between the annual equivalent costs of the alternative and traditional solution of 2·0 and a rate of interest of 5 per cent, and the assumption that the ratio will fall linearly with time, the pairs of values which satisfy the equality can be read from Figure 8.1, for example:

$R_f = 0.5$ and $t = 15$, $R_f = 0.7$ and $t = 9$, and $R_f = 0.8$ and $t = 6$.

The values can then be related to the actual annual equivalent costs and the equivalent changes in the variable element of cost, for the condition of equality in costs; the cost changes implied can be worked out and the probability of their being reached can be tested. It is clear that the running costs of the alternative must fall, in relation to the traditional either by a very large factor or in a very short period of time.

THE UNCERTAINTY OF FUTURE REQUIREMENTS

Another type of problem in which some aspects are very uncertain arises in deciding to what extent to provide for future contingencies in designing a building. It may be necessary to consider not just changes in methods of carrying out operations but possible total changes in the use of the building. For example, consideration might be given to converting an office building for domestic purposes or to converting a multi-storey car park to production, storage or selling. Many cinemas have been converted to retail stores. Some features of buildings are costly to change in relation to their cost of installation at the time the building is first erected. Additional space, better forms of heating and particularly floor bearing capacity and clearance heights can all be provided at the required level more cheaply during the original construction than they can subsequently. Usually, however, additional facilities not only add to the costs of construction, but also add to the running costs. As a result, it is not always cheaper to provide the facilities ultimately required initially; sometimes it is cheaper to wait until the need for them arises. Moreover, there must always be some uncertainty as to whether facilities not required initially will be ever required, and uncertainty about the time which will elapse before the need arises.

The choice between initial provision of facilities thought likely to be necessary in the future and conversion when the need materializes is therefore a choice between a certain expenditure now and a contingency expenditure in the future. The main element of uncertainty lies in the period likely to elapse before the need arises. Since the need may never arise, this period may stretch to infinity. The problem therefore needs to be formulated so as to expose the period, the element of greatest uncertainty. The prediction is therefore treated in terms of finding the period at which the two equivalent costs break even.

Example 8.5 The costs of anticipating a future requirement
Consider the case of a single-storey factory building for which a clearance height of A is considered adequate. It is thought that in ten years' time the production process will be changed and a greater clearance height B will be necessary. The elements of the building affected by decisions on the clearance height are expected to cost £16 000 for height A and £4000 more for height B. For a building with clearance height A the maintenance and heating costs are predicted to cost £100 and £540 respectively, while for a building of height B the figures would be £160 and £800 respectively. The cost of raising the storey height to B after completion of the building is predicted to be £10 000. This figure includes both the costs of taking down and re-erecting the roof to the new height and the costs of disturbance, including inevitable losses of output. The rate of discount will be taken to be 5 per cent net.

The comparative costs are set out below (Table 8.1).

In this case the discounted costs over 10 years would be £332 less to build to meet current needs than future needs, even although this would involve large-scale alterations in ten years' time. The difference in costs is relatively small, only about 5 per cent, and might be a result of errors of prediction. There are therefore no very strong grounds for choosing one solution rather than the other. The choice really depends on the likelihood of the additional height being required in ten years' time. The longer the period before the

TABLE 8.1 COMPARATIVE COSTS OF INITIAL AND SUBSEQUENT PROVISION OF ADDITIONAL CLEARANCE HEIGHT £'s

Initial provision of height			Capitalized
Additional capital costs	4000		4000
Additional costs of maintenance and height	320	a^{10} 7.722	2471
Total additional costs			6471
Subsequent provision of height			
Costs of alterations	10 000	v^{10} 0.6139	6139

extra height is needed, the greater the advantages of building for current needs only. The need for the alteration may never arise. The change in needs may take quite a different form and any advance provision may be largely a waste of resources. Thus, allowance for the likelihood of the additional clearance height being required should be made. If there were only a one in two chance the contingency cost would be that much less.

Compromise solutions are, of course, possible. The foundations and frame could be constructed so that they were capable of supporting the additional loads which would result from greater height. This would add to the initial costs of construction, but reduce the subsequent costs of alteration should this prove necessary. Such a solution would add to the certain costs, but reduce the contingency costs. Another solution would be to build for present requirements only, on the assumption that there would be a move to another building should needs change. It would be necessary to compare the costs of moving — selling and other disturbance costs — against the costs of alterations.

This type of comparison can, of course, also be stated in general terms, so that the break-even point can be readily obtained for any problem of this type by plotting a range of values on a decision diagram. There are four variables to consider:

(1) the additional cost of building for flexibility;
(2) the additional running costs associated with a building for flexibility;
(3) the costs of conversion;
(4) the period expected to elapse before conversion is necessary.

Cost items (2) and (3) can be expressed as a ratio of cost item (1).

Thus

$$R_s = \frac{\text{additional annual running costs}}{\text{additional costs of building}}$$

$$R_c = \frac{\text{costs of conversion}}{\text{additional costs of building}}$$

t = no. of years to elapse before conversion is necessary.

The cost of building for flexibility can be taken as unity. The costs of building for flexibility expressed as capitalized equivalent costs are:

$$1 + \sum_{r=1}^{r=t} v^r . R_s$$

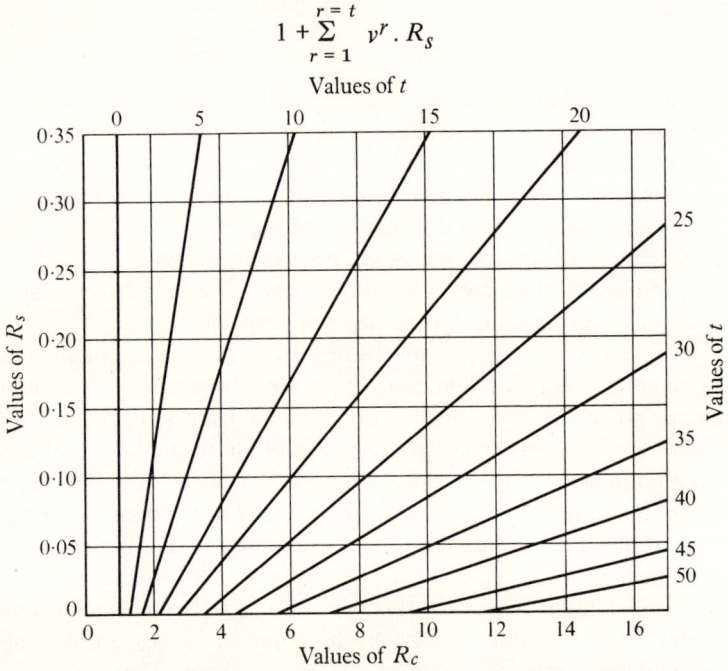

Figure 8.2 Decision diagram II. Values of R_s, R_c and t which satisfy the equation

$$1 + \sum_{r=1}^{r=t} v^r . R_s = v^t . R_c$$

where the rate of discount is taken as 5 per cent net.

while the costs of conversion also expressed in capitalized equivalent value are:

$$v^t . R_c.$$

Thus, the break-even point between the costs of the two methods is given by the equation:

$$1 + \sum_{r=1}^{r=t} v^r . R_s = v^t . R_c.$$

Usually it is possible to predict the values of R_s and R_c. The solution is, therefore, that of finding the value of t which satisfies the equation for the given values of R_s and R_c. A range of values of R_s, R_c and t with a rate of interest of 5 per cent net have been plotted (Figure 8.2). An example will make this clear.

Example 8.6 The use of decision diagram II
If this method is applied to the problem set out in Example 8.5, we have:

$$R_s = 320/4000 = 0.08$$

$$R_c = 10\,000/4000 = 2.5.$$

These equate when t is about nine years.
Decision diagrams can readily be constructed at other rates of discount and for other problems.

9
Prediction Errors and Interpretation

PREDICTION ERRORS

Inevitably the problems of prediction errors and interpretation have been touched upon in the earlier chapters. The problems must now be considered at greater length.

Cost analysis of buildings and developments can only be based on predictions, since with perhaps the exception of exhibition buildings, all buildings will remain in use for many years. No one can know with any certainty how the buildings will be used in the future or how they will function. Frequently requirements change substantially even during the building process. Inevitably, the costing can only be based on predictions about the future and many assumptions have to be made. This is unavoidable whether or not a conscious effort is made to evaluate the designs. Often no thought is given to the assumptions implicit in any decision about design. This is tantamount to assuming that current conditions will continue without change into the future: a most unrealistic assumption. The design can only be evaluated if the assumptions are made explicit. If the assumptions are explicit the effects on the costs of choosing given values for the parameters can be analysed and the results arising from the assumptions can be isolated.

The accuracy of the actual estimated costs is not of importance in itself, provided that the errors do not conceal significant differences or are themselves interpreted as significant differences. It is, therefore, necessary to use a technique which enables the analyser to differentiate between the effect of prediction errors and real differences.

Prediction errors are statistical errors and should not be confused with mistakes which arise from incompetence and carelessness. Broadly there are three types of prediction errors to be considered. These are errors of measurement, sampling errors, and errors in the assumptions.

Errors of measurement arise from the limitations of the measuring techniques. For example, if lengths of about 5 centimeters are measured with the aid of a ruler accurate to 1 millimeter, the results can only be accurate to 1 per cent. Hence, no significance can be attached to differences between pairs of measurements of 1 per cent or less. Sampling errors arise because no sample is ever completely representative of the population from which it is drawn. Hence there will always be some degree of uncertainty as to the exact value of the parameter in the population; this is the sampling error. Obviously assumptions, by definition, are always uncertain; there will be other possible assumptions which might have been made, although their likelihood may be less. The errors which could arise as a result of the assumptions need examination to determine to what extent they may invalidate the inferences drawn.

SAMPLING ERRORS

Usually data can only be obtained from samples; for example, samples of Bills of Quantities, samples of maintenance costs and samples of labour rates. Even when the items whose values are being measured are homogeneous, values vary from case to case. For example, the times taken by different bricklayers, and even the same bricklayers, to lay a thousand bricks under similar conditions, usually vary quite considerably. No estimate of the average time to carry out the task can be obtained from a single sample since there would be no way of determining whether the value was an extreme one. An estimate of the variability of the values can be obtained where the sample contains more than one item. The variability can be used to provide an estimate of the range of values about the sample mean within which the population mean is likely to lie. The greater the number of items in the sample, the narrower the limits within which the mean can be placed with equal confidence. The limits are also affected by the variability of the data and the degree of certainty with which they are to be fixed (Appendix D).

Thus, both in the case of measuring and sampling, errors will be present and results can only be correct to a certain percentage. Clearly, cost assessments based upon such figures are themselves subject to error. In the worst possible circumstances, in which all the errors were in the same direction, the percentage error in the final figure could be extremely large (Appendix D). The way in which errors aggregate can be seen by working the cost estimates using both the maximum and minimum values. Usually, however, errors are compensating and the errors in the final figures are not excessive. The rules for the propagation of errors are explained in Appendix D.

Example 9.1 The errors in an absolute difference in design costs
Consider the capital costs of two types of roof suitable for a given light factory building (Table 9.1).

(1) Suppose each figure is correct to ± 10 per cent, but no knowledge is available as to how the errors arose. It is then necessary to assume the most unfavourable circumstances; that is that each figure may be in error to the

Building design evaluation

TABLE 9.1 COMPARATIVE COSTS OF TWO ROOFS (£'s)

Building element	Design A (Flat roof)	Design B (Pitched roof)
(1) Columns and beams	31 800	37 200
(2) Roof trusses	33 600	34 800
(3) Roof covering, supports and rainwater goods	63 000	50 000
(4) Roof finish	34 000	–
(5) Roof insulation and lining	15 800	43 800
(6) Gable ends	–	2 400
Total	178 200	168 200

full 10 per cent in the same direction. This would give:

$$178\ 200 \pm 10/100\ (178\ 200) = 178\ 200 \pm 17\ 820$$

and similarly $168\ 200 \pm 16\ 820$

The difference between them is:

$$178\ 200 - 168\ 200 \pm (17\ 820 + 16\ 820) = 10\ 000 \pm 34\ 640$$

Clearly, the possible error is greater than the difference between the totals and no significance can be attached to the difference in their totals.

(2) Suppose, however, that although the errors in the figures are equally large, each estimate is derived from an independent sample so that the errors can be regarded as independent and likely to be compensating. The values for the two designs and their errors become:

$$178\ 200 \pm 10/100\ \sqrt{(31\ 800^2 + 33\ 600^2 + 63\ 000^2 + 34\ 000^2 + 15\ 800^2)}$$
$$= 178\ 200 \pm 8670$$

and similarly the value for the other design is

$$168\ 200 \pm 8380$$

The difference between them is

$$178\ 200 - 168\ 200 \pm \sqrt{(8670^2 + 8340^2)} = 10\ 000 \pm 12\ 060$$

The error is still greater than the difference and no significance can be attached to it.

(3) Suppose all the figures were taken from a price book which was thought to overestimate the prices for this type of work by about 10 per cent. The difference in the costs of the two designs would then be:

$$178\,200 - 168\,200 - (17\,820 - 16\,820) = 10\,000 - 1000$$

The difference would be significant.

(4) Suppose the figures for Design A were taken from a Bill of Quantities in which it was thought that the prices were overstated by 10 per cent while the prices for Design B were thought to be understated by the same amount. The difference in the costs of the two designs would then be:

$$(178\,200 - 17\,820) - (168\,200 + 16\,820)$$
$$= (178\,200 - 168\,200) - (17\,820 + 16\,820)$$
$$= 10\,000 - 34\,640$$

not be significant.

Examples of other cases can readily be worked out. Often it is convenient to compare in relative terms rather than in absolute terms. The same type of procedure is followed.

Example 9.2 The errors in a comparative difference in design costs
Suppose the costs-in-use of the two designs are as for Example 9.1. It is required to know by what percentage Design B is cheaper than Design A.

The relative difference in the most unfavourable circumstances is:

$$178\,200/168\,200\,[1 \pm (10/100 + 10/100] = 105 \cdot 9\,(1 \pm 20/100)$$

In this case the relative difference between the two costs is less than 6 per cent, whereas the possible error is 20 per cent. Clearly the result is not significant.

ERRORS AND COMMON ELEMENTS IN THE ITEMS COSTED

Frequently the building elements in the designs being compared contain common items. These do not, of course, add to the errors. As already stressed, elements which are common should not be included in the analysis. The presence of common items can only be exposed by analysing the operations which have been costed; this is, of course, a part of the costing process itself. For example, the heating costs of wall and roof units are frequently obtained by estimating the heat loss in therms and costing at a unit price per therm. As a result, several factors have common multipliers; for instance, the price per therm, the length of the heating season and the average internal to external temperature difference. The difference in the heating costs lies mainly in the U-values and in the exposed areas, both of which can be established within given and usually small margins of error. Steelwork is made up of standard units of structural steel, the erected prices of which are readily obtainable and not affected by limited differences in the work specified. Often a large part of the steelwork in alternative designs can be taken as common and hence excluded from the error term. Again, frequently the materials in walls, roofs and ceilings for design alternatives are similar. While the quantities are different, they do not differ sufficiently to change the unit price, so that the common element of material can be excluded from the cost comparisons. While labour differs, limits may be set to such differences. The unit price per hour of labour will usually be the same for each design.

A similar analysis of most items of running costs will reveal common materials and similar types of labour. The largest sources of error probably lie mainly in predicting changes in future costs and in the frequency with which operations need to be performed. Labour rates and earnings tend to move in related fashion, as do the prices of some materials. Special attention is necessary where materials have price levels which tend to move in isolation from general price levels, for instance, the prices of metals, fuel and of new materials.

Example 9.3 The effect of common elements in design comparisons
If Example 9.1 is re-examined it will be seen that element (1) Columns and beams, (2) Roof trusses, and (5) Roof insulation and lining, each contain large common items. There are also common items in (3) Roof coverings and rainwater goods. It will be assumed for the purpose of the Example that for Elements (1), (2) and (5) the whole of the materials and labours in Design A are also common to Design B. Only the rain-water goods are common to Element (3). It will be seen that after the elimination of these common items and allowing for independent errors the costs of the two designs appear to be significantly different. The net cost for Design A is:

$$94\,000 \pm 10/100 \sqrt{(60\,000^2 + 34\,000^2)}.$$

The net cost for Design B is:

$$84\,000 \pm 10/100 \sqrt{(5400^2 + 1200^2 + 47\,000^2 + 28\,000^2 + 2400^2)}$$

The difference between the costs of the two design is:

$$94\,000 - 84\,000 \pm \sqrt{(6000^2 + 3400^2 + 540^2 + 120^2 + 4700^2 + 2800^2 + 240^2)} = 10\,000 \pm 8820.$$

Prediction errors and interpretation   91

ERRORS FROM INCORRECT ASSUMPTIONS

Errors can also arise as a result of incorrect assumptions. It is often difficult to predict how long a building will remain in use, or how long a material or component will function. It is particularly difficult to predict durability for a new material or component. It is perhaps even more difficult to predict changes in comparative price levels. Difficulty is also experienced in predicting how buildings will be used in the future.

One method of dealing with the problem of uncertainty has already been discussed. This was to relate the costs-in-use to the factor about which most uncertainty was felt. The use of decision diagrams was illustrated.

Another approach to the problem of uncertainty is to examine how sensitive the cost comparisons are to changes in the predicted future values. This involves working with upper and lower limits for the factors whose values are uncertain. This, of course, makes the analysis more arduous. Often, however, the factors which are particularly subject to uncertainty, are those which affect the costs of all the designs more or less equally. Where this is so, absolute costs change when the values of the factors change, but the relative costs remain much the same. Thus, if the difference between two costs is being tested for significance, the error term is increased in the same ratio as the difference. This type of result is often obtained when a range of values are used for the life of the building, for the lives of materials and for the rate of interest. The extent to which the results are affected depends on the composition of the costs and in particular on the relationship between the initial and the running costs. It is worth while to explore the situations in which changes in the value of factors have little effect on the cost comparisons.

It will be supposed that there are two designs, A and B, (*a*) with initial cost to running cost ratios of 100:1 and 100:2 and (*b*) with initial cost to running cost ratios of 100:25 and 100:30. These sets of cases will be considered; for Set 1 the life will be varied but the rate of interest will be constant and no allowances will be made for taxation; for Set 2 the life will be taken as constant and the rate of interest varied, and for Set 3 the life and the rate of interest will be taken as constant and the net tax effect will be varied.

Set 1. The rate of interest will be taken as 5 per cent net and the life of the building as 100, 48, 28 and 14 years, giving present worths of future payments of 20, 18, 15 and 10 respectively (Table 9.2).

It will be seen that the length of life taken for the building does not have very much effect on the comparative capitalized costs-in-use of the two designs, unless the life is taken to be very short. It will be noticed that this is true whether the initial cost is extremely large compared with the running

92 *Building design evaluation*

costs, or only three or four times as large. The length of the life would never, of course, vary as much as it does between these four cases. The life of the building will generally be known within a few years. The shorter the life, the more accurately it is likely to be known and hence the range of comparative values will be reduced. Where the life of the building is taken to be a short period, the building will either be temporary and hence known within a few years, or an allowance will need to be made for the resale value which will offset the effect of the period of the life on the comparative values. Further, it will be noticed that where the initial costs are equal the effect of the life on the comparative values declines as the ratio of initial costs to running costs declines.

Set 2. The rates of interest will be taken as 7 per cent net, 5 per cent net net and 3 per cent net and the life of the building as sixty years, giving present worths of future payments of 14, 19 and 28 respectively (Table 9.3).

Reductions in the rate of interest have more effect on the comparative capitalized costs-in-use of the two designs when initial costs are equal and the ratio of initial to running costs is low than when it is high, although, of course, the comparative capitalized costs-in-use increase as the rate of interest falls. Thus, the lower the rate of interest and the higher the ratio of initial to running costs, when initial costs are equal, the greater the comparative difference between two designs and the more likely the difference is to appear significant.

Set 3. In this case the effect of taxation will be studied. The life of the building will be held at sixty years and the rate of interest at 5 per cent net. Three taxation situations will be considered; (1) the case of buildings in the public sector or in charitable or private occupation for which no taxation allowances will be assumed for buildings; (2) the case of buildings in industrial use for which allowances equivalent to about 25 per cent of initial costs, and 50 per cent of running costs will be assumed, and (3) the case of other buildings in business use for which allowances of about 50 per cent on running costs, but no allowance for initial costs will be assumed (Table 9.4).

The effect of allowances for taxation purposes on the comparative capitalized costs-in-use depends on the relationship between allowances on initial costs and those on running costs, on whether it is the initial or running costs which are closest, and on the ratio between initial and running costs. Clearly, the comparative difference in equivalent costs will fall if the effect of tax allowances is to reduce the cost of one type of element as compared with another, and if initial costs are equal or nearly so. In this situation, the higher the ratio of initial to running costs, the greater the effect of tax allowances on the comparative costs. Where it is running costs which are equal or nearly so, the reverse is true; the higher the ratio of initial to running

TABLE 9.2 EFFECT ON COMPARATIVE CAPITALIZED COSTS-IN-USE OF THE LENGTH OF LIFE

	Case 1a		Case 1b	
Life 100 years	Design A	Design B	Design A	Design B
Initial	1.0	1.0	1.0	1.0
Running	0.2	0.4	5.0	6.0
Total	1.2	1.4	6.0	7.0

Design B is 16.7 per cent more expensive than Design A in both cases.

	Case 2a		Case 2b	
Life 48 years	Design A	Design B	Design A	Design B
Initial	1.0	1.0	1.0	1.0
Running	0.18	0.36	4.5	5.4
Total	1.18	1.36	5.5	6.4

Design B is 15.3 per cent and 16.4 per cent respectively more expensive than Design A.

	Case 3a		Case 3b	
Life 28 years	Design A	Design B	Design A	Design B
Initial	1.0	1.0	1.0	1.0
Running	0.15	0.30	3.75	4.5
Total	1.15	1.30	4.75	5.5

Design B is 13 per cent and 15.8 per cent more expensive than Design A.

	Case 4a		Case 4b	
Life 14 years	Design A	Design B	Design A	Design B
Initial	1.0	1.0	1.0	1.0
Running	0.1	0.2	2.5	3.0
Total	1.1	1.2	3.5	4.0

Design B is 9 per cent and 14.3 per cent respectively more expensive than Design A.

TABLE 9.3 EFFECT ON COMPARATIVE CAPITALIZED COSTS-IN-USE OF THE RATE OF INTEREST

	Case 1a		Case 1b	
Interest 7% net	Design A	Design B	Design A	Design B
Initial	1.0	1.0	1.0	1.0
Running	0.14	0.28	3.5	4.2
Total	1.14	1.28	4.5	5.2

Design B is 12.3 per cent and 15.5 per cent respectively more expensive than Design A.

	Case 2a		Case 2b	
Interest 5% net	Design A	Design B	Design A	Design B
Initial	1.0	1.0	1.0	1.0
Running	0.19	0.38	4.75	5.70
Total	1.19	1.38	5.75	6.70

Design B is 16.0 per cent and 16.5 per cent respectively more expensive than Design A.

	Case 3a		Case 3b	
Interest 3% net	Design A	Design B	Design A	Design B
Initial	1.0	1.0	1.0	1.0
Running	0.28	0.56	7.0	8.4
Total	1.28	1.56	8.0	9.4

Design B is 21.9 per cent and 17.5 per cent respectively more expensive than Design A.

costs, the less effect tax allowances have on the comparative costs and the greater the differences of tax allowances for the two types of costs, the greater the comparative cost differences.

It will be appreciated that the extent of the effect of changes in the life of the building, the lives of components, the rate of interest, tax allowances and rates and future cost levels on the comparative costs depends on the ratio between initial and running costs and between the corresponding types of costs for the comparative designs. The more fundamentally the ratios vary,

TABLE 9.4 EFFECT ON COMPARATIVE CAPITALIZED COSTS-IN-USE OF TAX ALLOWANCES

	Case 1a		Case 1b	
Public	Design A	Design B	Design A	Design B
Initial	1.0	1.0	1.0	1.0
Running	0.19	0.38	4.75	5.70
Total	1.19	1.38	5.75	6.70

Design B is 16 per cent and 16.5 per cent respectively more expensive than Design A.

	Case 2a		Case 2b	
Industrial	Design A	Design B	Design A	Design B
Initial	0.75	0.75	0.75	0.75
Running	0.095	0.19	2.375	2.85
Total	0.845	0.94	3.125	3.60

Design B is 11.2 per cent and 15.2 per cent respectively more expensive than Design A.

	Case 3a		Case 3b	
Commercial	Design A	Design B	Design A	Design B
Initial	1.0	1.0	1.0	1.0
Running	0.095	0.19	2.375	2.85
Total	1.095	1.19	3.375	3.85

Design B is 8.7 per cent and 14.0 per cent respectively more expensive than Design A.

the more sensitive the comparative costs-in-use tend to be to changes in the factors listed above. Special care needs to be exercised where one design has a high initial cost to running cost ratio, and the other the reverse, especially where the ratios between like elements also vary. This type of situation is particularly apt to arise in comparisons of heating systems, mechanically and manually operated systems and long- and short-life materials. For example, installations designed to operate on natural fuels, such as coal and oil, tend to be expensive as compared with those designed to operate on

96 *Building design evaluation*

processed fuels such as gas and electricity, while the natural fuels themselves tend to be cheap in relation to their calorific values as compared with the processed fuels.

Generally, of course, the cost relationships of the elements will not be as variable as the cases examined in the previous paragraphs, not will the range of possible assumptions be as wide. Moreover, in practice the number of items will be large, the size of the effects of changes in assumptions on each one will therefore tend to have only a small effect on the comparative costs-in-use and often the changes will offset each other. Usually it will be found that quite large changes in assumptions will have comparatively little effect on the ratios between the costs-in-use, even although substantial changes occur in the absolute costs. Nevertheless, it is advisable always to examine the effect of possible changes in the assumed values in order to ensure that apparently significant differences are not the result of the values chosen for the factors rather than the true differences in the costs-in-use of the designs. Some idea of the effect of changes in assumptions in a typical costs-in-use comparison can be seen (Example 9.4).

Example 9.4 Effect of changes in assumed values on cost comparison
A comparison was made between two roof designs for the same factory building. Design A was for a flat roof with a covering of a decking, built up from asbestos cement sheets, covered with a felt finish on fibre board with mineral chippings, and with a soffit of plasterboard. Design B was for a pitched roof with a covering of asbestos cement sheets and lined with plasterboard. The initial costs of these two designs has already been studied in Example 9.1. The difference in the costs-in-use was found to be negligible. Variation analysis was the applied to ascertain whether a significant difference would exist if the assumed values of the factors were changed (Table 9.5).

As will be seen, the relative differences between the costs-in-use are comparatively small and it seems unlikely that changes in assumed values would be large enough to lead to the costs-in-use being accepted as significantly different.

The problem of errors from incorrect assumptions is perhaps most difficult where one of the design alternatives is based on a new material, component or technique for which there can be no relevant experience. In such cases it is usually necessary to work with the limits of the values assumed for the innovation. No difficulty will arise if the design based on the innovation is less expensive than alternatives when minimum values are taken for its life and costs and maximum values for its maintenance programme, or when it is more expensive when all the values are set at the

TABLE 9.5 EFFECT OF CHANGES IN ASSUMPTIONS ON COMPARATIVE COST RATIOS

Change in assumptions	Costs-in-use ratio Design A/Design B%
Basic assumptions	100.0
Life of building 80 instead of 60 years	99.9
Life of building 40 instead of 60 years	104.4
Period of prediction 20 years (50% resale value)	100.8
Interest at 7% instead of 5%	101.1
Interest at 3% instead of 5%	98.6
Tax relief 25% on initial costs and 45% on running costs instead of no relief	101.1
Increase renewal and annual cost of asbestos products by 50% and reduce renewal and annual cost of felt by 50%	104.3

most favourable levels. When the comparative costs break even for intermediate values, the decision can only be based on the probabilities of the relevant values.

ERRORS IN DRAWING WIDER INFERENCES

Building design evaluations have a wider interest and a wider value than derived from a single case study. Frequently inferences are drawn from one case to another and general rules are established on the basis of inferences drawn from a group of cases. In making such inferences care is necessary to ensure that basic assumptions and conditions are not overlooked. It is necessary to consider each factor which has entered the cost evaluation to ensure that none have been inadvertently changed in making inferences to a new situation. One of the most important set of conditions affecting the costs-in-use is the way the building is to be used. The hours of use and the time of the day and year in which they occur, the required level of heating and lighting, the climatic conditions, the patterns of internal movement and floor loadings are some of the factors to be considered.

Much better use can be made of natural light in a building that is used during all the hours of daylight than in one used only in the middle of the day or at night. Natural light will be less strong and of shorter duration in winter than in summer. More space for heating and heating for a longer period will be necessary in some parts of the country than in others. In some types of factory the volume of process heat is so high that it is not worth while providing much insulation in the walls or roof. In other buildings where there is little or no process heat, the volume of space heating is important and a high degree of thermal insulation is worth while. The higher the level of lighting required, the more likely a large area of roof glazing will be worth while, even though the load of heating is thus increased. The best shape, storey height and span sizes often depend on the way the operations are performed in the building, and the ideal dimensions may be very different even for a firm producing much the same products.

10
The Optimum Design and the Type of Client

THE ECONOMIC DESIGN

The most economic design is not necessarily the cheapest; it is the one which gives the best value for money. In the productive sector of the economy, the object is to produce goods and services, not for their own sake, but in order to make a profit. The final criterion for the entrepreneur is the difference between revenue and expenditure and the relationship of this difference to the capital employed. The building is one of these expenses. Since the building interacts with the other costs of production, activity or process carried on in the building, it is not sufficient simply to minimize the costs of the building itself. The object is to minimize the costs of the process as a whole; the costs-in-use being interpreted in a wide sense to include all the expenses of operating within the building which are associated with it, as well as the costs of operating the building itself. The value of the building as such does not arise; it is simply a production cost. In contrast in the consumption sector of the economy, the building is the final product which has a cost on the one hand and a value on the other. The value of a building is inevitably subjective and hence difficult to assess. However, since the determination of the optimum design is a comparative exercise, it is only necessary to compare the value features which differ and this is usually rather easier. The difference in value between two buildings can then be compared against the difference in their costs-in-use. Thus, the final choice between alternative designs can be made in terms of the differences between the ratios of value and cost.

TYPE OF CLIENT AND COSTS TO BE CONSIDERED

The items of costs which go into the costs-in-use analysis and the form of treatment depend on the type of client. Differences arise partly from the differences in the responsibility of clients for costs arising from their use of buildings and developments, and partly from the differences in the incidence of taxation, subsidies and grants. Such differences especially of the latter type, arise to a large extent from legal considerations.

The private client, whether an individual, firm or non-profit-making organization usually only has to consider such costs as arise within the curtilage of the site and from communication with the site. The costs to be considered are usually the costs of acquiring the site, the costs of construction, of maintenance and servicing the building, and some of the costs of operating in it and of communicating with it. The prices to the private client are the market prices which he incurs less the allowances against them which he can obtain as a result of the incidence of tax allowances and grants. The costs to be considered are much the same for public boards, for charitable bodies and for other non-profit organizations, since they have a duty to balance their accounts within specified limits. Government authorities, whether central or local, are in a rather different position. While they may balance their accounts in certain sectors, particularly in their trading sectors, they usually have a responsibility over a wide field and there is little advantage in balancing one set of accounts at the expense of another set. Moreover, in the last resort, government authorities exist only as machinery for satisfying the requirements of the community and have no function to operate particular sectors against the interests of the community. The community is concerned with all the values produced and with all the resources used and is not concerned with the way resources are transferred from one sector to another, except in so fas as the values are affected.

These points can most easily be made clear by examining the costs of building as they arise directly and indirectly to various groups of people in the economy.

The developer
As indicated in Chapter 2, the developer is concerned with the costs which he must bear and with the costs the purchaser will consider in determining the price he is prepared to pay for the property in question. The developer will normally purchase the land either freehold or leasehold and will bear all the costs of developing the site and of erecting the buildings upon it. The costs to the developer erecting for sale are thus all the initial costs of development and construction. Generally the purchaser is more concerned with annual than with initial costs and may take into consideration not only the rent, or its equivalent, but also the costs of maintaining, heating, lighting and generally servicing the building. Thus the purchaser will usually be more concerned with the costs-in-use than with initial costs. In these circumstances, the developer would need to take the ultimate costs into account if he is to be able to sell at the best prices in relation to his costs. The developer will also consider the incidence of tax on his profits; this may affect the price at which he is prepared to develop, even if it does not affect the design.

The investor
The investor is concerned with the difference between annual expenses and annual revenue and its relation to the capital tied up in the building. His annual expenses will normally include a ground rent or the equivalent annual cost of the land, the equivalent annual cost of erecting the building and the cost of the services he provides. The services may include some or all of maintenance, heating, lighting and such services as cleaning and portering. Whether or not all the building services are supplied by the building owner, there is still a need for him to consider them, since the tenant may include their cost in assessing the rent the building is worth. The investor will also take into account tax incidence.

The occupier
The occupier is clearly concerned with all the ways in which the building affects his costs. The ultimate costs to him will include the rent or the equivaient annual costs of developing and erecting the building, all the costs of servicing it and costs which arise as a result of interactions between the building and the way he uses it. The latter type of costs tend to be individual to the occupier; in some forms of use they may be of greater importance than for others. Clearly, buildings for which the design and layout have an important effect on the costs of operating within them and for which costs vary to a large extent from user to user, will be those which need to be tailored closely to the user's requirements and will not be very suitable for speculative development or investment.

The site will tend to affect the costs of using the building through transport costs to and from it — these costs will be related to distances and to congestion — and through access, circulation and storage of vehicles and goods. Circulation between and within the buildings on the site will tend to affect the costs of internal transport and communication, and the materials and parts which need to be stored: there may also be interactions with the volume of labour and with materials consumption. Shape, layout, floor, loadings, column spacings, room sizes, storey height and similar factors may all affect the degree of intensity with which the spaces can be used and hence the total space required. The internal environment; lighting, heating, noise, cleanliness and similar factors may affect the quality and speed of work. The appearance of the buildings may affect the attitude of the employees to their work and hence their efficiency, and the attitude of the public to the firm and hence the sale of the firm's products.

Where the building is used for consumption rather than production, the interest of the occupier will be comparatively less in terms of costs and more in terms of values. The occupier will still be concerned with the costs of operating the building, but instead of a concern with the interaction between the building and the costs of carrying out the activity within it, he will be concerned with comfort, convenience, appearance and other consumer satisfactions.

Private occupiers; persons, firms and private bodies have interests somewhat different from those of public bodies; government and other state institutions. The differences lie mainly in the breadth of the field of costs to be considered and in the treatment of transfer costs. Both types of occupiers are concerned with the costs which affect them and the differences in outlook relate to the extent of the costs which are considered to be within their interest.

Private occupiers. The private occupiers are concerned with the costs and values which enter into their cost-value equations. Consumers are concerned with the value for money to them and producers with profit on their capital, or in the case of non-profit-making concerns with revenue and expenditure and with the values they exist to create. Thus, they tend not to be concerned with the interests of persons and organizations outside their corporate activities. Within the limitation of the law, individuals and organizations will not usually be concerned with the way their buildings and their use affects other buildings and sites and their use. They will not generally site or develop their building so as to reduce costs and increase benefits to other building users and will tend to be indifferent to costs which they cause but which others bear; for example, the costs of traffic congestion and accidents, air pollution, noise, unsightlines and loss of business. Generally, charitable and similar bodies will act in a similar way as far as the interests affected lie outside the field which they were promoted to serve. In general this attitude is rational and inevitable. Apart from a few obvious consequences of their actions, for example, obstructing the public highway when parking and unloading, air pollution and the creation of noise and clutter, which public-spirited persons and organizations will seek to avoid, at least in their grosser form, the occupier can have little idea of the extent to which his building, and the use to which it is put, creates costs for others.

Public occupiers. In many respects public occupiers are in a similar position but their field of activities is wider. Public boards often have the duty either of making a certain level of profits in relation to capital, or of breaking even after certain costs are taken into consideration. Generally it is not their function to make losses themselves in order to protect others from losses. In fact, public boards, because of the scale and nature of their activities, frequently cause more public nuisance than many private occupiers; for example, airport noise and the disfigurement of the landscape as a result of mineral working and power lines.

Direct government bodies are in a rather different position. Three types may be distinguished. First, local authorities: they usually provide a wide range of services, some of which are financially self-balancing but many of which are at least partly paid for out of taxation, part of which is raised locally. Secondly, central government authorities; they also provide a wide range of services which they finance from taxation. Thirdly, government agencies; they provide specialist services using funds provided by the central government from the proceeds of taxation.

Local authorities broadly provide three types of service. First, trading services for which revenue and expenditure must usually be kept in balance; for example, bus services and catering services. Secondly, semi-social services for which, while revenue and expenditure must be kept in balance, a part of the revenue is in the form of central or local government subsidies; for example, housing. Thirdly, social and administrative services which are financed entirely out of taxation such as highways, refuse collection and libraries.

In so far as buildings are concerned two factors affecting their costs must be considered. First, the extent to which central government grants and subsidies are related to factors of design and, secondly, the extent to which decisions about design affect the costs of other services as well as the cost of the services for which they are designed. Central government specific grants and subsidies are usually given towards the finance of initial construction rather than towards running costs. They are usually fixed in relation to size and provide no encouragement towards economic designs. Often, in fact, the subsidies have the effect of reducing incentive towards economic design by operating so as to limit the amount spent on initial costs. In the case of housing subsidies in Britain, the subsidies have often provided incentive towards the use of uneconomic forms of structure.

In the long run local authorities meet the balance of their expenditure, not covered by rate support grants, from taxation levied locally. Politically it is desirable to limit the amount of these taxes. This cannot be achieved simply by balancing the building account. It is necessary to trace the consequences of the development through all the accounts of the authority. For example, a new housing development is likely to affect not only the costs of construction and maintenance of the housing but also the costs of servicing the estate roads and sewers, of handling the refuse of the estate, of creating improved roads from the estate to other parts of the town, of providing local authority and social services such as education and libraries, and sometimes of providing public transport services.

Central government authorities usually provide an even greater range of services than local authorities. The effect of their decisions about buildings can therefore have an even more profound effect on the costs incurred. For example, if government offices are located in the central area of the metropolis, locally they add to congestion and to the need for expensive highway works, and nationally they add to the need for commuter transport services and encourage central metropolitan growth. In so far as they result in increases in the use of subsidized materials, they increase costs on other accounts.

Goverment agencies such as hospital boards, provide services to the public and draw their revenue from the central government. In many respects they are in a similar position to the central government departments. If they limit their concept of costs to their own costs they may thereby raise the costs to other sectors of the government. For example, central hospital sites may generate traffic congestion while peripheral sites may lead to additional transport costs. In cases where building construction is met from grants not directly related to costs; the incentive is to design to minimize running costs even if this raises initial costs.

The community
Government bodies are only organizations set up by the community to act for them. The costs which matter to the community are costs measured in terms of resources, that is factor costs, costs which represent real goods and labour as distinct from market prices which include elements of taxation and subsidies. The community is concerned with the total use of resources and not just with the use and cost directly involved to the client authority. It is the total costs-in-use in this sense which the community requires to be minimized in relation to the values created.

TAXATION, SUBSIDIES AND OTHER GOVERNMENT INTERVENTIONS

If the national accounts are considered as a whole, the amount paid in subsidies can be set against the amount paid in taxes to give the net taxation. In this sense the collection of taxes and the payment of subsidies can be regarded as a transfer from one part of the community to another. The payment of a subsidy, or the addition of a tax, does not of itself change the amount of resources used to create a particular asset. Thus, from the point of view of the community, taxes and subsidies merely result in a transfer of payments from one part of the national community to another, and hence cause no direct drain on the resources.

To the client for a building, whether public or private, the incidence of transfer payments can be very important. Generally taxation enters into the costs-in-use of private buildings and subsidies into the costs-in-use of public buildings. The incidence of transfer payments varies from one country to another and from one period to another in accordance with changes in tax laws and with subsidy arrangements.

In the public sector, buildings for the central government are, of course, financed directly while those for local authorities and government agencies are either financed indirectly or subsidized or both. Often maximum prices are laid down by the central government which control the expenditure possible for constructing the buildings. Ceiling prices are fixed centrally in Britain for such buildings as schools, universities, hospitals and public authority housing. The ceiling prices are often fixed in terms of some unit of use such as pupil place or hospital bed, or in terms of prices per square foot. Such ceiling prices do not directly interfere with the designer's freedom to find the best solution except in so far as they are too low to allow the design offering the best value for money to be afforded. In great Britain, subsidies in the housing sector have often been related to the number of storeys and to total costs and as a result of the levels fixed have provided an incentive to multi-storey flatted construction as compared with houses on the ground, and to small as compared with large dwellings. Other general grants and subsidies sometimes have had the effect of encouraging local authorities to retain their population in circumstances in which this was not economic and have indirectly provided incentives to high density construction. Such subsidies and grants thus tend to distort the use of national resources, and to lead to local authorities acting against the community interest.

BUILDING SITES

Building sites (development land) are different from the other resources used in the construction of buildings, since they are not produced goods. Whereas all forms of construction use labour either directly, or indirectly in terms of labour used for producing materials, the land upon which construction takes place is not produced by labour, but is a natural product. Of course, labour is needed to convert it from one use to another, but the cost of any such conversion is included in the development costs. Thus, of all the factors of production used in providing buildings and works, land alone is not a produced resource.

The price paid for building sites is a real cost to the developer and to the occupier, whether public or private and its cost is an element in the costs-in-use of developers and occupiers. However, from the point of view of the community the price paid for building sites represents not the value of produced resources used in its development, but the transfer of money from one member of the community to another.

Nevertheless, the use of land as sites for building has a real cost to the community, but the cost must be reckoned, not in terms of the price paid to the owner, but in terms of the produced resources which must be used to replace the value of output lost as the result of using the site in one way rather than another. For example, if a piece of land is taken from agriculture the produce lost must be replaced by production elsewhere. This will involve production on marginal land or marginal farms where production costs in real terms, including delivery to the market, will be higher than on the piece of land used as a building site. When an urban site is taken for development, or for development in a different way, often traffic congestion will be increased; amenities will be lost, and need to be replaced elsewhere. Thus again conflicts arise between the best use of land for particular public or private purposes and its best use from the point of view of the community.

COSTS-IN-USE AND THE TYPE OF CLIENT

Clearly, in working out the optimum design for a development, it is necessary to take account of the economic circumstances of the person or organization for whom the building is intended. The nature of the optimum design will vary with the types and level of costs which they bear and with the way taxation, price limits and subsidies affect them. The designer will try to produce the design most suitable for their needs and circumstances. In fulfilling this function he may generate costs which other members of the community will bear and use resources in a way which, from the point of view of the comunity, is very wasteful. The individual client and his advisers cannot visualize the many ways in which the design may cause extra costs to others and can hardly be expected to increase their costs to save costs to others, or to ensure a better use of the national resources. The community can be protected in two ways; by laws which impose standards of behaviour and maintain a balance between conflicting interests, and by framing taxes and subsidies, and where necessary fixing price ceilings, so that there is some inducement to use national resources to the best advantage.

11
Design Evaluation in Practice

DESIGN AND DESIGN EVALUATION

A general discussion of the way design details affect the costs-in-use of a building has already been given in Chapter 3. Subsequent chapters have been concerned with the techniques of costs-in-use analysis. In the final chapters design cost consequences will be considered in relation to a range of design problems which arise in practice. Use will be made of knowledge built up from costs-in-use analysis to provide an appreciation of general design cost consequences and of the factors which need special attention.

NEW BUILDING OR ADAPTATION

The need for additional building or for a new building is often more apparent than real. The volume and form of space may be adequate for the process to be carried on in the building if the function is reorganized to make a better use of the space. Excessive space may be devoted to storage or circulation, the arrangement of work places may not make the best use of the natural light and some space may only be used for brief periods during the day. Frequently some changes to the building will be necessary; while no more may be necessary than the removal of partitions, often more radical changes will be needed such as the rearrangement of spaces, the lowering of floors and raising of beams, the removal of columns and the construction of extensions. In other cases no amount of redevelopment of the existing building will be adequate and either it will be necessary to rebuild or to move to different premises.

Thus theoretically three types of solution are possible. While in practice one or more of the alternatives may appear unsuitable, usually each alternative has advantages and disadvantages. A quantitative evaluation is necessary before a rational decision can be reached.

Usually the first step is to study the process and its organization. Often, as a result, machinery and equipment can be rearranged in a smaller space. Inevitably there will be a temporary loss of production — the term is used here to cover the provision of services as well as the output of goods. Of course, alterations are usually relatively expensive as compared with the equivalent amount of new construction. Alterations and the gradual reconstruction of a building often result in more interference with the production process than development elsewhere and subsequent removal. New buildings are usually less expensive to maintain and service than existing ones. Moreover, more labour and even materials and capital may be necessary to produce the same output in an adapted building than in a new one.

Supposing an existing complex of buildings, while adequate for the function in its current form, provides no suitable space for a new process. The new space might be for a group of automatic machines, a computer for an office, a laboratory for a school or an operating theatre for a hospital. The following types of solution might be possible:

(1) the reorganization of existing functions to release a space large enough to house the new process and its redevelopment to meet the new requirements;

(2) the building of an addition to the complex and the provision of communications with other parts of the complex;

(3) the splitting off of certain functions and their removal to a building purchased on another site together with partial redevelopment on the original site;

(4) the gradual redevelopment of the whole complex of buildings on the existing site; and

(5) development on a new site for the whole complex and subsequent removal from and the sale of the old site.

The present site might be either owned freehold or leasehold and paid for by the user, or owned and subject to a mortgage. In either case its cost is already contracted and it will not be affected by future decisions. The cost comparisons required relate to future costs, not to those contracted in the past.

The items of costs to be considered would include the following:

(1) the costs of reorganizing the function;
(2) the costs of adapting the building in the cases of alternatives (1) to (3);
(3) the costs of building additions in the case of alternative (3);
(4) the cost of complete redevelopment in the case of alternative (4);
(5) the costs of new construction in the case of alternative (5);
(6) the costs of purchasing additional property in the case of alternatives (3) and (5);
(7) the proceeds from the sale of property in the case of alternative (5);
(8) changes in maintenance and service costs — these will be slight in the cases of alternatives (1) and (2) and should show a saving in the cases of alternatives (4) and (5);

(9) the costs of the process carried on in the building — if the new process is successful a saving will be shown — this will be greatest in the case of alternatives (4) and (5);

(10) the costs of inter-site communication in the case of alternative (3);

(11) the costs of the loss of production during reorganization — this is likely to be highest in the case of alternative (4); and

(12) the costs of professional advice, loans to cover the costs of reorganization, rates and insurance.

Comparatives tables can be set out for the alternatives covering the types of costs listed above.

Example 11.1 Reorganization within the existing space as compared with the provision of extra space on the same site

Suppose that the annual equivalent cost of reorganizing the existing space is £10 000 a year but that as a result of replacing partitions, fittings and so on, maintenance and other running costs are reduced by £2000 a year. The annual equivalent cost of a new building, taking into account its longer life, would be £7000 with annual running costs of £3000. The costs of plant on an annual basis will be taken as £10 000 in the reorganized building and £8000 in the new building but annual operating costs will be reduced as a result of replacements of some existing plant by £1000 but splitting the functions will add £3000 a year (Table 11.1).

Thus reorganization, solution type (1) would in this case be £4000 cheaper than adding to the complex, solution type (2). Given that £8000 represents the annual costs of plant common to both solutions, the difference in costs exceeds 40 per cent and is unlikely to arise from errors in costing, especially as these other costs are of a common kind.

Solution type (3), additional development on a new site, would be even more expensive than solution type (2) on the assumptions given, since additional costs would arise for land and transport, and communications between the sites.

In the situation assumed, solution type (4) would not need to be considered since the reorganization of the existing space would be adequate and cheaper unless, quite apart from the additional space needs, there was a case for redeveloping the existing complex of buildings, quite apart from needs created by expansion.

Again in the circumstances assumed, solution type (5), would not need to be considered from the point of view of additional space needs, unless it would be likely to bring gains, either because the new complex possible on a new site would be cheaper, or because financial benefits could be obtained as a result of a change of sites. Such a possibility might be investigated at a time at which some redevelopment was necessary.

110 *Building design evaluation*

TABLE 11.1 COMPARATIVE ANNUAL EQUIVALENT COSTS OF REORGANIZING AND PROVIDING EXTRA SPACE (£'s)

Element of cost	Reorganisation	Extra space
Reorganizing existing space	+ 10 000	–
Savings on running costs on existing building	–2 000	–
New building construction	–	+ 7 000
Annual running costs of new building	–	+ 3 000
Purchase of new plant	+ 10 000	+ 8 000
Reduction of existing operating costs	–1 000	–
Additional operating costs from splitting functions	–	+ 3 000
Total	+ 17 000	+ 21 000

Example 11.2 Reorganization on the existing site as compared with new development on a new site
Suppose the annual equivalent savings of selling the existing site and purchasing a new one in a less expensive area were £100 000; the annual equivalent costs of erecting a new building with fees and interest were £120 000; costs on the same basis for new plant less the second-hand value of the existing plant and including for expansion were £80 000; that the equivalent savings in operation costs were £100 000; and that removing, loss of production and other once and for all expenses were the annual equivalent of £5000 on the existing site and £10 000 on the new site (Table 11.2).

Thus on the assumptions given it would cost an additional £25 000 a year to move to the new site — the costs of plant and the savings in operation costs would be the same in both situations. The most variable item is the gain from selling one property and purchasing another. This gain would depend on the purpose for which the existing site could be sold and, where and at what price a new site could be obtained. Other costs might vary with the site chosen. A comparatively cheap site might carry expensive development costs and poor accessibility; the latter would affect transport and staff costs, and perhaps the ability to obtain staff at all.

Of course, in some sectors of the economy the selling of one site and the purchase of another might make it possible to obtain capital by way of a mortgage, not otherwise available, and result in tax savings.

TABLE 11.2 COMPARATIVE ANNUAL EQUIVALENT COSTS OF DEVELOPMENT ON A NEW SITE AS COMPARED WITH REORGANIZATION (£'s)

Element of cost	Development on new site
Gain from selling existing site and purchasing new one	+ 100 000
Erecting new buildings including fees and interest	−120 000
Additional costs of moving	−5 000
Total additional costs of moving to new site	−25 000

GEOGRAPHICAL LOCATION

The geographical location of a building usually depends more on its purpose than on factors associated with the planning and design of the building. Some buildings serve tightly localized purposes, for example, buildings serving small communities and buildings associated with existing building complexes. The location of all buildings serving local communities is restricted to the locality. Perhaps only buildings serving national or international purposes have a wide choice of locality. Broad location is determined in relation to the comparative costs of communications with the sources of materials and labour, and with the consumers. The development of more efficient forms of transport and telecommunications tends to reduce the importance of location.

The determination of the economically best location in the commercial sector of the economy is relatively straightforward since this depends on the comparative costs of bringing together the factors of production. In the case of industrial sites this involves the prices of materials and labour at the site, including the costs of any special inducements to labour, and the site value of the products after allowance for transport costs to the markets. For service industries, such as retail trade, allowance is necessary for the volume of potential custom at the site. Sites for the buildings providing public services can be evaluated in relation to the real costs to the community of obtaining the services offered. For example, convenience for labour is more important than convenience for the public served in the case of tax offices, since most communications are by post and telephone. In the case of hospitals, however, the patients and their friends spend a great deal of time visiting the building and the real costs of this need to be set against the costs of staff travelling. While primary schools need to be located centrally to the housing area where the pupils live, residential colleges can be located almost anywhere in the region they serve. Again the cost consequences of location at different sites can be compared in terms of the factors described.

SITE COMPARISONS

Geographical location cannot be determined completely without taking account of the physical attributes of the sites themselves, since costs associated with the attributes of the site may be as important as general location. The price of the site is a real cost to the developer and to the user, although not to the community. Site prices are, of course, extremely variable. The extra cost of a site in a central area over a peripheral area may outweigh the effect of the costs of transport. The quality of the land also affects the costs of its development and the construction of the building. Running costs may be affected by the micro-climate and by the degree of atmospheric pollution. Transport costs may be affected by the local concentration of traffic as well as by the distances to be covered.

The cost items to be considered in evaluating sites include:

(1) the price of land;
(2) the cost of a building of the shape and form possible on the given site;
(3) the cost of the foundations and site works;
(4) the cost of providing the site with mains services;
(5) the cost of cleaning and maintenance;
(6) the cost of heating and light;
(7) rates and insurance;
(8) the costs of transport to and from the site for goods, labour, customers and other people who need to visit the site; in the case of buildings serving a public purpose this will include the social value of travelling time; and
(9) the social costs of the building other than on people who use the building; these costs include the consequences for other road users and for the supply of town facilities.

Example 11.3 The comparison of two sites for office blocks of a similar size and function

It will be supposed that Site A is a restricted site in a town centre currently consisting of three shops with accommodation above, while Site B is the large garden of a house now in bad condition at the periphery of the town centre. In terms of annual equivalent costs Site A costs £100 000 and Site B £50 000. Building on Site A involves a tall building and expensive foundations to overcome the problems of made-up land, while on Site B the office can be of two storeys on land behind the existing house; the annual equivalent costs of development on Site A will be £70 000 and that on Site B £40 000. Annual service and management costs will be much the same on both sites, about £50 000. However, because Site B is less accessible than Site A and provides less convenience for the staff, being both more difficult for travelling and less convenient for lunchtime shopping, additional inducements will need to be offered such as a free canteen and a bus to convenient points to public transport; these will add £40 000 a year to operation costs. Fares and other costs of meeting clients might add another £10 000 a year to operation costs (Table 11.3).

TABLE 11.3 COMPARATIVE ANNUAL EQUIVALENT COSTS FOR SITES A AND B (£'s)

Element of cost	Site A	Site B
Acquiring site	100 000	50 000
Construction	70 000	40 000
Additional operation costs	–	50 000
Total	170 000	140 000

On balance Site A is £30 000 more expensive in annual equivalent costs than Site B. This represents a difference of 15 to 20 per cent, much greater than the possible error, especially given the common elements on both sides. Thus the peripheral site would appear to be the better proposition.

The social costs would depend on the local circumstances. The costs of acquisition and most of the difference in option costs represent transfer costs. More profit and less public transport would be likely to be used in the case of Site B as compared with Site A. On the other hand, development on Site A might to enhance the town centre and remove derelict shops, while Site B would be left to provide more space for housing. These considerations might be reflected in the granting of planning consent.

SPACE REQUIREMENTS

Generally, the costs of constructing and servicing a building do not rise proportionately with the amount of facilities and space provided. A dwelling for eight persons costs only about twice as much as one for one person. The costs-in-use of factory buildings also show significant falls per unit area as the total area is increased, costs falling about 20 per cent when areas increase by a factor of ten. Moreover, it is often more expensive to operate in a limited space than in a slightly larger area. Needs change: buildings are usually more

114   *Building design evaluation*

flexible the more generous the spaces provided. For instance, a three-bedroom dwelling can accommodate a household of up to five or six people and smaller households of a range of compositions, whereas a two-bedroom dwelling will normally only accommodate households of four persons at the greatest. A large stock of small dwellings, costing only a little less, may need to be supplemented on a large scale as a result of quite small changes in household size. It may prove cheaper to provide generous space, for instance, dwellings with sufficient rooms for the needs of households slightly larger than average, than to closely tailor space to current needs.

The costs of extra space can usually be set against reductions in operation costs, or the costs providing for flexibility in some other way. Techniques for handling this type of problem have already been considered in Chapter 8.

BUILDING SHAPES AND FORMS

The geometry of buildings is well known and has been the subject of various studies; few of them, however, have extended the costing to the total costs-in-use. All things being equal, the costs-in-use tend to be at a minimum when the shape is as near as possible to a sphere and the enclosing surfaces are themselves at a minimum. But walls, ground floors and roofs have different costs-in-use per unit area and the cost relationships are complicated by the problems of structure and lighting.

For single-storey buildings, for which top lighting is acceptable, costs-in-use tend to fall as the plan ratio falls. The evaluation of the design for such buildings usually involves consideration of the costs of the structure, heating and lighting. As the plan ratio rises from 1:1, costs-in-use increase by about 10 per cent. Where top lighting is not applicable and natural lighting is to be provided, the depth of the building is limited by the strength of the light at the back of the room. This can be increased by raising the height of the windows and hence raising storey heights. This increases building and maintenance costs, the costs of heating and window cleaning. Problems of glare often arise; such solutions as baffles and supplementary lighting tend to add to building, maintenance and lighting costs. Raising storey heights can be avoided by making use of permanent supplementary lighting; this increases the costs of the lighting installation and its running costs. Usually it is thought necessary to provide levels of lighting higher than normally required for the tasks to be performed in spaces largely lit by artificial means and this naturally increases further the costs of installing and running the lighting. With very deep rooms and with internal rooms conditioned air usually becomes necessary. The additional costs of installing and running air conditioning plant and permanent artificial lighting can be set against

...ch might cease to be usable as a result of changes in the use of the ...g or in the way the function is carried out. The value of complete ...bility is often far less than the additional costs of providing it.

As spans are increased, the depth of the beams tends to rise and this increases the storey height and the area of walling to be built, maintained and heated. Of course, the space between beams may be utilized for fixing mechanical equipment, wiring and pipes and hence save space elsewhere. Alternatively, if the beams are left open, additional clearance height becomes available which might be useful for the accommodation of individual pieces of tall plant or for raising the height of glazing and increasing the depth of the room reached by natural light. The form of the roof frame may affect the form of top lighting where this is provided. For example, in one case it was found that a two-way system of beams was far more expensive than a one-way system, mainly because of the effect on the costs of providing natural top lighting. The type of beams used affect their maintenace costs as well as their initial costs and often the costs of the construction and maintenance of the soffit. The type of columns used also affect both initial and running costs, and the amount of floor space available for productive use. In some cases there are arguments for providing a floor area unencumbered by columns and this is, of course, quite feasible where the distances to be spanned are not too great but beyond a certain point increasing spans raises costs.

Example 11.4 Suppose a single storey area of 30 metres square is to be roofed; it is economic to support the roof entirely from the perimeter of the building?

It will be assumed for purposes of illustration that the buildings is in continuous use. Some form of space frame would be necessary. Two possibilties would be one based on a tubular steel frame with a deck and an internal covering, and a two-way post-tensioned concrete frame. Since the space could be lit from identical roof lights and lighting would cost the same, these can be ignored (Table 11.4).

The tubular steel design is about 8 per cent more expensive than the concrete plate design; in terms of initial and maintenance costs the difference is about 15 per cent. The cost of fabric heat losses per unit is common to the total costs-in-use and the common portion could be eliminated giving about a 10 per cent difference. (It is possible that the U-Value of the concrete plate could be made as good as that of the tubular steel design at little extra cost.) Overall evidence, therefore, suggests that the concrete plate is significantly less expensive than the tubular steel design. This would be even more true if the building was used for only a part of each day.

Design evaluation in practice 117

TABLE 11.4 CAPITALIZED 'COSTS-IN-USE' FOR A STEEL OR CONCRETE SPACE FRAME (£'s)

Building element	Tubular steel trusses (boarded and lined with insulated plaster-board)		Post-tensioned concrete plate (Two way)	
	Initial costs	Maintenance costs	Initial costs	Maintenance costs
Columns	1 800	—	34 000	—
Beams	29 200	800		
Cover support	5 200	200	—	—
Insulation	—	—	800	—
Internal finish and support	2 600	200	—	—
Subtotal	38 800	1200	34 800	—
	40 000		34 800	
Replacing fabric Heat losses (24 hour use)	7 400		9 000	
Grand Total	47 400		43 800	

Example 11.5 Another possible alternative would be to use a one-way post-tensioned concrete plate instead of the two-way system. These could be compared

This would be more complicated comparison than the previous one (Example 11.4) because the most efficient form of roof lights would differ as between the two designs (Table 11.5).

The two-way system is about 25 per cent more expensive than the one-system — a very significant difference without even making allowance for common elements. Thus the one-way system is not only the more economic form of concrete plate but a cheaper form of space frame in this case than the tubular steel trusses. Again the period of use of the building would not significantly affect the cost comparison.

Before proceeding with a space frame the client may still desire to know what if anything extra is being paid for an unencumbered floor area. One sensible test would be to compare the most efficient of the space frames, the one-way post-tensioned concrete plate with a conventional steel frame.

118 *Building design evaluation*

TABLE 11.5 CAPITALIZED 'COSTS-IN-USE' FOR A ONE OR TWO WAY CONCRETE SPACE FRAME (£'s)

Building element	One-way post-tensioned concrete plate		Two-way Post-tensioned concrete plate	
	Initial costs	Maintenance costs	Initial costs	Maintenance costs
Columns and beams	30 000	–	34 000	–
Rooflights	11 000	2 400	12 600	2 400
Insulation	800	–	800	–
Covering	5 200	200	4 800	200
Decoration	1 200	4 800	1 600	5 200
Lighting	3 200	2 800	5 000	4 600
Subtotal	51 400	10 200	58 800	12 400
	61 600		71 200	
*Replacing fabric Heat losses				
Roof cover	8 400		8 000	
Glazing	8 600		12 000	
Cleaning rooflights and lighting	6 000		10 000	
*Power for lighting	31 600		44 400	
*Tube replacement	8 200		10 600	
Grand Total	124 400		156 200	

* 24 hour day.

Example 11.6 A 'costs-in-use' comparison between a one-way post-tensioned concrete plate and a steel frame on a grid of 15 × 10 metres
The difference in costs-in-use exceeds 10 per cent without allowing for common elements other than those which are identical. Thus the conventional roof would be significantly cheaper. Again the length of working day for the building is not significant. The justification for spending an additional £3300 therefore rests on the effective costs of two internal columns. (A grid on a 10 metre basis, involving four internal columns, would be substantially cheaper still.) The amount worth paying to avoid an internal column would depend on the use to be made of the floor space and anticipated future uses. Some pieces of plant may be so large that no obstruction is feasible, while in other cases the inconvenience of internal columns may be negligible. An

TABLE 11.6 CAPITALIZED 'COSTS-IN-USE' FOR A CONCRETE PLATE AND CONVENTIONAL BEAM FLAT ROOF (£'s)

Building element	One-way concrete plate post-tensioned		Steel frame 15 × 10 metre grid	
	Initial costs	Maintenance costs	Initial costs	Maintenance costs
Columns	30 000		11 600	200
Trusses	–		6 400	200
Cover support	–		6 000	200
Insulation	800		–	–
Internal finish and support	–		3 200	200
Decoration	1 200	4 800	1 400	5 200
Rooflights	11 000	2 400	8 000	1 800
Subtotal	43 000	7 200	36 600	7 800
	50 200		44 400	
Replacing fabric Heat losses (24 hour use) Roof cover		9 200		8 400
Grand Total		59 400		52 800

estimate of the effect on operation costs is necessary. Clearly the removal of internal columns, should this become necessary, would be expensive. Whether or not it is worth providing a column free floor area in case this should subsequently become necessary is a probability problem – this type of problem has already been considered in Chapter 8.

The nature of the frame reacts with the fixings of claddings, partitions, soffits and plant, and hence affects both initial and running costs. While a frame makes it possible to consider a wider choice of other components, wall claddings, roof claddings, partitions and floors, as well as a greater freedom to plan and change spaces within the building, it may be more expensive in the long run to use a frame than some form of loadbearing walls. Except for tall buildings, loadbearing masonry is often practicable for blocks of flats and offices, as well as houses and small shops. In such cases neither large spans nor flexible spaces are usually necessary. The sizes of the openings will affect the costs of loadbearing external walls. Where the openings are large any cost advantages of not using a frame will be reduced. Loadbearing walls take more space than some forms of curtain walling and will reduce the area of useful space. Thus could be costly on expensive sites, where the loss of rentable space would be important.

In most cases brick tends to be the cheapest form of wall cladding both to construct and to maintain; its thermal value is usually adequate. Cheap, lightweight walling, such as asbestos cement sheets backed with insulating plasterboard, are often cheaper where the walling has to be supported over openings, since the support of lintels and beams may become unnecessary or a lighter structure may be adequate (Chapter 5). The weight of walling can also be important in buildings of many storeys. Since it is usually relatively simple to add sufficient insulation to obtain a given U-value, the comparison of the costs-in-use of walling can usually be made in terms of initial and maintenance costs. Many curtain walling materials are both more expensive to erect and to maintain than more traditional forms of walling. Generally, painting and cleaning costs add considerably to the costs-in-use, and quite large additional initial costs can be incurred without the off-setting advantages of an easily maintained material. The benefits from using expensive wall claddings are often mainly in terms of prestige and appearance; benefits difficult to evaluate. It is, however, useful to know the relative cost differences and to compare these with the benefits, even if they cannot be directly evaluated.

Roof claddings and coverings affect the costs-in-use through the costs of construction, maintenance and heating (Chapter 5). They tend to interact more with the rest of the structure than wall claddings. Whereas the latter interact with the columns and beams and with the foundations, the former also tend to interact with the roof frame and lining. They also may affect the clearance height within the building and may necessitate a taller building. Some forms of roof have larger developed areas than others in relation to the area of building protected. Hence the heating costs will be affected through the area exposed as well as through the U-values. The difference between internal and external temperatures may be greater at the apex of a roof than at the height of the eaves because of the effect of the temperature gradient. The form of roof can also interact with the type of top lighting; this can be important for single-storey factory buildings which usually have this type of lighting. Often roofs cannot be seen from the ground and their appearance is of little importance.

Again, check lists can easily be prepared to cover the items giving rise to costs and values, and the costs and values of those which differ can be compared.

THE USE OF GLASS

The way glazing intereacts with other building components and with initial and running costs can be quite complex. Some discussion of these interactions has already been provided in discussing costs-in-use evaluations of other building components. As a cladding glazing tends to be expensive compared with other forms. Its initial costs are usually greater than the cladding in which it is set, its frame is usually expensive to maintain and glass usually needs frequent cleaning, if the planned light gain is to be obtained. While glass admits light and so reduces the necessity to use artificial lighting, it is a poor insulant against heat losses from the building and readily admits solar gain, which is often difficult to handle. Glass is a poor insulant against external noise. On the other hand, glass enables a view to be obtained, and often enhances the appearance of the building and improves the internal atmosphere. The balance of advantage from glazing depends to a large extent on the way the building is used. The value of the light admitted is proportional to hours of daylight during which the building is used. Thus the value of the light admitted in a building which is constantly occupied throughout the year, for example, a hospital, can be three to four times as great as for a building only occupied during the day-time for a part of the year, for example, a school. In contrast the heat lost through the glazing increases less than proportionately to the hours of use. This is because space heating is usually provided to some extent between the hours of use as otherwise it is not possible to provide the required temperature when the building is in use. Moreover, during the summer space heating is usually not necessary.

The value of the glazing depends on its position. Wall glazing tends to admit light of less and less value the closer it is carried to the floor, since it penetrates to less of the room. On the other hand, the heat losses are only marginally less closer to the floor. In most situations wall glazing has greater costs-in-use than the walling it replaces; these costs are increased in so fas as curtains and blinds are necessary and air cooling is required to offset solar gain. Where the hours of use are great enough and outside temperatures low enough, double glazing may give lower costs-in-use.

Example 11.7 Suppose a decision is to be reached about wall glazing for a rectilinear space of 225 square metres with two external walls
The external walls could be glazed continuously from floor to ceiling or from cill to ceiling, or be provided with conventional windows. Again it will be supposed that the building is to be in continuous use (Table 11.7).

If the common elements are removed the 100 per cent glazing solution costs £1480 compared with £880 for the 63 per cent glazing solution, the

TABLE 11.7 CAPITALIZED 'COSTS-IN-USE' OF WALLS WITH ALTERNATIVE GLAZING (£'s)

Building element	100% Glazing (continuous floor to ceiling)		63% Glazing (continuous sill to ceiling)		29% Glazing (conventional windows)	
	Initial costs	Maintenance costs	Initial costs	Maintenance costs	Initial costs	Maintenance costs
Solid cladding	—	—	720	160	1300	300
Windows and frames	2400	200	1800	120	440	60
Subtotal	2600		2800		2100	
Cleaning glass and wall	600		500		400	
*Replacing fabric heat loss	2900		2200		1200	
*Fuel for lighting	1800		1800		2000	
*Tube replacement	800		800		900	
Grand Total	8700		8100		6600	

* 24 hours per day

latter costs £2520 compared with £1040 for the 29 per cent glazing solution. The differences are clearly significant and substantial savings can be made by reducing the amount of glazing, conventional glazing being the cheaper of the three. Of course, it the amount of glazing was reduced too far artificial light would be necessary the whole time the space was in use. The costs for lighting and tube replacement would be substantially reduced if the building was used for the conventional working day but the pattern of differences would remain much the same. Under the same circumstances the costs of replacing fabric heat loss would be reduced proportionally. The differences in costs between the solutions would remain significant. Thus the conventional windows would have significantly lower costs even if the building were to be used for a conventional working day. Each solution would provide an adequate volume of light for most purposes; the costs indicate that little additional light of value is provided by the additional glazing. Generally the extra glazing would reduce the standard of comfort; unless continuous heating was provided along the windows in cold weather, cold off the glass might be unpleasant; the greater the area of glazing the greater the discomfort from glare and solar gain, and the greater the cost of blinds and curtains. In making a choice these disadvantages and the costs-in-use differences would need to be set against differences in aesthetic satisfactions.

The analysis of the costs-in-use of roof glazing is equally complex. Both the value of the light gained and the heat lost depends on the position of the glazing. Some types of roof design result in glazing with a much better balance between the value of light gained and the value of heat lost than others. While for some types of roof better value for money is obtained by omitting the glazing, generally it reduces the costs-in-use if roof glazing is provided. The greater the level of lighting required and the hours the building is used, the more glazing it tends to be worth using. The higher the difference between internal and external temperatures the less likely it is to pay to use glass in the roof. The higher the temperature differences and the longer the hours of use, the more likely it is that double glazing will lower the costs-in-use.

Example 11.8 Consideration of the cost effectiveness of glazing in a flat roof
It will again be assumed that the space to be lit is 30 metres square. Adequate side lighting is not possible because of the size of the space. The roof covering, support and finish is taken to be boards with felt covering and aluminium foil backed plasterboard to give a high U-value. The addition of roof lights adds to installation costs but reduces running costs. The question is whether the saving in the latter adequately off-sets the former (Table 11.8).

With a difference in costs-in-use of the order of 25 per cent, without

TABLE 11.8 CAPITALIZED 'COSTS-IN-USE' OF ROOF WITH AND WITHOUT GLAZING (£'s)

Building element	With glazing		Without glazing	
	Initial costs	Maintenance costs	Initial costs	Maintenance costs
Finishing and covering	2 600	600	3 200	800
Cover support	5 400	120	6 400	200
Internal finish and insulation	1 200	80	1 400	100
Decoration	800	3 000	1 000	3 700
Rooflights	10 600	2 200	–	–
Subtotal	20 600	6 000	12 000	4 800
	26 600		16 800	
Replacing fabric				
*Heat losses				
Roof		8 400		10 400
Glazing		8 600		
*Fuel for lighting		31 600		60 000
*Tube replacement		8 200		16 000
Grand Total		83 400		103 000

*24 hour day.

considering common cost elements, there is little doubt that the addition of roof lights in this case would be worthwhile. Suppose, however, that the building space was not used on a 24 hour day basis, but was used only in normal working hours. For every hour not used during the hours of darkness there would be an equal saving in fuel for lighting and tube replacement, thus the absolute difference in costs would be reduced, but the proportional difference would be increased. In the case of heating costs the reductions would be proportional and thus the cost gap would be reduced. However, even under extreme conditions where the building was used only when daylight was adequate and heating costs were halved, the difference in the costs woulf be about £24 000 and the non-glazed alternative would be nearly 70 per cent more expensive than the glazed. Thus the glazed alternative would provide good value for money in most circumstances. Attention in the design would need to be given to the problem of solar gain in the summer; the cost of blinds and openable side vents would not add substantially to the costs. Consideration would also be necessary to the possibilities of reducing heat losses through the glass by using double glazing.

Example 11.9 Would costs-in-use be reduced by using double glazing in the roof?
This example relates to the glazed roof examined in the previous example. In this case most of the building elements are identical and it is only necessary to cost the roof lights themselves, the costs of heat losses through them and the associated lighting costs (Table 11.9).

TABLE 11.9 COMPARISON OF THE CAPITALIZED COSTS-IN-USE OF SINGLE AND DOUBLE GLAZING (£'s)

Building element	Single glazing	Double glazing
Rooflights:		
Initial costs	10 600	14 000
Replacing fabric heat loss		
(24 hours day)	8 600	3 200
*Fuel for lighting	31 600	33 000
*Tube replacement	8 200	8 600
Total	59 000	58 800

* 24 hour day.

In this case the difference is marginal and well within possible prediction errors, in practice either might turn out cheaper. Double glazing would reduce the possibility of condensation but breakages would raise costs against the double glazing. Since shortening the working day would reduce heating costs proportionally double glazing would become relatively more expensive than single glazing as the length of the working day or required temperature were lessened.

It will be appreciated that in order to evaluate the comparative costs-in-use of different systems of glazing the costs are required of the following types of item:

(1) the extra over costs of introducing glazing into the fabric;

(2) the costs of maintaining and painting the frames and glazing bars and replacing glass as compared with maintaining the cladding replaced;

(3) the costs of cleaning the glass;

(4) the costs of summer colour wash to glass;

(5) the costs of installing, maintaining and cleaning blinds and curtains;

(6) the additional costs of the lighting installation, its maintenance, cleaning of fittings, tube replacement and electricity which would be incurred if no glazing were provided;

(7) the costs of replacing the heat lost through the glass — usually no addition will be required to the size of the installation and the additional costs will be mainly fuel costs;

(8) the costs of combating solar gain in the summer by forced ventilation or air cooling.

It is, of course, necessary to make allowance for the likely actual use of heating and lighting as distinct from the theoretical use. For example, usually solar gain is not sufficiently consistent to be used for heating purposes. The control mechanisms of heating plants are not generally sufficiently responsive to enable fuel savings to be obtained from this source. The use of methods of storing solar gain have been considered and can be analysed by the methods described here. The use of artificial light is not usually closely regulated in accordance with the levels of light provided naturally. In some cases, if no provision is made for lights to be switched off automatically when adequate light is being provided naturally, the expected saving from the use of windows will not be obtained.

HEATING SYSTEMS AND FUEL

Space heating is required to provide an environment suitable for working and for the process to be carried out. Active workers will not need such high temperatures as people sitting in their homes or in hospital. Heat is lost from a building partly through the fabric, particularly through glass, partly through ventilation, and partly incidentally through leaks in the fabric, entrances and materials, liquids and gases leaving the building. Heat is gained from the process carried on in the building, whether this is industrial, social or domestic, from the heat contained in materials brought into the building, from the lighting and other powered equipment, and from the bodies of people in the building. In so fas as the incidental heat load exceeds the heat losses, the problem will be to provide additional ventilation rather than space heating. Usually, however, additional heat is required in order to obtain the required temperature at the critical times. Where there is excess heat during the critical times of occupation the standards of thermal insulation can clearly be relaxed.

The critical times for heating vary according to the use of the building. While hospitals tend to require an even temperature for twenty-four hours a day throughout the heating season, most industrial and commercial establishments only have critical temperature requirements for about eight hours a day, five days a week. The critical heating period in some buildings, for example, some homes, doctors' waiting rooms and some places of entertainment, may be only for a few hours at a time. Some forms of heating have lower costs-in-use than others for continuous heating, while others have comparative advantages for intermittent heating. For intermittent heating, systems which are expensive per therm of heat may have lower costs-in-use than systems which, although less expensive per heating unit, lack flexibility. This is equally true for water heating. Electric fires may have lower costs-in-use for intermittent heating, such as the doctor's waiting room, or for intermittent topping up of background heating, than central heating systems based on cheaper fuels. However, oil- and gas-fired domestic pumped water radiator systems can often be operated on an intermittent basis.

The heating load may be critical to the size of the heating installation. A slight reduction in load may be sufficient to reduce the size and the cost of the heating plant. In such cases the saving resulting from a small increase in the U-value of the walling or roof, or a reduction in the area of glazing may be far greater than the average saving. The critical load may only arise intermittently and the costs-in-use may be reduced by providing a second form of heating for topping up at critical times. Where the heating load is critical for the sizing of the heating plant, a detailed analysis of the choice and siting of the heating units may be justified. Space is not always all in use throughout the critical period. In such cases the flexibility of unit heaters may lead to lower costs-in-use, even though their costs per therm of heat are greater than for a centralized system.

The form of heating interacts with the costs of constructing the building and with its maintenance and cleaning. Some forms of heating installation require special building constructions to house the plant and to store the fuel. Space may also need to be made available for the installation of the heating units and their connections and control units thus reducing the useful area of the building. The repair and replacement of some forms of heating installation is difficult without damage to the fabric of the building and its decoration. The costs-in-use are increased not only because of the builders' work, but also as a result of useful space being temporarily withdrawn from use. Moreover, cleaning is more difficult with some types of heating installation than others and some forms of heating necessitate more cleaning and decoration than others.

The costs of fuels are particularly likely to vary in relation to each other in the future and the form of heating with the lowest costs-in-use today may not be the cheapest in the long run. Changes in relative costs may not come soon enough to make it worth while to accept other than the current most economic form. Techniques for handling such comparisons were dealt with earlier (Chapter 8).

Changes in the price of basic fuels tend to affect each other; movements in the price of one tending to be followed by the prices of others either as a result of cutting profit margins or by allowing margins to rise, or through adjustments to output and hence to supply price. Since the basic fuels are used in the production of secondary fuels such as electricity, manufactured solid fuels and town gas, changes in the price of basic fuels, also tend to be reflected in the prices of secondary fuels. Thus fuel prices tend, at least in the long run to move together. What is important, of course, is not just the unit prices of fuel as purchased but the price per unit of heat consumed. This depends not only on the price of the fuel consumed but also on the annual equivalent of the costs of the heating appliance and the efficiency with which it converts fuel to heat and yields the heat where, when and how it is required. For example, while the generation of electricity from basic fuels is relatively inefficient and even though electric heaters are generally very efficient at converting electricity to heat, the direct conversion of the basic fuel to heat generally has a greater overall efficiency in terms of units of heat but not necessarily in terms of useful heat.

Fuel supplies and hence prices tend to be very volatile and forecasts of long term prices are hence very hazardous to make. The importance of accurate forecasts of future prices becomes less important as the rate of discount is raised, since less and less weight is given to future costs. When rates of discount themselves are volatile, it is safer to use a more normal rate of discount as a check, or at least to investigate the position if the rate were to fall after a few years.

HEATING AND VENTILATING SYSTEMS

Every building needs ventilation even if no heating is provided. Generally natural ventilation is present, the usually warmer air in the building escaping through door and window frames, flues and other vents, and the cooler air from outside being drawn into the building. A considerable proportion of the heat generated in the building is generally lost in this way. The amount of natural ventilation is usually much lower in buildings of modern construction than in buildings of an earlier period of construction. Doors and windows provide a more air-tight fit, flues are reduced in size or partly eliminated as the open fire gives way to central heating and electric heating. This can be a gain in the winter providing there are no sources of unwanted heat such as, process heat, an excessive number of occupants, an unduly high level of lighting or solar gain — it can, however, give rise to problems of condensation. Where there is excessive heat and there generally is in summer if not in winter, or air-movement is required, additional ventilation is necessary. In many buildings this can be obtained naturally by opening windows. This is not always possible or satifactory, for example, where the rooms are very deep, where external noise levels are excessive and where the buildings are tall and wind levels high. In some cases there is no choice but to use artificial ventilation by forced air or even air-conditioning; the latter would be necessary where a specially clean internal atmosphere was necessary or where for functional reasons the building had to provide wide spaces without roof openings, or where external noise levels were very high. However, in many cases there is a choice between a building designed to be satisfactory with natural ventilation or one for which artificial ventilation is necessary. Such a choice frequently occurs in the design of office buildings and sometimes schools and other buildings.

The decision to use mechanical ventilation or air-conditioning instead of natural ventilation tends to affect every aspect of the building; superstructure, engineering services and finishes. Buildings to be ventilated naturally must generally be narrow and not excessively high. The amount of glazing must generally be restricted to the amount necessary to provide acequate daylighting and artificial lighting levels kept to the levels necessary for functional purposes. The provision of mechanical ventilation or air-conditioning frees the designer from many design constraints. If a completely artificial environment is acceptable the building can be any shape and almost any weathertight cladding material can be used. The percentage of auxiliary space will generally be much greater where artificial ventilation is used, especially where air-conditioning plant is used, since this will take up much more space than purely heating plant. The loads on the building will also be much greater. Typically the cost additions for additional space for heating plant, heating and mechanical plant, and full air-conditioning are probably of the order of 2·5 per cent, 5·0 per cent and 7·5 per cent respectively. The costs of the heating and ventilation plants are two to three times as expensive as heating only and full air-conditioning plants four to five times as expensive. Thus mechanical ventilation may add something between an eighth and a twentieth to the first costs of an office building and full air-conditioning something between a third and perhaps an eighth to first costs.

Running costs are also affected partly because the volume of building and floor space to maintain is increased and partly because the maintenance of the heating and ventilating plant and fuel rise with the sophistication of the system. Maintenance costs rise broadly proportional to capital costs. Fuel for heating and mechanical ventilation is a third to half as much again as for heating only, and that for full air-conditioning is about three times as great.

Example 11.10 Suppose a commercial firm is considering the development of a new head office
It has narrowed its search down to two sites, one in a city centre and one in

TABLE 11.10 COMPARATIVE ANNUAL COSTS-IN-USE FOR OFFICE OPTIONS PER 100 SQ. METRES OF FLOOR AREA (£'s)

Type of cost	City centre site			Peripheral site		
	Mechanical ventilated	Air conditioned	Heating only	Mechanical ventilated	Air conditioned	
Land	1000	1000	400	400	400	
Capital cost	3000	3500	2000	2400	2900	
Maintenance	300	340	200	240	300	
Fuel and servicing of Mechanical installation	3840	4660	2610	3180	4020	
Fuel heating and ventilation	200	400	120	200	400	
Fuel lighting	100	100	100	100	100	
Servicing	240	320	200	240	320	
Communications	400	400	600	600	600	
Total	5240	6060	3620	4180	5020	

a private park at the periphery of the same provincial town. Suppose that the city centre is noisy and the site restricted but adequate in size given the plot ratio allowed, while the peripheral site is spacious and quiet but less accessible than the city centre site. On the city centre site a tall, deep building will be necessary and its windows will need to be sealed because of noise, involving either mechanical ventilation or air-conditioning. On the peripheral site the building must be kept low but otherwise can take any shape and form, and have natural or forced ventilation. Before making a decision the developer would require estimates of the costs-in-use. These would be based on the broad form and concepts of the site and building alternatives, and their operation, and would not be based on design details. The costing would aim to cover the major items of cost likely to be affected by the location and form of building and would not at that stage go into any detail.

The difference in costs-in-use both between building form and location are all substantial and are clearly likely to be statistically significant. Despite additional communication costs at the peripheral site, the saving in land costs are sufficient to make it the cheaper solution; savings on the costs-in-use of buildings add to the differences and other factors would need to be weighed very heavily to make the city centre site preferable, especially as a building with heating only would be feasible at the peripheral site but not at the city centre site. Again the additional costs of air-conditioning and to a lesser extent mechanical ventilation are sufficiently higher than those for natural ventilation to require considerable value to be placed on such forms of ventilation and on the differences in appearance in the building which they would make possible to justify their use.

LIGHTING LEVELS AND SYSTEMS

Today lighting installations usually provide a greater level of illumination than is strictly necessary for the tasks to be performed. Standards of lighting are concerned with more than levels of illumination. The quality of the lighting and the comfort it provides is also given attention. Some forms of lighting cause less glare than others, provide better colour rendering, warmth and brightness. While for some purposes special lighting qualities are required, generally high standard lighting is provided to raise comfort standards rather than to raise the efficiency level of the operations to be carried out in the building. It is, therefore, difficult to quantify the return obtained for the additional cost of a higher standard lighting installation. However, it is still of value to calculate the comparative costs-in-use of alternative lighting installations so that the differences can be related to the standards of comfort they are expected to provide.

Generally, the standard of the installation will be reflected in the number of lighting fittings, in their cost and in the units of electricity each will consume. Some forms of bulb and tube are less efficient at converting electricity into light than others. The more fittings required per unit of floor area, the greater the cost of cleaning, tube and fitting replacement. The range of costs-in-use for lighting for the same floor area is very considerable. An analysis of lighting systems suitable for a factory of a standard size indicated a range of over tenfold. The costs-in-use depend on the quality, the level of the illumination and the hours of use per year. The costs-in-use of some systems, quality for quality, are only half those of others. The most efficient system depends on the hours of use and the quality required.

The hours during which lights are used depend on the hours during which the building is used, on the natural light available and the use made of it. Hence, as explained earlier, the lighting system interacts with the form and quantity of glazing and with the physical attributes of the site; freedom from obstructions, atmospherical purity and freedom from cloud. The cleanliness of the glass, the absence of obstructions to light, and the cleanliness and colour of the surfaces in the building also affect the quantity of the light from each source which can be utilized.

The higher the level of illumination required the greater is likely to be the number of hours during which artificial lighting is required.

The cost of electricity for lighting varies considerably from one building to another with the tariff which is charged and with the way in which it is operated. In favourable circumstances industrial buildings obtain electricity for lighting much more cheaply than other types of buildings.

The higher the electricity consumption the greater the volume of heat generated. In some cases the level of lighting installed is so high that the heat generated becomes significant; additional ventilation may be necessary. Where the output of heat is consistent and in a suitable position it may be possible to make some use of it for space heating, but generally heating obtained from lighting is an expensive form of space heating.

Example 11.11 Suppose a decision is to be taken for the lighting system of an office with natural ventilation and use only during normal hours of work
The client is half persuaded by the arguments of advisers supporting the need for good quality of lighting and a high level of illumination. Before reaching a decision he wishes to examine the value for money provided by the alternatives and calls for comparisons over a range of systems and levels of illumination. Of course, the costs depend on the fitments required for the room layout involved; comparative costs between systems will not always be the same.

TABLE 11.11 COMPARATIVE EQUIVALENT ANNUAL COSTS-IN-USE OF LIGHTING INSTALLATIONS (£'s) PER UNIT OF FLOOR AERA

Type of system	Quality grading	Type of cost	Level of illumination			
			(1) 270	(2) 370	(3) 740	(4) 1480
Tungsten filament	A	Initial	100	130		
		Maint.	70	80		
		Fuel and lamps	100	200		
		Total	270	410		
Fluorescent Natural	A	Initial	250	320	400	
		Maint.	200	240	300	
		Fuel and lamps	60	100	370	
		Total	510	660	1070	
Fluorescent white	A	Initial	180	240	300	500
		Maint.	130	180	200	360
		Fuel and lamps	40	80	290	1000
		Total	350	500	790	1860
Fluorescent natural	B	Initial	140	180	260	
		Maint.	110	150	200	
		Fuel and lamps	50	80	300	
		Total	300	410	760	
Fluorescent white	B	Initial	120	140	200	340
		Maint.	100	110	150	250
		Fuel and lamps	40	60	240	900
		Total	260	310	590	1490
Cold cathode	B	Initial	180	220	400	780
		Maint.	120	140	250	500
		Fuel and lamps	50	100	250	1450
		Total	350	460	1000	2730

Not unexpectedly the costs-in-use rise substantially with the level of illumination, because the higher the level, not only does the number of fittings increase but the hours of use rise since the level of natural light is adequate for shorter periods. There is a considerable range in the cost levels which vary by a factor of ten. The relative costs with level of illumination are not consistent since some systems can be designed more economically for the particular building at some levels than others. Broadly the difference between quality grading is that quality A are glare corrected whereas quality B are not. There are, however, other differences related, for example, to colour distortion, which are generally not very important for offices. While the glare-corrected is generally more expensive than the other, some of the lower quality systems are actually more expensive than the better ones in some circumstances.

The relative costs would change if the lights were not used rationally. For example, if the lights were left on all day and nor regulated according to the level of natural light, the tungsten filament and cold cathode would compare less favourably in relation to the others than they appear to in Table 11.11. Comparative costing errors would generally not be very great since most of the cost elements contain large elements in common but cost errors could in effect arise because the most economic system for the particular situation had not been found. While the client would need to make up his own mind about the values he attached to the levels and grades of quality, he would need technical advice on the most economic system to meet his requirements.

FINISHES

As already mentioned, finishes interact both with lighting and with heating. They affect the insulation properties of claddings and their reflective properties. Generally, however, finishes are reflected in the costs-in-use mainly through their costs of installation, maintenance and cleaning. Floor finishes often have to withstand harsh treatment. Their costs-in-use arise from the need to repair and replace them, from the loss of useful space during maintenance, from the cost of accidents which can arise from slippery and uneven floors, from damage to decorative surfaces and goods arising from dusty floors and from the cost of their cleaning. Floors also affect the comfort of the building through absorbing noise, reducing fatigue and creating a sense of well-being. There is a considerable range of floor finishes which provide a large range of properties. The range in their costs-in-use is considerable. The range of other finishes is also considerable as are their costs-in-use. Decoration and cleaning use manpower rather than materials. Manpower is costly relative to manufactured goods and the cost relatives are likely to widen. Permanent surfaces which need relatively little attention are, therefore, likely to be economic even if expensive in initial costs. Moreover, maintenance and cleaning often interfere with the use of the space. Where a high standard of cleanliness is necessary as, for example, in hospitals, frequent thorough cleaning and redecoration could necessitate a large reserve of space for use during such operations. However, the actual life of a surface may in practice be much less than the physical life, since a change in decorative treatment may be required before the life is exhausted. Some finishes, for instance, some plastics and other permanent finishes, may have comparatively low costs-in-use even if only part of their potential life is used. Much depends on the way the building is used. Examples of estimating the costs-in-use of finishes have been given earlier (Chapter 4) and in a different context are given later (Chapter 13).

EQUIPMENT

Equipment not only costs money to install and to run, but takes space. On the other hand, it increases the convenience and comfort of a building and may help to reduce labour service costs. In some cases the choice of equipment has an impact on the design of the building itself. Lifts provide a good example.

The capitalized value of a lift operator over the life of a lift is usually quite large in relation to the initial cost of the lift, so that a significant addition to the cost of a lift installation is usually worth accepting to eliminate the need for a lift operator. The costs-in-use are worked out over the entire operation including the cost of the attendants who marshall people into the lifts. The elimination of lift operators might not reduce the costs-in-use if lift marshalls then have to be provided, or if the attendants can fulfil some other role, such as doorman, as well as operating the lift. In tall buildings a choice arises between alternatives based on different numbers of lifts of different sizes and different speeds. The choice can be critical during peak periods, when it affects the period passengers wait and the speed of the journey. The choice affects not only the costs of installing and running the lifts, but the space they occupy in the building and the costs of providing them. In some buildings, for instance, blocks of flats, the capacity of even the smallest practical size of lift (it usually needs to be large enough to accommodate furniture and stretcher cases) is large compared with the number of people to be carried at times other than peak periods. At such times the combination of size and speed may result in considerable real costs to those who live or work on upper floors. Erection and running costs can be reduced by grouping as many flats as possible around the vertical access core. This need can dominate the shape of the building. The comparison of alternative forms of providing vertical access hence involves the comparison of buildings of different shapes. There is also a range of methods for providing vertical access and handling of goods. Where the volume to be handled is small, a comparatively inefficient form of handling may have the lowest costs-in-use. Goods handling may again interact with the shape of the building.

Additional costs may not be justified even if time is saved. Time saving is only important if the time saved is sufficiently valuable. Some residents may have a high value on the time spent each week which might be saved by installing a more rapid lift: it is not certain however that they would value it sufficiently to be prepared to pay the additional rent to finance it. Short periods of time saved by staff are of no value if they are too short to be used for some other purpose. On the other hand, the cumulative time lost each week by staff waiting for lifts to take them to their place of work might be quite valuable and worth saving at a not inconsiderable capital and running cost. Again the cost of someone visiting a building each week, for example, to wind clocks, might be quite considerable over their life and it might be worth while to install electric clocks, even if they were much more expensive to install.

It will be appreciated that the principle of the costs-in-use comparison is widely applicable in the design of a building, in its equipment and furnishing. It has its place wherever lives, initial and running costs and benefits of alternatives differ. It can be applied to the choice between ranges of furnishings, for example, carpets and curtains, and used to determine to what extent higher prices should be matched with longer lives. Equally it can be applied to the choice of plantings, some of which provide a display much longer than others and which need less attention, although perhaps costing more to purchase.

12
Planning Evaluation

PLANNING COSTS AND BENEFITS

In the earlier chapters the emphasis has been on the interests of the developer, owner and user of buildings. No more than a passing reference has been made to the interests of neighbours either individually or collectively, that is to the community or social interest. Building developments inevitably confer benefits and losses on neighbours. Generally, neither the owners can obtain any return for benefits they confer on others, nor can neighbours obtain any compensation for inconveniences resulting from building developments. While some of the worst nuisances are prevented by Acts of Parliament and by local bylaws, generally the protection of the community interest is left to the official town planner and to the planning control which he exercises.

Official town planning is concerned with the development of the built environment in the interests of the community, that is with obtaining the best return for the national resources used. The maximization of social benefits in relation to the use of national resources is not necessarily achieved by maximizing the returns to the individual developers. There will be conflicts between the interests of the individual developers, the building users and the community at large. Methods of development which increase gains to the community may reduce the returns to the individual developers and building users. The costs-in-use to be considered by the town planner are the costs-in-use to the final consumer, that is to people as members of the community, rather than as producers or individual consumers. The interests of developers cannot be ignored because the powers of the town planner are largely negative. Planning can only guide development; development will only take place if it is in the interests of the individuals, firms and organizations wishing to develop.

The position of public developers is not as clear-cut as that of private developers. Public developers are as much agents of the community as town planners. There is no clear answer to the way in which conflicts between the interests of the public agency and the community interest should be resolved. Many public developers represent sectional interests, for example, the consumers of a fuel, telephone services, housing and road transport. The extent to which the consumers of particular services should make a special contribution to the built environment is no clearer than in the case of private developers, although there would appear to be no case for putting such public organizations in a specially favourable position. Local authorities have dual functions. Part of their function is to provide services to sectional interests. In functioning in this way they are not different from other public organizations. Local authorities also provide general services to all those living in their area. Town planning is one such service; other services are refuse collection, highways and sewerage. These are communal services; broadly they are supplied according to need and charged according to ability to pay. In providing such services there would seem to be little reason to give weight to the economy of the services where these conflict with the broad community interest. Conflicts arise, however, between the interests of the local community and those of the national community. The question is often raised as to the extent to which a local community should increase its expenditure in order to provide services largely enjoyed by people not contributing to local taxation. The strength of this argument is gravely weakened now that such a large proportion of local government revenue is met from the national exchequer. Where services are provided nationally out of general taxation, it would appear that the interests of these services should be subordinate to the interests of the national community.

It is clear that for many of the public developments the developer is in a similar position to the town planner. There is neither a revenue related to the services provided nor a set of personal satisfactions against which to set the costs of the development. In the absence of both a market test and a personal test of value, value for money can only be measured by evaluating the consequences of the development on the community. The benefit can be measured partly through the way other costs to the community are affected and partly through estimates of the consequences for the quality of living. Planning evaluations are particularly relevant to the development of roads, public transport, sewerage and water schemes and other developments for which market prices cannot be charged.

HOUSING DEVELOPMENTS AND DEVELOPERS' AND USERS' COSTS

The costs of a housing development to the developer usually includes the costs of the site, its development with roads and services, the costs of the buildings, landscaping, fees and interest. The revenue is either the price realized on selling the dwellings, or the rents (Table 12.1). Sometimes when the dwellings are leased the developer or owner provides for their maintenance and other services. The position of a public housing authority is not very different from that of a private developer, except that subsidies are usually provided by the national exchequer, by other tenants, and sometimes by the rate fund. The form of housing subsidies has been varied considerably from time to time. In the past they have generally been related to the dwellings actually developed but recent legislation has applied to the housing fund rather than actual housing developments. Subject to subsidies the public housing authority theoretically charges sufficient rent to meet the costs. Recent policy to hold down rents to control inflation has often resulted in rent revenue falling below expenditure even after allowance for central government subsidies; the loss is then borne by the rate fund. Often, however, the public housing authority pools all the expenditure and revenue from the housing it owns. Since the housing authority raises capital for housing by borrowing, the greater the rate of inflation and the greater the average age of their housing stocks, the lower the rents which need to be charged to balance the expenditure. The financial position thus often depends as much on the time pattern of development as on design. Private developers normally charge the market rent, subject to rent restriction, and try to ensure that each development yields a normal return.

It will be seen that the type of housing developed privately must largely conform to market requirements since the revenue, the rent, is the market price for that type of accommodation. If the expected costs of developing and servicing the dwellings, together with a normal profit, exceed the expected revenue, development will not take place in that form and on that site. For this reason there has been little private development for renting for the last half century. In contrast a public housing developer has far less market constraint on the type of housing to develop. National exchequer subsidies have in the past been scaled to offset, at least to a considerable extent, the additional costs of expensive sites and of using tall buildings. Authorities have also been able to use the pooled revenue from their housing account and grants from their rate fund to subsidize any dwellings whose development costs were unduly high. Thus the revenue account does not provide a test of value for money. One test of value for money would be to compare the market prices of the dwellings with the development and service costs. There are difficulties in using this approach. The market for the particular type of dwelling developed might be small or non-existent. For example, a small number of wealthy people are prepared to pay very high prices for quite modest dwellings in specially favoured areas. Because of this, private developers can afford to build expensively on high-prices sites. Most people cannot afford such high prices, and most dwellings would only fetch modest prices, even if they were developed expensively. Clearly, to price public authority dwellings at prices realized in only a few special cases, would be to over-value them. Moreover, it is difficult to price dwellings when the market is affected by rent controls and subsidized housing, and by the scarcity and falsification of values which these inevitably introduce. Some alternative method of valuing is therefore require.

One possible method is to value according to the attributes of the dwellings developed. These can be measured in terms of the number and size of rooms, the quality of the construction and finishes, the provision of equipment, the size and quality of private and public gardens and other external facilities, and the locality of the development. The last item could be measured in terms of the quality of the local amenities and the convenience in relation to the facilities provided by the town. The weights to be given to each attribute could be estimated in terms of the average values over all housing in the town or region. The object is to value according to the totality of the attributes and their reflection in the users' valuations and to avoid valuing in terms of costs. However, even on this basis the values accorded to the dwellings would not necessarily reflect the values of the community.

Example 12.1 Developers' costs and revenue
It will be supposed that there are two alternative ways of redeveloping a site near the town centre and rehousing the people living there. This area is a high density Victorian development of housing with local shops and other facilities and a few workshops. Most of the housing is unfit, but a few dwellings and most other property is sound. The site is not large enough to allow the provision of accommodation for everyone currently living there at densities acceptable today; some would need to be housed on a site at the periphery of the town; the number depending on the density of development adopted. Two alternatives are to be considered:

Case (1): high density development with only a small overspill, and
Case (2): low density development with a considerable overspill.

Alternative (1) requires less land than alternative (2), but involves the use of high blocks. It will be assumed that a small part of the central site would be set aside for non-residential uses; a small area would also need to be provided for non-residential purposes on the peripheral site.

The accounts set out in Table 12.1 relate only to the housing areas. They show the expenditure and revenue to private and public developers respectively. The rents charged by a public developer would be much less than those charged by a private developer, partly because of the effect of the various types of subsidies, including the power of the public authority to borrow at a lower rate of interest than a private developer, and partly because no one would accept the risks of private housing development for

TABLE 12.1 THE COMPARATIVE ANNUAL EQUIVALENT EXPENDITURE AND REVENUE OF TWO ALTERNATIVE HOUSING DEVELOPMENTS

	A. Annual equivalent expenditure and revenue to the private developer	£000's Alternative (1)	Alternative (2)
	1. Site	240	300
	2. Roads and sewers	52	70
	3. Buildings	984	670
	4. Landscaping	40	60
	5. Fees and interest	110	80
I.	Total expenditure to private developer	1426	1180
	6. Maintenance and services	260	200
II.	Total costs to private developer letting with full services	1686	1380
	7. Gross profit to developer including risk premium on cost of borrowing capital	380	296
III.	Rent to be charged by private developer	2066	1676
	B. Annual equivalent expenditure and revenue to the public developer	£000's Alternative (1)	Alternative (2)
	1–5. Costs of development	1426	1180
	6. Maintenance and services	260	200
IV.	Gross expenditure to public developer	1686	690
	8. Exchequer subsidies (Equivalents)	400	200
	9. Rate subsidies	100	40
	10. Contribution from housing account	86	40
V.	Net expenditure and rent charged	1100	1100

TABLE 12.2 ANNUAL COSTS TO TENANTS OF TWO ALTERNATIVE HOUSING DEVELOPMENTS

		£000's	
A. Annual costs to tenants of private housing		Alternative (1)	Alternative (2)
III.	Rents	2066	1676
	11. Rates (50p in the £ of annual capital cost equivalent)	844	674
	12. Travelling and other incidental costs	90	130
VI.	Total annual cost to private tenants	3000	2460
B. Annual costs to tenants of public housing			
V.	Rents	1100	1100
	11. Rates (as above)	844	674
	12. Travelling and other incidental costs	90	130
VII.	Total annual cost to public tenants	2034	1904

rent in preference to some other form of development unless there was an adequate margin over the costs. Whether such rents could be obtained would depend on the market valuation. If they were thought to be too high the development would not go forward or would result in a loss. If the rents satisfied the market conditions they would form the gross value from which reteable values would be calculated.

The costs of the alternative schemes to the tenants arise not only from the rents but also from servicing costs not covered by the rents, for example heating, from rates and from the effect of the location on living costs such as prices of consumer goods and travelling. The rents charged by private developers would need to be greater for Alternative (1) than Alternative (2) because of the greater expenditure involved. A public developer would normally levy the same rents as a matter of policy, spreading costs and subsidies over the entire stock of housing, or at least over the stock offering similar amenities. Since more people would need to be moved to the peripheral site under Alternative (2) than Alternative (1), the costs of travelling and other costs arising from a peripheral location would be greater for the latter alternative. Total user costs might be relatively less under Alternative (2) to the tenants of private developers than to the tenants of public developers. This would depend to some extent on the travelling resulting. The number of tenants subject to peripheral costs would be greater under Alternative (2).

Accounts in a similar form could be prepared for the non-residential parts of the development.

HOUSING DEVELOPMENTS AND COMMUNITY COSTS

As already explained, while the price of the site is a real cost to the developer and user, it does not necessarily represent the real cost to the community of changing the use of the site. This depends on the consequential changes which the change in land use involves. The development of housing would directly affect the costs of providing local authority services such as refuse collection, sewerage, education, social services and local roads. Often the local authority operates a bus service; the costs of this too might be affected by the development of the site. More than one local authority might be affected. This would depend on where the housing and the services required by the tenants were located. The real costs depend on the actual labour, materials and capital equipment used and are not affected by the origin of the revenue used to meet the expenses.

Similarly, the supply and cost of public utility services would be affected by the form of the housing development. Generally, costs will increase as density falls. The expenditure of such supply authorities as those for electricity, gas, telephone and water will be affected. Often no related charges will be levied on the developers or users, but the costs will be reflected in the charges for the services.

The form of the development may also affect the costs of other members of the community in various ways. Congestion on the roads and in public transport may be caused, particularly by differences in the densities and location. Similarly, effects may be felt in the costs of retailing and in providing other consumer services.

The value of the site itself in real terms depends on its previous use. If its previous use was for housing its real value can be measured in terms of the value of the accommodation it provided. The value would include allowance for the number of units of accommodation, their quality and their future expected life. The value of other buildings could be estimated in a similar way. Alternatively the value could be estimated in terms of the costs of providing accommodation elsewhere of a similar quality and quantity, and with a similar life expectancy. Since in practice new buildings would be provided, it would in that case be necessary to discount the additional value created by substituting new buildings for older ones with a shorter expectation of life. Where the land itself is used to provide a service, the value could be estimated in terms of the cost of obtaining the service elsewhere, for example, in the case of food production, of growing and delivering the same volume on other land at home or importing from abroad.

Again, while subsidies, grants and tax reliefs are real savings to the developers and users, they are only transfer payments from the point of view of the community and would not be included in the community's balance sheet.

Not all the consequences of housing development will be related to the use of resources; some will affect the levels of satisfaction enjoyed by tenants and others living in the area. In a free market the comparative satisfactions of tenants would be reflected in the relative rents they were prepared to pay. In the absence of a free market some attempt to assess the comparative satisfactions can be made as indicated earlier by awarding points for the attributes offered by the housing. It is even more difficult to evaluate the satisfactions of the rest of the community. Some progress might be achieved by means of social studies, but satisfactions are difficult to define and to measure. Moreover, it is difficult for people to compare their satisfactions about alternatives, especially where they may have had experience of only one of them. Designers and planners are better able to compare planning alternatives than the layman because they are trained to be able to visualize the appearance and working of developments from paper plans. It should be possible eventually to devise systems of pointing which would give reasonably uniform results. The evaluation of the experts might not, however, be in line with the mature evaluation of the users, and it would be necessary to compare the two sets of evaluations and to feed the experience back to those evaluating paper plans.

When a block of old housing is redeveloped, there is usually a considerable improvement in facilities and amenity. This is generally true whatever form of development is used. The new dwellings will normally provide better quality and housing for a longer period in the future than the previous dwellings. Thus a development normally results in a real increase in value. The size of the increase depends on the attributes of the existing housing as well as on those of the new housing. The major elements to be valued are the internal amenity of the dwellings, the effect of the form of the dwelling, the resultant effect on the amenity of the estate and the effect of the location of the estate. The value of the new dwellings therefore depends on the weight given to the form and location as well as to the basic value of housing space. The value of the existing housing is related to its amenity and expected life. Some allowance needs to be made for the gains and losses of satisfactions by the community at large, as well as by the housing users.

The better the quality of the existing housing, the greater its value and the smaller the net return from the development. In such cases the possibility of improving the housing rather than developing it will normally be considered. Since redevelopment will normally not interact with costs and benefits arising outside the estate, the evaluation is comparatively simple, and follows the lines discussed in previous chapters.

Example 12.2 Tracing planning consequences to the community
The cost implications of the two alternative developments considered in Examples 12.1 will now be examined further for the case of publicly provided housing. The analysis is extended from developers and tenants to other agencies which might be affected by the form of housing: local authorities and public utility authorities, and other members of the community. In the final account the social costs are abstracted from the earlier accounts in Tables 12.1, 12.2 and 12.3.

It is assumed for the purpose of this example that new schools and other amenities will be provided in connection with the new housing so that local government services to tenants will be more expensive after redevelopment than before. The extent of the revenue services provided by local authorities will not usually be much affected by differences in the form and location of the housing. Estate services will tend to increase in cost as the density falls and greater lengths of roads need to be cleaned, maintained and lit. Services are likely to be a little more expensive on outlying estates, although peripheral building might be on a very large scale. The costs of providing bus services will tend to arise in relation to revenue when outlying estates need to be serviced. Whether the net costs appear in Account A or B would depend on whether this service is provided privately or by a public transport authority. Additional roads and sewers would usually be necessary if outlying estates were developed. Public utility services also tend to be more costly when densities are lower and when outlying estates need to be serviced. The overspilling of people to the periphery and the extra movement involved might tend to add to the transport costs of other citizens. Other members of the community, that is members other than those living on the housing estates, would eventually bear extra taxation needed to cover grants and subsidies to those on the estates. They will also bear the extra costs to public utilities, not covered by charges to the users, and the rise in agricultural prices resulting from production being shifted from the land at the periphery (taken for housing) to other land which is less productive and convenient. In the final account D, all the transfer payments have been eliminated and only costs arising from the direct use of national resources are listed. This is the cost to

TABLE 12.3 THE COMPARATIVE ANNUAL EQUIVALENT COSTS-IN-USE OF TWO ALTERNATIVE HOUSING DEVELOPMENTS TO THE COMMUNITY (£000's)

A. Costs to local authorities (ex housing account)		Alternative (1)	Alternative (2)
	9. Rate subsidies for public authority housing	100	40
	13. Additional local government services to tenants	520	560
	14. Extra deficit on bus services	2	6
	15. Development of roads, sewers, etc., outside the estates	10	14
	Deduct		
	11. Rates on new property net of rates on existing property to be demolished	520	338
	16. Exchequer grants	100	100
VIII.	Net cost to local authorities	12	182

B. Costs to public utility authorities			
	17. Development of services	60	66
	Deduct		
	18. Excess service charges over supply costs	64	60
IX.	Net cost to public utility authorities	−4	6

C. Net costs to other members of the community			
	19. Transport and other incidentals	2	6
VIII.	Net cost to local authorities	12	182
IX.	Net cost to public utility authorities	−4	6
	20. Net addition to exchequer costs	500	300
	21. Rise in agricultural prices as a result of loss of land at periphery	4	10
X.	Net cost to other members of community	514	504

D. Net costs to the economy	Alternative (1)	Alternative (2)
2–5. Housing development	1186	880
6. Maintenance and services	260	200
12. Travelling and other incidentals	90	130
13–15. Local government services (net)	532	584
17. Development of public utility services	60	66
19. Transport and other incidentals	2	6
21. Rise in agricultural prices	4	10
XI. Net cost to economy	2134	1876

the community. It is, of course, the difference in costs which is of importance: inevitably there are included items which are common to both sides. Comparisons of other alternatives might involve not only different costs, but also different cost items, although the general form would probably remain much the same.

HOUSING DEVELOPMENTS, COSTS AND BENEFITS

In the above examples an attempt has been made to trace the cost consequences of the alternative housing developments right through the community. There remain differences in the consequences of the developments which do not affect the resources used, but do affect the satisfactions of those using the developments. Little is known about the way people evaluate forms of housing. Some evidence suggests that flats are generally valued lower than houses, but that the difference is probably relatively small, except, perhaps, in the case of flats in high blocks. On the other hand, there is evidence that centralness is valued. When most of the existing housing in a clearance scheme is unfit, the loss from the clearance will be small. The community at large might value high blocks at less than low blocks and houses, partly because they obtrude more, and partly because high density housing is usually associated with more noise. On the other hand, there might be objections to the loss of additional farmland at the periphery of the city, and those people living close to the additional development might object to the siting of the development. Overall it might be felt that the second alternative was worse than the first. In comparing the annual value of the satisfaction derived from the developments against the costs, an allowance must be made for the value of any additional local government services to tenants which are not directly related to the housing developments.

Example 12.3 Costs and benefits of housing

The main item is the value the tenants place on the housing itself. An allowance is also made for the value the rest of the community derive from the developments; this is particularly difficult to evaluate — in Table 12.4 it is shown as a difference. A deduction is necessary for the value lost as a result of the clearance of the original housing. Against the net value can be placed the real costs of providing the housing. The cost of local government services not provided directly in connection with the housing and hence not included in the tenants' evaluation of the housing is, of course, excluded. In the case of this example there is a small net loss in the case of Alternative (1). This indicates that the tenants' and community's valuation is less than the costs. In the case of Alternative (2) values created are markedly higher than real costs.

Because of the inter-relation between the various examples and the continuity of the argument, the need to consider errors has been left to one side. Clearly, however, the possible errors must be considered in each balance as in previous examples. The differences can generally be judged against far smaller totals than appear in the tables because of the large common elements.

HOUSING AND OVERSPILL DEVELOPMENT

Frequently housing is overspilled not just to the periphery of the home town but to that of another town. The consequences of such developments are naturally more far-reaching than in the situation considered above. Whereas in the case of a short distance move the people housed can normally use the same non-residential facilities as before, this is not possible where the move takes place over a long distance. Even for moves within the same town it may be necessary to develop new facilities, for example, shopping and primary schools, even although useable facilities are available near the former estate. This adds to the value lost and may reduce the net return. Often population is overspilled to new towns. In such cases non-residential facilities of every type need to be developed. Moreover, the costs of moving people, and commercial and social organizations and their effects can be quite considerable. During the period of movement and during the subsequent settling-in period considerable output is likely to be lost. On the other hand, new towns may function so much better than the large cities from which

TABLE 12.4 THE COMPARATIVE BALANCE OF COST AND BENEFIT TO THE ECONOMY

	Annual equivalents £000's	
	Alternative (1)	Alternative (2)
Tenants' evaluation of housing	1680	1616
Differential evaluation of community	16	0
Loss from clearance of existing housing	96	96
Net value of new development	1600	1520
Net cost to economy of redevelopment less cost of extra local government services	1602	1292
Net gain to community from development	−2	228

such overspill frequently comes, that there may be large reductions in the costs of operating the new town and of operating within it. However, costs of building services in the large city may not decline very much even in real terms because population has been marginally reduced; the facilities already exist and manpower may be little reduced. The revenue to support the services may fall to a greater extent than the costs of the services. Clearly the costs-in-use analysis needs to be very wide. The incidence of subsidies and grants to local authorities, and their expenditure, is also influenced in a complicated manner. These matters have been dealt with elsewhere and will not be considered further in this book.

COMMERCIAL AND INDUSTRIAL DEVELOPMENT

The social or community value of commercial and industrial development can be analysed on similar lines to that of residential development. The value to the developer and users can be estimated in objective terms since the development is required, not for itself, but for the contribution it will make to the profits of the firm. The costs-in-use analysis has already been discussed; but the development will also have consequences for the community. In particular it will affect the pattern of travel and transport. The siting will affect the distances which have to be travelled by workers and customers, and increase or decrase their travelling time and costs. The siting will also affect the congestion of traffic in the town, and hence the costs of transport and accidents, and the comfort of pedestrians and the users of the buildings in the areas affected. The form of the development will affect the costs of using buildings in the area, partly through the effect on traffic, as described above, and partly through atmospheric pollution, noise and other factors. Some of these effects can be measured in terms of their costs to the members of the community both individually and collectively, while others can only be expressed in terms of the value of the net change in satisfactions which results. These costs and values can be related to those accruing to the developers and users but, of course, all elements of transfer value are discounted. It may be found that the best solution from the point of view of the developers and users is not the best solution for the community as a whole.

PUBLIC DEVELOPMENTS

Much of development work falls into the public sector. Distinction can be made between public commercial development and public social development. Development by the nationalized industries, local government trading departments, and by other public utility organizations falls into the first class. Generally, developments of this class do not raise problems different from other commercial and industrial developments, although in some cases more attention may be given to the social implications. Public social development consists of developments undertaken for the community at large. Generally, the costs are met through taxation, few or no benefit-related charges being made. Benefits can, therefore, only be measured by studying the consequences on various parts of the community. Open spaces, roads, public health and public education facilities fall into this class.

For example, the open space for a given number of people of given ages might be provided in a number of locations and forms. Basically the need might be measured in terms of a given number of pitches, courts and acres of land for various purposes. These might be provided near the places of residence, the places of work or some distance away where, perhaps, land is cheaper and more easily obtained. The costs of developing the open space will vary from one site to another according to the nature of the site and the extent to which its size and quality necessitates drainage, levelling and perhaps decking. The cost of the site itself will depend on the uses displaced. The time and cost of travelling to the open space will be considered and the costs of any congestion resulting from its location. Generally, open space is accepted as an improvement to the locality, but it may create noise and other nuisances which will reduce its desirability. The benefit it provides will be reduced if its siting reduces the number of attendances.

The widening and development of new roads results in land being lost from other uses and in the use of resources for construction and maintenance. It benefits transport through providing a faster and safer route for traffic formerly using other roads, by reductions in the congestion on those other roads and by providing road capacity for journeys formerly not attempted. The development of the roads, however, may result in additional congestion on other parts of the route to which they contribute. Moreover, they may increase the difficulty of access to properties lying along them and reduce their amenity in this and other ways.

The development of roads can have other results as well as those on transport. For example, the development of a road may so improve access to the land through which it passes that it becomes possible to make a better use of it. A road through undeveloped land might provide better value for the resources spent than an alternative route along an existing road line, even if it cost more to construct. The extra costs might be more than offset by a smaller loss of existing value and a greater creation of new value. Alternative routes by the coast and rivers can sometimes be obtained by constructing banks in the water. Such a development may also provide additional areas of land or perhaps act as a barrage, behind which water can be stored. Conversely, the site for a road may be one of the results of a water storage scheme.

The provision of a road is only one way of increasing transport potential. The primary need to be met can often be stated in terms of the movement of people and goods, for example, the movement of city workers from the residential districts to the commercial centre. The transport of such commuters might be provided by means of private cars, buses, surface railways, underground railways or some form of overhead railway or monorail. Each type of transport system would make a different demand on land, and on construction and maintenance facilities. The resources required for operation would also be very different. Each system would also contribute differently to general transport needs, would affect the values of properties on the line of the route differently and would meet the personal needs of the travellers in different ways. The form of transport offering the best value for money would depend to a large extent on the existing development of the land. Subsequent development would be influenced to a large extent by the form of transport chosen and the form of development which was the most economic in that situation.

TOWN DEVELOPMENT

The town planner is concerned not just with the development of particular projects, but with the development of the whole town, region and even country. The objective of the development is the creation of facilities, and amenities for a given population. Neither the level of facilities, nor the population is constant; both are in a constant state of change. The task of the town planner is to find the form of development which meets the changing needs in the most economic way. He must accept the existing development as a starting point. Generally, his powers are purely negative; he can prevent undesirable development, but cannot insist on desirable development. Even his negative powers are circumscribed by the need to provide compensation for refusing certain types of development on some sites. Any development plan produced must be approved by the elected representatives of the community, and in the long run by the community itself. The planner is, therefore, concerned not only with developing the town so as to obtain the best value for the resources used from a social point of view, but with harmonizing the interests of the developers and the community. Unless the often conflicting desires can be harmonized, a plan is not viable. Hence the town planner needs to carry out a costs-in-use analysis for each type of developer, public and private, as well as from the point of view of the community as a whole.

Clearly, in practice the planner cannot make a full costs-in-use analysis for each possible way of developing the town. He must be content to sub-optimize, partly by selecting the best of general comprehensive plans, and subsequently choosing between the detailed alternatives for those parts of the town to be developed or redeveloped in the near future, and partly by choosing the best solution for dominant developments and then comparing the alternatives which remain possible. The methods of measuring costs and benefits for the alternative developments have already been discussed above and in earlier chapters in relation to individual developments. Their application for choosing between town development plans is inevitably affected by the difference in conditions. The choice between methods of carrying out a particular development is a choice between definite programmes of development. The choice between plans for town development is a choice between plans which at best may only be realized over a long period of years and often in a modified form, and which may never be realized at all. Because town development is a long-term process, it is geared to long-term needs. These can only be examined tentatively. The needs may change considerably before the time arrives to provide for them. Town planning can only strive to promote development which appears to meet needs as currently seen in a way which will not unnecessarily impede possible future development. Because future needs cannot be known with certainty, it is clearly desirable to provide for flexibility to the extent to which this is economic. The development of regional, and even more national plans, clearly proceeds at a more general level than town plans. Allowance can be made for only the broadest differences in the costs-in-use of development at different locations and of the communications between them.

Some town developments are carried out by a single landowner. This occurs when development is undertaken on land in single ownership or when the state takes powers to acquire all the rights in the land required for development. In such cases the planner is intermediate in position between the planner of a single development and the official town planner. While he is not inhibited by the need to persuade many separate developers to accept his plan, he is still inhibited by the market, that is by the need to meet the wishes of potential users of the properties his plan creates. He is still planning to create the conditions for unknown future needs and aims to create development which best meets needs as currently foreseen with the minimum use of resources without unduly impeding development in the future. Such a planner has, however, a greater opportunity of finding the best town form and of achieving it, than has the official town planner.

It is clear, however, that the costs-in-use techniques are just as relevant to the town planner in the broad sense as to the designer of individual buildings and the planner of individual developments. While the types of costs and benefits to be evaluated change, there is the same need to visualize the comparative consequences of alternatives possibilities in their totality and the same need to discount the flows of payments over time. The need to trace the incidence of costs and benefits to the various types of developers, users and other interests involved, as well as to the community, is even more compelling.

13
Renewals, Adaption and Other Uses of the Costs-in-Use Technique

FUTURE COSTS AND BENEFITS

It has been previously pointed out that 'bygones are for ever bygones'. Once a building has been constructed the resources used have been committed irrevocably. Past design analysis and decisions are of no relevance to the future. Future action can only be based on making the best use of what is available. Decisions depend on future costs and benefits, on comparisons between immediate and future costs and the values these will create.

THE RENEWAL OF EQUIPMENT

When a component is broken beyond repair and needs to be renewed there is often a choice between replacement with an identical component and replacement with some alternative. Several alternatives may be available and suitable as replacements. The comparative costs-in-use clearly embrace the initial and running costs of the alternatives and the value of any savings they may produce in the costs of carrying out the relevant operations. The analysis is no different from those carried out and discussed earlier.

Often, however, a component is repairable, although it might be replaced more easily. The cost of repairs may be less than its complete replacement, but the life of the repaired component may be less than that of a new component. In this situation a comparison of the discounted costs is not relevant, since the two alternatives provide services for different periods. It is annual equivalent costs which are compared.

Example 13.1 The repair or replacement of a component
Suppose a component can be repaired for £400 to give a future life of five years, or replaced £1200 when its future life will be fifteen years. It will be assumed that no further costs will be incurred in either case. Interest will be taken at 5 per cent net. The annual cost for the repaired component is:

$$£400(a_5)^{-1} = £92.4$$

The annual cost for the replaced component is:

$$£1200(a_{15})^{-1} = 115.6$$

Clearly the component is worth repairing.

Frequently, however, the component that would replace the damaged one is an improved model with perhaps lower running costs. These will need to be taken into consideration.

Example 13.2 Replacement by an improved component
Suppose the situation is as in Example 13.1, but that the existing component has running costs of £80 a year while the replacement would only have running costs of £60 a year. The comparison is then as follows:

The annual cost for the repaired component is:

$$£92.4 + £80 = £172.4$$

The annual cost for the replaced component is:

$$£115.6 + £60 = £175.6$$

The difference in costs is so small that it could be the result of prediction errors.

Again, improved models often become available long before the existing model is either physically or functionally obsolete. The existing component does not thereby automatically financially obsolete. This only arises if the annual running costs of the existing model exceed the annual running costs of the replacement model by more than the annual equivalent of the initial cost of the replacement model minus the resale value of the existing model; that is:

running costs of the existing model $>$
running costs of replacement model
$+ 1/a_n$(initial costs of replacement model $-$
resale value of existing model)

This is clearly a stringent test to pass and is only likely to be satisfied either if the existing model is very inefficient as compared with a replacement model of the same type, or if there has been a really significant advance in the design of such models with a considerable increase in their efficiency. Unless the reduction in running costs is large, situations in which it is worth while to replace physically sound models will only occur where the annual equivalent of the initial costs of the model are small compared with the running costs. This is likely to be true for models which use a fuel, for example, for heating, lighting, or power, and for those which need an operator. If, for example, the running costs of a model amounted to 10 per cent of the initial costs and the life was about fifteen years, the equivalent of the initial costs calculated at 5 per cent net would be about equal to the running costs. For it to be worth while, in this situation, to replace an existing model by another during its life, the replacement would need to have a combined annual equivalent of initial costs and running costs of less than half the combined costs of the existing model. This would normally entail a substantial reduction in the initial costs of the model as well as in the running costs.

Example 13.3 Replacement by a model that provides a different service
Except when the hours during which the lights are used are small, white fluorescent lighting tends to be cheaper than tungsten filament lighting. Is it then worth while to replace a tungsten filament lighting installation by fluorescent lighting? Suppose that the lights are used for 1000 hours a year. The running costs for the existing installation are assumed to be:

Maintenance	£ 256
Electricity and lamp replacement	£1532
Total running costs	£1788

The costs of installing and running a comparable white fluorescent installation are assumed to be:

Annual equivalent of net installation costs	£ 708
Maintenance	£ 516
Electricity and tube replacement	£ 592
Total equivalent annual costs	£1816

It is just not worth while in the circumstances but would be worth while if, for instance, the hours for which the lights were used were a little longer.

In some cases maintenance costs will increase with age; this would favour replacement. The new component might be smaller than the old and offer some saving in space which might be of value. Labour might also be saved. Such factors can easily be taken into account.

ALTERATIONS

Decisions as to the economic value of the replacement of models or components are rather similar to those relating to alterations. In both cases the initial cost of change in terms of their annual equivalent, together with the future running costs, need to be less than the existing running costs in order to justify the change. Alterations are not usually considered unless as a result either new values will be created or the function to be carried out in the building will be facilitated and costs reduced. Thus the conditions are usually more easily satisfied in the case of alterations than in the case of the replacement of components.

Example 13.4 The value of an alteration

Suppose that as a result of improving a loading bay and access to it, and by providing mechanical handling plant, it is possible to reduce the labour force by three men. Is this a worth-while proposition? The building is expected to have a further fifteen years' life. The cost of the alterations and of providing the handling plant is expected to be £90 000; running costs are expected to be £1600 a year as against £400 now. The gross cost of the labour is £3400 a man. The saving in costs by making the alterations would be (interest at 5 per cent net):

Saving in labour costs per annum		£10 200
Costs of alterations £90 000$(a_{15})^{-1}$	£8670	
Additional running costs	1200	
Total additional costs		9 870
Saving as a result of alterations		330

The relative saving could be more apparent than real and could arise from prediction errors; the usual tests would be applied.

In some cases alterations to a building would enable savings to be obtained in materials used in production or servicing as well as in labour. For example, changes in the layout of space in a hotel might make it possible to bring together bars, dining rooms and kitchens. By reducing the distance between them it might be possible to consolidate the storage of food and drinks and to undertake all the cooking in one central kitchen. This might lead to a saving in staff, in the size of stores and in wastage. The value of the savings might be quite considerable. Whether or not they would be sufficient to offset the costs of alterations would depend in part on the period over which the solution would be satifactory. This is often uncertain. Leases run

158 Building design evaluation

out and cannot always be renewed on satisfactory terms. Demotion for road widening may be anticipated some time in the future. It might be felt that large-scale reconstruction would eventually be necessary or removal to a new site with more room for development. In fact the future period of use might be the most uncertain factor in the project. In these circumstances it is convenient to apply a test of the decision in terms of this factor, as in Chapter 8.

The value of n, the minimum period for which the alteration should be satisfactory, is given by the equation:

$$\text{change in running costs} = (a_n)^{-1} \text{ (the costs of alteration)}.$$

The first item may be a complex one involving costs of maintenance and servicing, and the labour and material costs of the function performed in the building. In the example this would be the costs of providing the food and drink, its preparation and serving. This item can be written as the difference between the running costs prior to alteration, A, and the running costs subsequent to alteration, B, that is as $(A-B)$. These values could be standardized by expressing them as ratios of the running costs prior to alteration. The equation for determining n becomes:

$$R_s = R_c$$

where $R_s = (A-B)/A$ and $R_c = (a_n)^{-1}$ (the costs of alteration)$/A$. The values of R_s and R_c lie between 0 and 1 and can be plotted on a decision diagram against n (Figure 13.1).

Example 13.5 Using a break-even chart for testing alterations
Suppose that the original cost of carrying out a function in a building is £80 000 a year, that alterations are suggested which would cost £40 000 and that subsequently the cost of carrying out the function is expected to fall to £65 000 a year. Is the period before which further attention would be necessary likely to be long enough for the costs to break even?

$$R_s = (A-B)/A = (80\ 000 - 65\ 000)/80\ 000 = 0 \cdot 175.$$

$$R_c = (a_n)^{-1} \text{ (costs of alterations)}/A = (a_n)^{-1}\ 40\ 000/80\ 000$$

$$= 0 \cdot 5\ (a_n)^{-1}.$$

Since R_s equals R_c at the break-even point, the value of n is that which

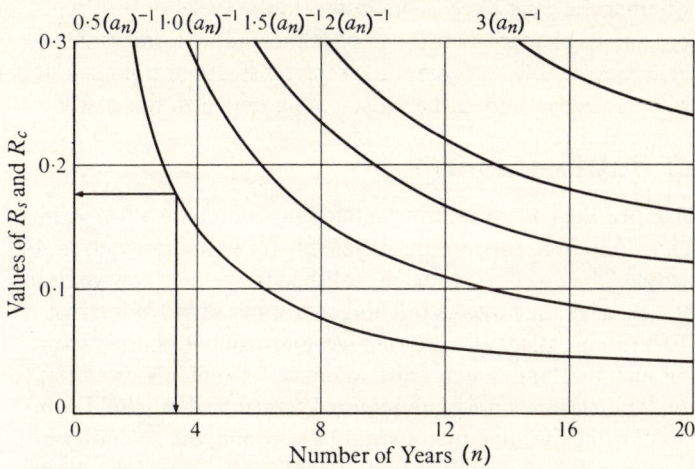

Figure 13.1 Decision diagram III. Relation between R_s, R_c and n with interest at 5 per cent

corresponds to $R_c = 0.175$ and the curve $0.5(a_n)^{-1}$. Reading from Figure 13.1 the period n is found to be about 3.25 years. This is a short period, so that there should be very little doubt as to whether this period of life could be obtained from the alteration.

Sometimes the savings will be less than the annual equivalent of the costs of the alterations. The alterations may still be worth while if the value of the appearance and comfort are high enough. This type of situation is quite usual outside the commercial sector. For example, the annual equivalent cost of installing central heating in a house over its expected life may exceed the saving in fuel costs and the expected reduction in the costs of maintenance and decoration. Suppose the extra annual equivalent costs were £104; that is £2 a week, or nearly £4 a week over the heating season. The householder can compare this sum with the advantages obtained and not already included in the cost analysis. These will include greater thermal comfort, less dusting and cleaning and less time spent, perhaps considerably less, on attending to heating appliances.

Similar problems arise in social buildings where alterations are undertaken to provide greater comfort as well as to improve the efficiency with which the service of function is carried out. Clearly the period over which the satisfactions provided by the alteration can be enjoyed is important. For example, the question frequently arises as to whether it is worth while to spend money on a building to be demolished or largely rebuilt in a few years. In the commercial sector the cost consequences can be calculated to

160 *Building design evaluation*

determine whether the gains exceed the losses. In the social or private sectors the equivalent annual change in costs can be compared with the value obtained. While it may be difficult to evaluate the satisfactions obtained, it is rather easier to consider whether the satisfactions are worth the cost.

A TEST OF COMPARABILITY

In the social sector the cost of improving buildings with only a few years of life is often a reduction in the resources available for new construction. For example, many of the dwellings to be demolished in the next few years in this country lack such amenities as hot and cold water services, internal toilets and bathrooms. Many are not even weather-tight. Resources spent on improving such dwellings are not also available for building dwellings to replace them. While less resources are required to make a household comfortable in an existing dwelling than to build a new one, the amenities of improved dwellings may be less than that of new dwellings and the life of the improved dwellings will generally be less than that of new dwellings. In order to reach a decision between the alternatives a method is required for comparing the returns obtained from the use of the resources; this will need to include allowances for differences in life and amenities. One test is to compare the return from the resources used to improve existing dwellings with that from resources spent on building new dwellings. The test is to compare the annual equivalent cost of alterations and improvements over the remaining life of the existing dwelling against the annual equivalent cost of constructing a new dwelling over its life. The new dwelling used as the basis of the comparison would have similar amenities to the improved existing dwelling. Allowance can also be made for differences in running costs, although the difference in running costs between a recently improved existing dwelling and a new dwelling might be quite small.

Example 13.6 Comparing an adaptation with a replacement
Suppose that the cost of alterations, improvements and repair to an existing dwelling is £6000 and the dwelling is expected to be demolished in ten years' time and that to provide a new dwelling of the same size and providing the same amenities would cost £18 000 but would have a life expectation of at least sixty years. The equivalent annual cost of the improved dwelling is:

$$£6000(a_{10})^{-1} = £769 \text{ (Interest 5\% net)}.$$

The equivalent annual cost of a new dwelling is:

$$£18\,000(a_{60})^{-1} = £951 \cdot 0 \text{ (Interest 5\% net)}.$$

The annual equivalent cost of improving the dwelling is less than that of building a new dwelling. In other words a better return is obtained from the resources spent on improving the existing dwelling than would be obtained from resources spent on building a new dwelling. In some cases it would be necessary to make allowance for differences in maintenance costs. The returns would break even if the improved existing dwelling provided amenities only about 82 per cent as good as assumed or if the expected life was only about eight years. Of course, under present legislation in this country grants are obtainable for the improvement of dwellings and owners would make allowance for these grants and for the costs of borrowing and for the values created or for the rent revenue.

REBUILDING AND MODERNIZATION

In many cases there is a choice between demolishing the existing building, replacing it, and modernizing it. While the costs of replacement are normally greater than the costs of modernization, running costs and the costs of operating in a new building may be less than in a modernized building. Generally the new building will remain functional longer than a modernized building. Since the periods over which returns would be obtained would differ, comparison is made in terms of the equivalent annual costs.

Example 13.7 Comparing rebuilding with the modernization of a commercial building
Suppose that the costs of demolishing and rebuilding are £400 000 and the costs of modernization £40 000 but that the running costs of the new building will be £2000 less than for the modernized building and the operating costs for the function £12 000 less. The new building would be expected to have a life expectation of sixty years, while the life expectation of the modernized building would be fifteen years. The net costs-in-use of the modernized building would be:

Annual equivalent costs of modernization = £40 000$(a_{15})^{-1}$	= £ 3 852
Additional running costs as compared with new building	= £ 2 000
Additional costs of operating within the building as compared with new building	= £12 000
Total net annual equivalent costs	£17 852

Annual equivalent costs of a new building

$$= £400\,000(a_{60})^{-1} = £21\,132$$

Thus in this case the costs of modernization are substantially lower than those of rebuilding. The difference is large in relation to the probable errors of prediction.

The types of costs which would need to be considered have already been discussed earlier (Chapter 11) and will not be considered again here.

THE NO-ACTION TEST

It will be appreciated that while it may be more economic to adopt one of the solutions for rebuilding or modernization for which comparison has been made, there may be other alternatives which would provide better value for money, or it may be better to portpone action to a later date. The costs-in-use of the alternatives already examined can be compared with those of taking no action. In this case there would be no initial payment to spread over the future life, but both the running costs and the costs of operating within the building might be greater.

Example 13.8 A comparison between modernization and no action
Suppose that the modernization was expected to have annual equivalent costs of £3852, to result in a reduction in the running costs of £400 and in the costs of operating within the building of £4000. This would be a saving in annual costs of £4400 against an annual equivalent cost of £3852. Clearly it would pay to modernize but there still might be better ways of achieving the modernization than the method costed. If, however, the annual savings from modernization had only been £2800 then it would have been better to take no action. It might be suspected that the situation would change fairly rapidly; a reappraisal the following year might indicate that modernization would then be worth while.

MAINTENANCE POLICIES

Often there is a choice of policies for the maintenance of a building or a building component. Some require the use of relatively more labour and some relatively more materials. Less frequent treatment may be more expensive in the end. Methods of maintenance based on remedial treatment and early scrapping can be compared with methods based on regular maintenance and long life. The actual costs of maintenance work are often less important than the effect of the disturbance cause by maintenance on the service provided in the building. Comparisons of this kind are made in terms of the usual analysis of the equivalent worth of sums of money payable at different points in time. An example will help to clarify the points which arise.

Example 13.9 A comparison of painting and washing cycles for a hospital ward

Hospital wards need to maintain a high degree of sterility. The walls, ceilings and other surfaces are frequently washed down. This tends to reduce the durability of the paint film but it is essential to maintain this film if sterile conditions are to be provided. While washing down the paint can be carried out without removing the patients, repainting cannot. To empty a ward of patients, it is usually necessary either to gradually run down the number of patients in the ward or to transfer them to a spare ward. Both methods lead to a waste of bed capacity and to inconvenience.

Suppose that washing down is carried out every six months at a cost of £240 a year. Every three years the wash down is followed by the application of one coat of paint at a cost of £400. At the end of the ninth year a full repainting is carried out at a cost of £800. This policy involves clearing the ward of patients every three years. Suppose a higher quality paint was available which provided a satisfactory surface for six years without intermediate repainting. Would this be worth using at a cost of £1200?

It will be noticed that the cycles are of different periods. Initial cost equivalents will not, therefore, provide a basis of comparison unless sufficient cycles are taken of each policy to provide equal periods of time. The comparison would need to be based on eighteen years, two cycles of the first policy and three cycles of the second policy. Comparability can be obtained on the basis of different cycle times if annual equivalent costs are used.

Method 1

$$£240 + (a_9)^{-1} (£800 + £400(v^3 + v^6)) = £444$$

Method 2

$$£240 + (a_6)^{-1} £1200 = £476.$$

At the rate of interest used (5 per cent net) the second method is more expensive than the first method. The difference in costs is large enough for it to be accepted with some certainty that the result was not a chance one, since the £240 washing down programme is common to both. But a policy based on the first method implies that the ward must be emptied every three years, whereas a policy based on the second method only implies emptying the ward every six years. Suppose it was estimated to cost £200 to maintain spare ward capacity for the days over which the painting takes place and to meet the costs of the additional work of moving patients to temporary accommodation and back. In the first case this cost would arise every three years and in the second every six years. The annual equivalent difference would be about £34. This would raise the cost of the first policy to over £476. The difference in cost between the two methods would not be significant. The second policy is less inconvenient and would seem to be the best, although consideration of the quality of the surfaces before they were repainted would need to be given some weight.

Much thought is now given to the value of planned maintenance as compared with remedial maintenance. While planned maintenance usually results in a greater rate of replacement of components and more routine servicing than remedial maintenance, it usually provides a more reliable service from the buildings and equipment, and perhaps reduces the number of separate visits by service engineers and the need to have stand-by equipment. Usually there is less disturbance to the users of the building and a greater opportunity to plan the maintenance work ahead so that a more efficient use can be made of the labour and the work can be planned to take place when it is most convenient from the point of view of the users of the building.

The comparative costs of planned and remedial systems of maintenance can be estimated in the normal way. Usually comparison would be made over a period of one year.

INNOVATION OF BUILDING COMPONENTS AND TECHNIQUES

New building components and techniques are frequently in some way a substitute for existing ones. Their acceptance depends on their ability to compete with existing alternatives. Cost comparisons should clearly be on a basis of initial and running costs. This is another situation for which costs-in-use analysis provides the technique required. The only important difference between comparing existing materials and methods, and existing methods against new materials and methods lies in the treatment of errors. In the comparison of new against existing materials the greatest element of uncertainty clearly lies with the new alternative for which there may be no practical experience and hence no adequate basis for estimating costs. The comparison can be arranged so as to indicate the conditions which the new product must satisfy if it is, at least, to break even with established products. The errors arising from uncertainty can be left with the costs-in-use of the innovation where they mainly belong.

Example 13.10 Ascertaining the competitive price of a new material
Suppose a manufacturer develops a form of plastic sheeting which can be

fixed to plastered walls and which is tough enough to withstand frequent washing for a period of thirty years. It will be supposed that the sheeting can equally well be fixed to ceilings. The manufacturer wishes to know within what price level he would need to sell in order to break even with painting the wall and ceiling surfaces. Redecoration would be necessary every six years. It is assumed that the costs and frequency of washing down would not change and that the joinery work would still need to be painted. Under these circumstances the saving is expected to be about £800 every six years for thirty years. This would be worth (at 5 per cent net) £2424 in terms of equivalent initial costs. Since the joinery would still need to be painted and the room cleared while this is done, there would be no appreciable saving in that direction. The potential users might be sceptical of the manufacturer's estimate of durability. Until this was proved he might need either to sell at a lower price than £2424, so as to break even at a shorter period of life, or provide a guarantee against a failure in performance during the period necessary for costs to break even.

It will be appreciated that in order to find the break-even price for a new material or component it is only necessary to find the initial cost at which the innovation has costs-in-use equal to that of existing materials or components. Conversely, given the production costs of a component, it is simple to find the performance standards which would need to be reached in order to compare favourably with rival products.

PROTECTION AGAINST HAZARDS

Buildings and building developments inevitably introduce hazards and are themselves subject to hazards. While it is usually difficult if not impossible to eliminate completely any particular form of hazard, it is possible to reduce hazards. Usually the closer the approach to the complete elimination of a hazard the greater the costs. Decisions are required on the level of hazard to be accepted. This depends on the cost of protection compared with its value. Again, this is a problem involving streams of costs and values arise at different moments in time.

Hazards take many forms. For example, lighting bulbs and tubes have fairly short lives. While it is not possible to know when a failure will occur, it is possible to estimate the average life and the chance of a failure occurring in relation to the age of the component. The replacement of the component has an establishable cost. This is likely to be much more for individual replacements than for replacements made on a group basis. The failure of a component usually results in additional operation costs — workers' time is wasted or materials spoilt. The cost of a failure can be set against the cost of its avoidance. The earlier in the lives of the bulbs or tubes the replacement is made, the higher the cost because the lower the effective life but the lower the chance that a failure will occur, and hence the cost of failures. The life at which to replace is obviously that which minimizes the costs of the component and its replacement and the operational costs resulting from a failure.

For some building components the lives are quite long but replacement is expensive both in building costs and in operation costs. For example, most industrial floor surfaces need to be replaced several times over the life of the building. The cost of replacement cannot usually be avoided whatever is used for surfacing but the operation costs can be avoided or reduced if the replacement is carried out at a time convenient for the operation of the factory. This will usually be during the annual period of shut-down or while production is being reorganized. Again, in order that the inconvenience and cost of an unplanned floor replacement may be avoided, it is necessary to sacrifice some of the potential life of the floor. The increase in the equivalent costs of shortening the life of the floor can be set against the additional costs of production and other costs which would result from an unplanned replacement.

Hazards also arise from breakdowns of equipment and from their effect on the costs of the operations carried out in the building. Some items of equipment are large and costly and the provision for stand-by equipment is considerable. Boilers are a good example. There are a number of possible approaches. The first step is to obtain some measure of the frequency of failure. If this is very low the costs of a failure in terms of production may be small compared with the comparative costs of stand-by equipment. The relevant comparison would be between the average annual cost to production from a failure and the annual equivalent cost of stand-by equipment. The costs of repairing the main equipment cannot, of course, be avoided. While fortunately breakdowns are usually rare, they can be very expensive when they occur. Because the risk of a breakdown tends to be very small, its incidence is uncertain. The equivalent cost of stand-by equipment is often very high compared with the average cost of failures over the same period but any one failure is likely to be very expensive compared with the cost of stand-by equipment. The most economic solution is to pool the risks with others and to convert an uncertain risk into a small certain cost. This is, of course, the function of insurance.

Whereas it is generally acceptable to cost hazards relating to plant and material, and to limit precaution in accordance with the comparative costs, the same approach is often unacceptable where the hazard affects people. Hazards can be reduced but seldom completely eliminated. Usually costs rise disproportionately as the risk is further and further reduced. The costs of human injuries and deaths can be evaluated either in terms of the costs of insurance or the costs to the firm or the nation of the loss of their productive capacity. While too much weight cannot be put upon valuations they can be useful as a guide to where resources can best be applied to the reduction of hazards. For example, the designer might wish to know whether better value for the money spent would be obtained from an additional staircase for emergencies resulting from fire or from dividing the building into fireproof cells. The risk of a casualty from fire might be so small as compared with casualties from slipping on floors that a better return could be obtained by providing non-slip floors, than by providing additional emergency exits. Again it is a question of comparing the costs of the special equipment over their life against the cost of the expected accidents over the same period. Because accidents are usually comparatively rare the cost of a single one is usually large compared with the average over any period of time. The cost of accident reduction is hence often expensive compared with the cost of pooling the very small risks with others, that is, with insuring.

INSURANCE

While insurance theoretically has the merit that it enables large uncertain risks to be reduced to small certain losses, in practice insurance may not always provide good value for money. The insurance premium depends on pooling the uncertainties and converting them to a measurable certainty; this is only possible if the pool of uncertainties is large enough for them to average out. Where the pool is small a premium larger than justified by the risk is necessary to cover the uncertainties. Often the risk to be covered is small compared with the costs of operating the insurance fund. Again the method of assessing the risk is often rather crude and takes account only of the average risk. For these reasons it sometimes pays to accept risks rather than to insure against them, or to pay higher premiums rather than to meet the cost of reducing the risks. Large undertakings with many small unrelated risks may find it cheaper to accept the risks rather than to insure them. For example, a firm owning a large chain of small shops may be able to pool the normally insurable risks and meet such costs as arise more cheaply than insuring. Similarly, it may not pay to install sprinklers or automatic fire alarms because the annual equivalent cost of their installation and maintenance is greater than the reduction which would be allowed in the insurance premiums. Structural fire precautions similarly may or may not be worth while. The effect of the design of a building on insurance premiums should be considered at the design stage. Guidance as to the best design can be obtained by making the normal costs-in-use comparisons.

CODES OF PRACTICE AND STATUTORY STANDARDS

In practice the design of a building or engineering works is closely circumscribed in certain fields by statutory codes of practice and building standards. These prohibit certain possible design solutions for reasons of safety or to protect the interests of third parties. Clearly, in setting such standards it is important to take into account the relationship between the resources required to implement them and the benefit which they bring. The comparative costs of alternative ways to improve the standards of safety can be compared. Similarly, comparisons can be made between the cost consequences of higher and lower standards to find the point at which the best value for money will be obtained. Such cost analyses will usually be required over a wide range of circumstances since cost relations vary according to the circumstances in which the standards are to be operated. Such cost studies involve the comparison of streams of payments over time and are no different in form from the examples of costs-in-use technique already given elsewhere in this book.

TAXATION

It has already been explained in earlier chapters how tax regulations interact with the design cost relationships. In particular, the difference in the treatment of capital and running expenses for tax purposes often leads to the waste of resources from the national point of view. Fuller studies of the effect of taxation can be made by the use of the technique of costs-in-use. While various types of expenditure are taken into account for tax purposes their net effect on retained profits depends, of course, on the revenues obtained in relation to allowable expenses. It is usually simpler to examine the effect of business decisions in relation to the gross profits before tax. The problem created by the differences in the basis of tax reliefs can be overcome by adjusting reliefs on capital expenditure to the same basis as those for current business expenses. The effect of the delay before the expenditure on capital goods can be completely set against revenue can be thought of as an interest-free loan to the government. The cost of this loan to the tax payer can be calculated by discounting the differences between the reliefs which could be claimed on a running costs basis and those which could be claimed on an investment basis. The cost of the loan can be added to the annual equivalent cost of the building or building component. The net return can be obtained when required by deducting the tax relied as for current expenditure. This method is simple to understand and minimizes the error from assumptions about the future level of taxation and profits. The method is, of course, generally applicable equally to buildings, building components and movable and mobile plant of every type.

14
Decision Techniques Compared

COSTS-IN-USE

The technique of costs-in-use is concerned with means and not with ends; it is concerned with the choice of means to a given end and with the problem of obtaining the best value for money for the resources spent. While the technique has been primarily developed to provide a means of comparing building designs and planning alternatives, it is clearly applicable to any comparison of alternative means to a given end. Again, while it provides a method of handling both first and running costs, it is equally applicable to comparisons which only involve first costs.

The concept of ends can be interpreted very widely. The end product can be as narrow as a lighting system or as a plant for producing a given output of concrete per hour. At the other extreme the end can be a building designed to fulfil a given function or even a town planned to provide complete facilities for a certain group of people. The size need not necessarily be identical for each alternative, since adjustments can be made for small differences in size. A limitation to the scale of the end arises when the project becomes so large that the method of obtaining it would change the complex of outputs and prices in the economy.

Of course, the wider the interpretation of the end, the more complex the differences in values and the more difficult they are to evaluate. The value of this or any other technique for comparing costs and values naturally declines as the proportion of costs and values which can be quantified declines. The argument that quantified comparative techniques are of little value because not all differences can be quantified is more a criticism of the way they are used than of the technique itself. It is an odd logic that argues that some information should be ignored because complete information is not available. It is more logical to make the best use of what information is available, but keeping in mind the limitation of the factors which have been quantified. Clearly, factors which have consequences in the use of resources are easier to evaluate in quantified terms than factors which only affect levels of satisfaction. Factors such as appearance, comfort, convenience and atmosphere can generally only be subjective. It is difficult to measure the likes and dislikes of building users but it is often possible to guess whether they would be willing to spend a given sum to secure a given quality. In this way the probability of reaching the right decision is increased by the use of a comparative technique, even though not all the values can be quantified.

The costs-in-use approach has been adopted in a number of countries and in various disciplines under a range of names, such as ultimate costs, life cycle costs and even terotechnology.

COST-EFFECTIVE ANALYSIS

Cost-effective analysis is another technique which is concerned with comparing different means to the same end. This technique has been developed in the field of weapons analysis where the end is not a flow of values, but a weapons system with a given purpose. Some basis is required for comparing the costs of alternative weapons systems to ascertain which gives the best performance for the least costs. Naturally this technique, which has been designed for a special purpose, has developed differently from the costs-in-use technique, which has been developed particularly to facilitate the comparison of design and planning detail.

DISCOUNTED CASH FLOW

Discounted cash flow is a technique developed for use in the business sector of the economy for comparing alternative investment projects. In the business sector, the scarce factor is capital, usually only fixed capital, and it is the returns on capital which the business man wishes to maximize. Within limits the individual entrepreneur is not greatly concerned with what he produces as long as the return on the capital employed is adequate. In fact, of course, he is more likely to obtain a satisfactory return by staying within the limits of his experience and by using the machinery, expertise and markets built up in the course of his existing business. The individual entrepreneur is not concerned with trying to produce what the community requires but only what the market indicates it requires. Hence the individual entrepreneur can usually assume that neither the supply of the factors of production, nor the market prices of his products will be affected by his decisions. Maximizing the returns on capital is therefore a valid criteria for the individual entrepreneur. The market forces will tend to act so as to produce the best balance between demand and supply.

The application of this criterion involves comparing the returns on capital from alternative investment possibilities. The most accurate method is to discount the flow of expenditures and revenues at the rate of interest at which the sum of the discounted values of the surpluses exactly equals the discounted values of the capital expenditures. This can be found by discounting at a range of rates of interest either side of the true rate; the actual rate can then be found by interpolation. The usual practice is to set a minimum rate below which no investment project will be accepted. The critical rate can be varied according to the supply of investment alternatives. There is, of course, still the problem of choosing the best combination of investment projects. This problem arises because earlier projects may be accepted which use the capital which might have been used on projects examined later.

COST-BENEFIT ANALYSIS

The principal behind the discounted cash flow technique has also been applied to the evaluation of social projects. The arguments is that national resources should be invested so as to obtain the best returns and that these should be calculated on the basis of the capital used for the project. In dealing with social projects it is necessary to evaluate not only the revenue which accrues directly to the project, but also all the side effects, both those which increase the revenue to other projects and those which increase general welfare and satisfactions even if no corresponding payments are made. Thus values or benefits are quantified in the same way as in the costs-in-use technique.

The validity of the application of the discounted cash flow technique to social projects is open to question. The use of this principal assumes that capital is the only scarce factor of production and that all other factors, for instance, labour, materials and management, are freely available. As argued earlier, this is valid for an entrepreneur, for once he has secured his capital, and particularly fixed capital, he can purchase the other factors of production from the market without influencing their prices. Capital is not necessarily the most scarce factor in a national economy. In an advanced economy labour, or at least skilled labour, is often the most scarce factor. To judge projects in terms of the return on capital is to accept that labour and other factors of production should be used relatively uneconomically in order to save capital. The higher the required minimum return on capital the greater the extent to which the capital equipment to be purchased would need to reduce operating costs and buildings and their equipment result in lower running costs. Hence, the higher the required rate of return, the less it would appear worth-while to economize on construction even if this resulted in high running costs.

The selection of projects on the basis of the rate of interest earned on the capital employed is tantamount to rejecting projects for which the benefits do not substantially exceed the cost during the early years. The higher the rate of discount, the shorter the period over which benefits are considered. For example, at a rate of discount of 3 per cent, half the face worth is still accorded to benefits and costs arising in twenty-three years' time, while at a rate of 7 per cent discount the period has dropped to ten years. Looking at it another way, whereas at 3 per cent discounted costs and benefits due in twenty-three years' time have a half face worth, at 7 per cent discount their equivalent worth if only about a fifth of their face worth. At a discount rate of 15 per cent, even costs and benefits acruing in four to five years are only worth a half their face value and in sixteen to seventeen years they are only worth a tenth of their face value. Thus the higher the rate of interest to be earned on the capital, the shorter the period for which costs and benefits are considered, and the smaller the chance of a project being accepted which does not produce a balance of benefits over costs in the early years. Hence, the higher the rate of the return on the capital, the more future interests and generations are likely to be sacrificed to short-term advantages.

These criticisms do not affect the validity of the comparison of one project against another or of trying to quantify benefits. They only bring into question the method of making the final comparison. An alternative method which does not suffer from the objections discussed is to use as the basis of comparison the ratio of discounted revenues to discounted expenses. This method treats all expenses as of equal importance. The rate of discount has still to be fixed. If a very high rate of discount is taken this tends to dominate the cost-benefit ratio. The higher the rate of interest the less important are costs and benefits which do not arise until some years after the project is started. The use of a high rate of interest is in effect just another way of expressing the dominating importance of capital. Often a social rate of interest is taken as the basis of discounting. This is usually taken to be the pure rate of interest; sometimes an even lower rate is taken. In this form the cost-benefit ratio comparison is not dissimilar in concept to costs-in-use comparisons. The latter, of course, can be made in terms of comparisons of totals. Ratios are usually necessary in the case of cost-benefit comparisons because the scale of the projects differ, since they are not all for the same end. Sometimes the annual expenses are deducted from the value of the benefits before these are discounted. If these discounted net benefits are then compared with the discounted value of capital expenditure the ratios take the form of a measure of the return on capital. Again capital is regarded as the scarce factor.

The importance of quantifying all the benefits is clearly of much greater importance in the case of cost-benefit comparisons than it is in the case of costs-in-use comparisons. This is partly because cost-benefit analysis is applied to the choice between different ends, not just between different means, and hence the benefits usually vary considerably and partly because it is much easier to misinterpret a comparison of ratios with missing elements than a comparison of sums with missing elements. In the latter case, as shown earlier, it is usually possible to set the cost differences against the difference in values and judge whether the additional cost is worth while even where the values cannot be completely quantified.

The cost-benefit method of comparison is hence both more difficult to apply and often more difficult to interpret than the less ambitious costs-in-use comparison. Clearly the latter is to be preferred where the choice is between different means to a common end. This is often the case since the need is for some particular facility and the choice relates to the best way to achieve this rather than a choice between different facilities which provide different amenities. For instance, a block of housing is no substitute for a road improvement scheme, nor is a new sewerage works a substitute for a block of housing. It is useless to choose the facility with the best returns if it is not capable of fulfilling the most urgent need.

The facility required may not be a building, but some form of service. For example, the end required may be a method of transporting a given number of people from their homes to their places of work each day and to return them in the evening. A number of alternative means may be available as, for example, private transport, buses and a railway system. Concomitant with each method of transport are systems of road or tracks and the provision of these will have various consequences on the urban settlement through which they pass. Clearly, the cost consequences of all the ramifications of the alternative means to the end of moving people should be included. The costing can be extended to include the value of the time and effort of people travelling. The benefit can then be taken as common to all the alternatives, that is the benefit of being transported. This does not need to be evaluated because it is the common end. Small differences of comfort and convenience which often defy efforts to quantify can be related to the cost differences to test the possible scale of differences in relation to the cost differences.

Similarly, alternative ways of providing town developments can be regarded as different means to the common end of providing towns for people to inhabit. Comparisons can be made of different types of urban form. In each case the end is towns for perhaps a million people. The means may be twenty towns of 50 000, ten towns of 100 000, or two towns of 500 000. The alternative means can embrace various types of layout, density, shape and transportation system. The complete cost consequences of constructing, operating and living in the towns can be compared, allowance being made for consequences of the forms of the towns on every aspect of life. Again, if the end is common, the benefit it brings does not need to be quantified.

Resources are, however, limited and it is rarely possible to provide all the facilities which are desirable. Some facilities are more desirable than others and priorities are unavoidable. Hence a choice between ends is necessary. Theoretically all the desirable facilities could be listed in descending order of returns. They could then be carried out in that order until all the available resources at that time had been used. In practice such a system would be difficult to operate. Comparing all possible and desirable facilities and their returns would be a large task. Some of the facilities are more than just desirable and would need to be given priority even if the returns were low. Many projects are linked with others and particular combinations might need to be carried out if the best results were to be obtained. Thus, up to a point, additional housing, sewerage schemes and hospitals would be given priority, because however poor the returns, they are essential facilities. If, however, such facilities already exist, their replacement is less urgent and comparison might be made between their renewal and the provision of some other type of facility. For less essential facilities such as open space and other recreational activities, the replacement of existing buildings and the preservation of historical buildings, comparative returns would seem to provide a useful index of priorities.

It might be argued that the returns from essential projects would be high enough to place them at the top of the list without the need to segregate them as essential. In practice this is not necessarily so. The values of benefits derived from essential projects may be low compared with those from socially less important projects either because they are benefits which carry low prices generally, or because they are intended for people with low incomes and hence low valuations. For example, the value of land used for agriculture is extremely low compared with land in town centres or even with land used for most building purposes. Again, the benefits derived from a development of low-cost houses will have a low value compared with the benefits from an office development.

It is necessary to consider the boundaries of the projects whose returns are to be compared. If these are drawn too narrowly the project may not be very valuable even though the returns as calculated are high. Where the object is to maximize returns there is always a temptation to draw the boundaries so as to include only those features which contribute to high returns. For example, the kernel of a shopping centre will usually provide much higher returns than the facilities which need to accompany it. The order of the returns may be reversed if all the consequences are included in the analysis of costs and benefits. The siting of a new shopping area either in the town centre or out of town would affect the travel pattern of the whole town for many years and it would be necessary to consider the future patterns of travel in the town and hence the expected future pattern of development in the town and in the region around. In such a case the comparison is, in fact, a comparison of means to a given end and might be better handled as a costs-in-use comparison.

It is not easy to ensure that allowance is made for every consequence of a project. For example, resources spent on recreational facilities will not only benefit the people living in the area but may attract people to settle in the area and perhaps attract visitors. Such consequences may raise costs as well as benefits. Again, a road improvement in a remote area may have a low rate of return as compared with a road improvement in a large town. But the road improvement in the remote area may be necessary to prevent depopulation, the consequences of which would be very expensive in terms of the provision of facilities for the former inhabitants elsewhere.

However, despite difficulties and the care necessary to avoid wrong conclusions, the cost-benefit technique is useful for analysing comparisons of the returns offered by alternative projects. It provides a useful tool when resources are limited, and where there is no overriding necessity for one project rather than another or priority for one project as compared with another.

THRESHOLD ANALYSIS

This is a technique of application to planning regions or towns. In developing regions or towns limitations arise from topography, land uses and the infrastructure. As a result, one settlement may be more expensive than another, for example, one settlement may only be able to expand on hilly land, or on a marsh, or sewerage capacity may be nearly exhausted. Similarly constraints may be found in developing a settlement in one direction rather than another. Clearly the alternatives need to costed and allowance made for their comparative benefits this is the purpose of threshold analysis which is closely related to the other techniques considered.

NATIONAL PROJECT COMPARISONS

The assumption underlying all these techniques is that the choice of project does not affect the complex of outputs and prices. This is likely to be true as long as the individual projects are small in relation to the national economy. The larger the projects the more likely it is that the choice of

176 Building design evaluation

project would involve a switch of resources resulting in a change in the pattern of the economy and in the relative prices. Hence, if cost-benefit techniques were used for general resource allocation, it would probably be necessary to develop weights for resource unit evaluation instead of market prices. The weights would need to be calculated to take account of shifts in the use of resources both currently and at future times. While this would be a large task and increase the uncertainty of the measurement of the returns, it would help to promote a thorough understanding of the consequence of the choices which were open.

The problem of national project comparisons lies outside the scope of this book, and it is sufficient to point out the problems which would arise if the decision techniques discussed here were used for comparisons of national projects. Probably the greatest difficulty arises in evaluating the imponderable benefits when the whole pattern of consumer goods and services is free to change. It would not be possible to assume that the existing price relationships would hold good. In these circumstances it would not be possible to determine which pattern of consumption would be most valuable or hence which sets of projects would give the best value for money.

APPENDIX A
Compound Interest Functions

SIMPLE AND COMPOUND INTEREST

The difference between simple and compound interest lies in the treatment of the interest. If a sum of money is invested at interest and the interest is paid to the depositor as it falls due, the capital remains constant and the interest payable is the same each year. This is understood as simple interest. If, instead, the interest is retained by the borrower, it is equivalent to borrowing further capital and interest must be paid on the extra increments of capital, as well as on the original capital. This is known as compound interest. Clearly, if a comparison is being made between the different uses of money over time, interest and capital must be treated together.

THE ACCUMULATION OF A FIXED SUM

Suppose £1 is invested at 5 per cent for three years, the interest being retained by the borrower. At the end of this period the lender will be paid £1·157625 by the borrower. The arithmetic is as follows:

At the end of the first year the borrower owes capital of £1 plus interest of 5/100. £1 = £0·05   i.e. *Total £1·05*

At the end of the second year the borrower owes £1·05 plus further interest of 5/100. £1·05 = £0·0525   i.e. *Total £1·1025*

At the end of the third year the borrower owes £1·1025 plus further interest of 5/100. £1·025 = £0·055125   i.e. *Total £1·157625*

It is unnecessary to calculate compound interest functions in this tedious manner. The mathematical formula can easily be derived.

Suppose an investment at 1 at interest of i.

At the end of year   1   the sum owing is $(1 + i1) = (1 + i)$
2    $(1 + i) + i(1 + i) = (1 + i)^2$
3    $(1 + i)^2 + i(1 + i)^2 = (1 + i)^3$
$(n - 1)$ $(1 + i)^{n-2} + i(1 + i)^{n-2} = (1 + i)^{n-1}$
n $1(1 + i)^{n-1} + i(1 + i)^{n-1} = (1 + i)^n$

Thus the sum of 1 at interest i for n years is $(1 + i)^n$; that is if £1 is invested at interest i for n years and no interest is paid to the lender in the meantime, the borrower has to pay the lender £$(1 + i)^n$ at the end of n years.

It will be seen that at 5 per cent interest the worth of the investment doubles in about fifteen years and trebles in about twenty-three years (Figure A.1). In about sixty years its worth is increased nearly 19 times.

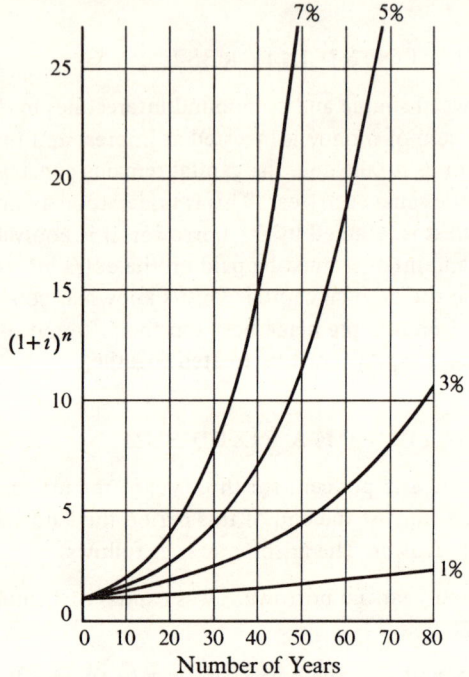

Figure A.1 The value of £1 accumulated at i per cent interest for n years

The rate at which £1 accumulates is very sensitive to the rate of interest. The accumulated worth at the end of forty years is less than 1·5 times the original investment at 1 per cent, 3·3 at 3 per cent, over 7 at 5 per cent and nearly 15 at 7 per cent (Figure A.1).

THE PRESENT WORTH OF A SINGLE PAYMENT PAYABLE IN THE FUTURE

If £1 invested at 5 per cent is worth £7 at the end of forty years, then £1/7th is worth £1 at the end of forty years. Hence if £1 is required in

TABLE A.1 PRESENT WORTH OF A SINGLE PAYMENT OF £1 PAYABLE IN n YEARS (IN £'s)

No. of years	Rate of interest							No. of years
	4%	5%	6%	7%	8%	9%	10%	
1	0.9615	0.9524	0.9434	0.9346	0.9259	0.9174	0.9091	1
2	0.9246	0.9070	0.8900	0.8734	0.8573	0.8417	0.8264	2
3	0.8890	0.8638	0.8396	0.8163	0.7938	0.7722	0.7513	3
4	0.8548	0.8227	0.7921	0.7629	0.7350	0.7084	0.6830	4
5	0.8219	0.7835	0.7473	0.7130	0.6806	0.6499	0.6209	5
10	0.6756	0.6139	0.5584	0.5084	0.4632	0.4224	0.3855	10
15	0.5553	0.4810	0.4173	0.3625	0.3152	0.2745	0.2394	15
20	0.4564	0.3769	0.3118	0.2584	0.2145	0.1784	0.1486	20
25	0.3751	0.2953	0.2330	0.1843	0.1460	0.1160	0.0923	25
30	0.3083	0.2314	0.1741	0.1314	0.0994	0.0754	0.0573	30
35	0.2534	0.1813	0.1301	0.0937	0.0676	0.0490	0.0356	35
40	0.2083	0.1421	0.0972	0.0668	0.0460	0.0318	0.0221	40
45	0.1712	0.1113	0.0727	0.0476	0.0313	0.0207	0.0137	45
50	0.1407	0.0872	0.0543	0.0340	0.0213	0.0134	0.0085	50
55	0.1157	0.0683	0.0406	0.0242	0.0145	0.0087	0.0053	55
60	0.0951	0.0535	0.0303	0.0173	0.0099	0.0057	0.0033	60
70	0.0642	0.0329	0.0169	0.0088	0.0046	0.0024	0.0013	70
80	0.0434	0.0202	0.0095	0.0045	0.0021	0.0010	0.0005	80
90	0.0293	0.0124	0.0053	0.0023	0.0010	0.0004	0.0002	90
100	0.0198	0.0076	0.0030	0.0012	0.0005	0.0002	0.0001	100

TABLE A.1 PRESENT WORTH OF A SINGLE PAYMENT OF £1 PAYABLE IN n YEARS (continued)

No. of years	Rate of interest					No. of years
	11%	12%	13%	14%	15%	
1	0.9009	0.8929	0.8850	0.8772	0.8696	1
2	0.8116	0.7972	0.7831	0.7695	0.7561	2
3	0.7312	0.7118	0.6931	0.6750	0.6575	3
4	0.6587	0.6355	0.6133	0.5921	0.5718	4
5	0.5935	0.5674	0.5428	0.5194	0.4972	5
10	0.3522	0.3220	0.2946	0.2697	0.2472	10
15	0.2090	0.1827	0.1599	0.1401	0.1229	15
20	0.1240	0.1037	0.0868	0.0728	0.0611	20
25	0.0736	0.0588	0.0471	0.0378	0.0304	25
30	0.0437	0.0334	0.0256	0.0196	0.0151	30
35	0.0259	0.0189	0.0139	0.0102	0.0075	35
40	0.0154	0.0107	0.0075	0.0053	0.0037	40
45	0.0091	0.0061	0.0041	0.0027	0.0019	45
50	0.0054	0.0035	0.0022	0.0014	0.0009	50

forty years' time, it is only necessary to invest £1/7 at present to secure this sum when it is required. The £1/7 is known as the present worth or the discounted value of £1 payable in forty years' time. The present worth is normally denoted by v^n and is the reciprocal of $(1 + i)^n$

i.e. $v^n = 1/(1 + i)^n$.

It will be seen that the discount value falls sharply as the period increases and then flattens out (Figure A.2). The higher the rate of interest the more

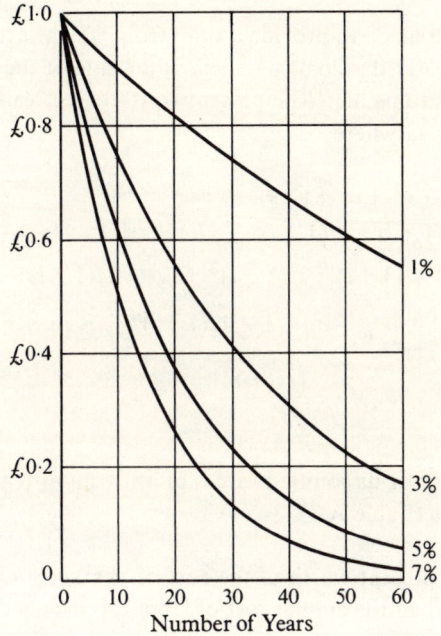

Figure A.2 Discounted values of £1 payable in n years at i per cent interest

the present worth falls in relation to the face value. At a rate of interest of 1 per cent the present worth of £1 payable in forty years is £0·67, at interest of 5 per cent it is £0·14 and at 7 per cent £0·07.

A range of present worths, or discounted values are given above (Table A.1). It will be seen that the differences in the present worths decline as the rate of interest (discount) increases and it is difficult to show the difference graphically.

Example A.1 Find the present worth of the cost of a renewal of plant costing

£200 which is expected to be carried out in fifty years' time. Interest to be taken as 5 per cent.

$$\text{Present worth is } £200 (0.0872) = £17.44$$

Thus if £17.44 is invested now at 5 per cent it will be worth £200 in fifty years' time when the renewal is necessary.

THE PRESENT WORTH OF REGULAR ANNUAL PAYMENTS

A single payment can be made to provide a fund from which regular annual payments are made. Clearly the single payment is the sum of the present worths of the payments to be met. The present worth of a stream of annual payments is denoted by a_n where

$$a_n = v^1 + v^2 + v^3 + v^4 + \ldots + v^n$$
$$= 1/(1+i) + 1/(1+i)^2 + 1/(1+i)^3 + \ldots + 1/(1+i)^n$$
$$(1+i)a_n = 1 + 1/(1+i) + 1/(1+i)^2 + \ldots + 1/(1+i)^{n-1}.$$

Hence
$$(1+i)a_n - a_n = 1 - 1/(1+i)^n$$

and
$$a_n = \frac{1 - 1/(1+i)^n}{i}$$

A range of the present or discounted values of a stream of regular annual payments is given below (Table A.2).

Example A.2. Find the present worth of the cost of operating a lift over a period of thirty years when the annual cost of labour, power and insurance is £10 000. Take the rate of interest as 4 per cent.

$$\text{Present worth is } £10\,000 (17.292) = £172\,920$$

Thus if £172 920 is invested at 4 per cent it will be possible to withdraw £10 000 at the end of each year for a period of thirty years to meet the annual operation costs.

It will be noticed that the higher the rate of interest the smaller the sum which needs to be invested to provide the annual amounts required (Figure A.3). Hence the higher the rate of interest the more it is economic to spend on the running costs as compared with the intial costs.

TABLE A.2 THE PRESENT WORTH OF REGULAR ANNUAL PAYMENTS OF £1 FOR n YEARS (IN £'s)

No. of years	Rate of interest							No. of years
	4%	5%	6%	7%	8%	9%	10%	
1	0.962	0.952	0.943	0.935	0.926	0.917	0.909	1
2	1.886	1.859	1.833	1.808	1.783	1.759	1.736	2
3	2.775	2.723	2.673	2.624	2.577	2.531	2.487	3
4	3.630	3.546	3.465	3.387	3.312	3.240	3.170	4
5	4.452	4.330	4.212	4.100	3.993	3.890	3.791	5
10	8.111	7.722	7.360	7.024	6.710	6.418	6.145	10
15	11.118	10.380	9.712	9.108	8.559	8.061	7.606	15
20	13.590	12.462	11.470	10.594	9.818	9.129	8.514	20
25	15.622	14.094	12.783	11.654	10.675	9.823	9.077	25
30	17.292	15.373	13.765	12.409	11.258	10.274	9.427	30
35	18.665	16.374	14.498	12.948	11.655	10.567	9.644	35
40	19.793	17.159	15.046	13.332	11.925	10.757	9.779	40
45	20.720	17.774	15.456	13.606	12.108	10.881	9.863	45
50	21.482	18.256	15.762	13.801	12.233	10.962	9.915	50
55	22.109	18.633	15.991	13.940	12.319	11.014	9.947	55
60	22.624	18.929	16.161	14.039	12.377	11.048	9.967	60
70	23.395	19.343	16.385	14.160	12.443	11.084	9.987	70
80	23.915	19.597	16.509	14.222	12.474	11.100	9.995	80
90	24.267	19.752	16.579	14.253	12.488	11.106	9.998	90
100	24.505	19.848	16.618	14.269	12.494	11.109	9.999	100

TABLE A.2 THE PRESENT WORTH OF REGULAR ANNUAL PAYMENTS OF £1 FOR n YEARS (continued)

No. of years	Rate of interest					No. of years
	11%	12%	13%	14%	15%	
1	0.9009	0.8929	0.8850	0.8772	0.8696	1
2	1.7125	1.6901	1.6681	1.6467	1.6257	2
3	2.4437	2.4018	2.3612	2.3216	2.2832	3
4	3.1024	3.0373	2.9745	2.9137	2.8550	4
5	3.6959	3.6048	3.5172	3.4331	3.3522	5
10	5.8892	5.6502	5.4262	5.2161	5.0188	10
15	7.1909	6.8109	6.4624	6.1422	5.8474	15
20	7.9633	7.4694	7.0248	6.6231	6.2593	20
25	8.4217	7.8431	7.3300	6.8729	6.4641	25
30	8.6938	8.0552	7.4957	7.0027	6.5660	30
35	8.8552	8.1755	7.5856	7.0700	6.6166	35
40	8.9511	8.2438	7.6344	7.1050	6.6418	40
45	9.0079	8.2825	7.6609	7.1232	6.6543	45
50	9.0417	8.3045	7.6752	7.1327	6.6605	50

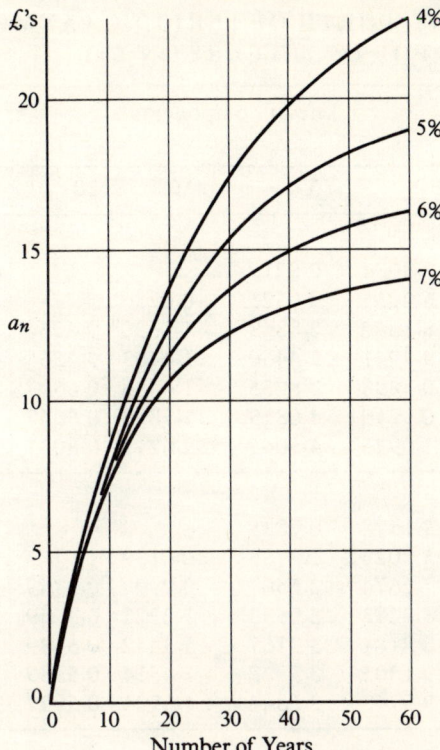

Figure A.3 The discounted value of annual payments of £1 at i per cent interest

THE PRESENT WORTH OF FUTURE PAYMENTS

It was shown in the last section that the present worth of a stream of regular annual payments was a_n. Frequently, however, it is necessary to evaluate streams of payments arising at other intervals of time and not necessarily regularly. As before, the present worth is simply the sum of the present worths of each separate payment; i.e.

$$v^1 + v^3 + v^6 + v^{10}, \text{etc.}$$

However, usually the payments arise at regular intervals, even if not every year.

$$\text{e.g. } v^5 + v^{10} + v^{15} + v^{20} + \ldots + v^n.$$

TABLE A.3 PRESENT WORTH OF PERIODIC PAYMENTS OF £1 EVERY t YEARS FOR $(n-t)$ YEARS (IN £'s)

Life of building	Life of components					
	1	2	5	10	20	30
Rate of interest of 4%:						
10	7.4353	3.3004	0.8219			
20	13.1339	6.2055	2.0528	0.6756		
30	16.9837	8.1682	2.8843	1.1320	0.4564	
40	19.5845	9.4941	3.4460	1.4403	0.4564	0.3083
50	21.3415	10.3898	3.8255	1.6486	0.6647	0.3083
60	22.5285	10.9949	4.0819	1.7893	0.6647	0.3083
100	24.4852	11.9925	4.5045	2.0212	0.8031	0.4327
Rate of interest of 5%:						
10	7.1078	3.1528	0.7835			
20	12.0853	5.7022	1.8785	0.6139		
30	15.1411	7.2674	2.5507	0.9908	0.3769	
40	17.0170	8.2283	2.9633	1.2222	0.3769	0.2314
50	18.1687	8.8181	3.2167	1.3642	0.5189	0.2314
60	18.8757	9.1803	3.3722	1.4514	0.5189	0.2314
100	19.8404	9.6743	3.5844	1.5704	0.5927	0.2973
Rate of interest of 6%:						
10	6.8017	3.0144	0.7473			
20	11.1581	5.2561	1.7229	0.5584		
30	13.5907	6.5078	2.2677	0.8702	0.3118	
40	14.9491	9.2068	2.5719	1.0443	0.3118	0.1741
50	15.7076	7.5971	2.7418	1.1415	0.4090	0.1741
60	16.1311	7.8150	2.8367	1.1958	0.4090	0.1741
100	16.6186	8.0638	2.9449	1.2578	0.4488	0.2097
Rate of interest of 7%:						
10	6.5152	2.8847	0.7130			
20	10.3356	4.8595	1.5838	0.5084		
30	12.2777	5.8633	2.0265	0.7668	0.2584	
40	13.2649	6.3737	2.2515	0.8981	0.2584	0.1314
50	13.7668	6.6331	2.3659	0.9649	0.3252	0.1314
60	14.0219	6.7650	2.4240	0.9989	0.3252	0.1314
100	14.2681	6.8922	2.4801	1.0316	0.3469	0.1509

TABLE A.3 PRESENT WORTH OF PERIODIC PAYMENTS OF £1 EVERY t YEARS FOR $(n - t)$ YEARS (IN £'s) (*continued*)

Life of building	Life of components					
	1	2	5	10	20	30
Rate of interest of 8%:						
10	6.2468	2.7628	0.6806			
20	9.6035	4.5057	1.4590	0.4632		
30	11.1584	5.3129	1.8196	0.6777	0.2145	
40	11.9186	5.6869	1.9866	0.7771	0.2145	0.0994
50	12.2121	5.8601	2.0639	0.8231	0.2606	0.0994
60	12.3666	5.9403	2.0997	0.8445	0.2606	0.0994
100	12.4938	6.0063	2.1292	0.8620	0.2726	0.1103
Rate of interest of 9%:						
10	5.9952	2.6482	0.6499			
20	8.9501	4.1893	1.3469	0.4224		
30	10.1982	4.3402	1.6413	0.6008	0.1784	
40	10.7255	5.1152	1.7656	0.6762	0.1784	0.0754
50	10.9482	5.2313	1.8181	0.7080	0.2103	0.0754
60	11.0422	5.2804	1.8403	0.7215	0.2103	0.0754
100	11.1089	5.3151	1.8560	0.7310	0.2170	0.0815
Rate of interest of 10%:						
10	5.7590	2.5404	0.6209			
20	8.3649	3.9054	1.2459	0.3855		
30	9.3696	4.4316	1.4868	0.5342	0.1486	
40	9.7569	4.6345	1.5797	0.5915	0.1486	0.0573
50	9.9193	4.7126	1.6155	0.6136	0.1707	0.0573
60	9.9638	4.7513	1.6293	0.6221	0.1707	0.0573
100	9.9991	4.7698	1.6344	0.6273	0.1745	0.0608

where the payments are for regular maintenance, repairs or decoration, no payment arises for the year in which the life of the building is deemed to end. For example, if the building is to be repainted externally every five years over a life of sixty years, repainting would be necessary at the end of the fifth, tenth, fifteenth . . . to the fifty-fifth year.

Example A.3. Find the present worth of the annual payments necessary to cover service charges for a lift in a building with a life of sixty years. The stream pf payments is

TABLE A.3 PRESENT WORTH OF PERIODIC PAYMENTS OF £1 EVERY t YEARS FOR $(n-t)$ YEARS (continued)

Life of building	Life of components					
	1	2	5	10	20	30
Rate of interest of 11% :						
10	5.5370	2.4388	0.5935			
20	7.8393	3.6499	1.1547	0.3522		
30	8.6501	4.0764	1.3523	0.4762	0.1240	
40	8.9357	4.2268	1.4219	0.5199	0.1240	0.0437
50	9.0362	4.2797	1.4464	0.5353	0.1394	0.0437
Rate of interest of 12% :						
10	5.3282	2.3432	0.5674			
20	7.3658	3.4196	1.0721	0.3220		
30	8.0218	3.7662	1.2346	0.4257	0.1037	
40	8.2330	3.8778	1.2869	0.4591	0.1037	0.0334
50	8.3010	3.9136	1.3037	0.4698	0.1144	0.0334
Rate of interest of 13% :						
10	5.1317	2.2529	0.5428			
20	6.9380	3.2112	0.9973	0.2946		
30	7.4701	3.4935	1.1312	0.3814	0.0868	
40	7.6268	3.5767	1.1707	0.4070	0.0868	0.0256
50	7.6730	3.6011	1.1825	0.4145	0.0943	0.0256
Rate of interest of 14% :						
10	4.9464	2.1678	0.5194			
20	6.5504	3.0223	0.9292	0.2697		
30	6.9830	3.2528	1.0398	0.3425	0.0728	
40	7.0997	3.3149	1.0696	0.3621	0.0728	0.0196
50	7.1312	3.3317	1.0776	0.3674	0.0781	0.0196
Rate of interest of 15% :						
10	4.7716	2.0871	0.4972			
20	6.1982	2.8502	0.8673	0.2472		
30	6.5509	3.0388	0.9588	0.3083	0.0611	
40	6.6380	3.0853	0.9814	0.3234	0.0611	0.0151
50	6.6596	3.0967	0.9870	0.3271	0.0648	0.0151

TABLE A.4 ANNUAL EQUIVALENT OF AN INITIAL PAYMENT OF £1 (IN £1's)

No. of years	Rate of interest							No. of years
	4%	5%	6%	7%	8%	9%	10%	
1	1.04000	1.05000	1.06000	1.07000	1.08000	1.09000	1.10000	1
2	0.53020	0.53781	0.54544	0.55309	0.56079	0.56847	0.57620	2
3	0.36035	0.36721	0.37411	0.38105	0.38805	0.39507	0.40212	3
4	0.27549	0.28201	0.28859	0.29523	0.30200	0.30867	0.31576	4
5	0.22463	0.23098	0.23740	0.24389	0.25046	0.25710	0.26380	5
10	0.12329	0.12951	0.13587	0.14238	0.14903	0.15582	0.16275	10
15	0.08994	0.09634	0.10296	0.10980	0.11683	0.12406	0.13148	15
20	0.07358	0.08024	0.08719	0.09439	0.10185	0.10955	0.11746	20
25	0.06401	0.07095	0.07823	0.08581	0.09368	0.10181	0.11017	25
30	0.05783	0.06505	0.07265	0.08059	0.08883	0.09734	0.10590	30
35	0.05358	0.06107	0.06897	0.07723	0.08580	0.09464	0.10369	35
40	0.05052	0.05828	0.06646	0.07501	0.08386	0.09296	0.10226	40
45	0.04826	0.05626	0.06470	0.07350	0.08259	0.09190	0.10139	45
50	0.04655	0.05478	0.06344	0.07246	0.08174	0.09123	0.10086	50
55	0.04523	0.05367	0.06253	0.07174	0.08118	0.09079	0.10053	55
60	0.04420	0.05283	0.06188	0.07123	0.08080	0.09051	0.10033	60
70	0.04275	0.05170	0.06103	0.07062	0.08037	0.09022	0.10013	70
80	0.04181	0.05103	0.06057	0.07031	0.08017	0.09009	0.10004	80
90	0.04121	0.05063	0.06032	0.07016	0.08008	0.09004	0.10002	90
100	0.04081	0.05038	0.06081	0.07008	0.08004	0.09002	0.10001	100

TABLE A.4 ANNUAL EQUIVALENT OF AN INITIAL PAYMENT OF £1 (continued)

No. of years	Rate of interest					No. of years
	11%	12%	13%	14%	15%	
1	1.1100	1.1200	1.1300	1.1400	1.1500	1
2	0.5839	0.5917	0.5995	0.6073	0.6151	2
3	0.4092	0.4163	0.4235	0.4307	0.4380	3
4	0.3223	0.3292	0.3362	0.3432	0.3503	4
5	0.2706	0.2774	0.2843	0.2913	0.2983	5
10	0.1698	0.1770	0.1843	0.1917	0.1993	10
15	0.1391	0.1468	0.1547	0.1628	0.1710	15
20	0.1256	0.1339	0.1424	0.1510	0.1598	20
25	0.1187	0.1275	0.1364	0.1455	0.1547	25
30	0.1150	0.1241	0.1334	0.1428	0.1523	30
35	0.1129	0.1223	0.1318	0.1414	0.1511	35
40	0.1117	0.1213	0.1310	0.1407	0.1506	40
45	0.1110	0.1207	0.1305	0.1404	0.1503	45
50	0.1106	0.1204	0.1303	0.1402	0.1501	50

$$v^1 + v^2 + v^3 + \ldots + v^{59}.$$

Instead of summing the series the sum can be obtained as

$$a_{60} - v^{60}$$

with interest at 5 per cent this is 18·8757.

Since many evaluations of this form are necessary and these cannot be easily evaluated from standard tables special tables are worth preparing. A range of these are given above (Table A.3).

THE ANNUAL EQUIVALENT OF AN INITIAL PAYMENT OF UNITY

If a_n is the present worth of a stream of annual payments of unity payable for n years, £1 will purchase a stream of annual payments of $1/a_n$ for n years. A range of the annual values which can be obtained for an initial payment of £1 are given above (Table A.4).

It will be seen that the annual equivalent worth of an initial payment of unity at first declines very rapidly as the period over which payments are to be made increases but that it levels off after a few years (Figure A.4). The annual equivalent value is a very useful relationship since it relates initial and annual costs. Over a long life, sixty to seventy years or more, the annual equivalent is about equal to the rate of interest. The higher the rate of interest the more rapidly the annual equivalent value reaches stability.

Example A.4. Find the annual equivalent over forty years of an initial payment of £100, taking interest at 5 per cent.

This is $\qquad$ £100·$1/a_{40}$ = £5·8 .

METHODS OF EVALUATING STREAMS OF PAYMENTS

Two methods of evaluating streams of payments over time have now been discussed: (1) by bringing all payments to their present worth and (2) by bringing all payments to their annual equivalent worth.

The first method is of special value when the person who is interpreting the results is used to thinking in terms of capital costs, for example, designers and developers. The second method is of particular value for interpretation by such people as property owners and building users who normally think in terms of annual costs.

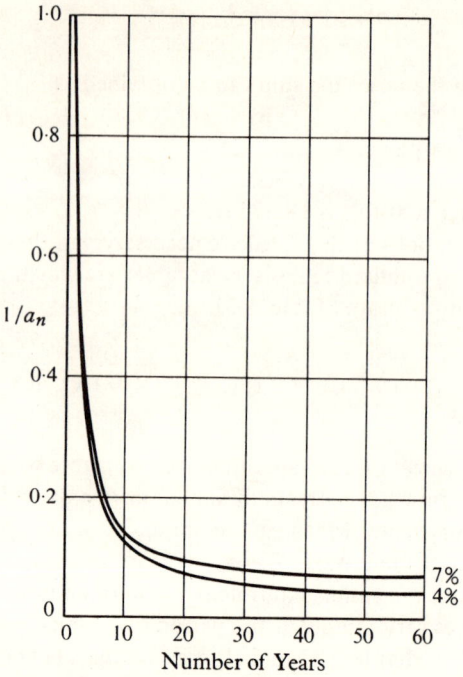

Figure A.4 Annual equivalent value of a present payment of £1 at i per cent interest

Streams of payments can, of course, be equated at any point in time, during, prior to, or after the life of the building. In fact, the equivalent worth at the end of the life has been suggested as a third way of evaluating streams of payments. However, values at that point in time do not correspond to any significant standard of comparison. Of course, the comparative values are the same at whatever point in time the comparisons are made. For instance, the annual equivalent is simply the present worth divided by a_n. Hence the relative relationship between the ultimate costs is the same whatever basis is used, while the absolute values are changed by a constant factor.

ADJUSTMENTS FOR THE ANNUAL TIME PATTERN

In the above tables and examples the underlying assumption is that all payments arise at the end of the year. It might be thought that on average payments would fall in the middle of the year. If this assumption were correct an adjustment would be necessary since the period during which

Appendix A 193

interest could accrue would be six months less than the period assumed and the present worth of such payments would be increased by $(1 + i/2)$. Again some periodical payments are payable more than once a year, being payable: half yearly, quarterly, monthly or even weekly. Adjustments can easily be made. For example, in the case of quarterly payments the adjustment to the value on an annual payments basis would be:

$$1/4 \,[1 + (1 + i/4) + (1 + 2i/4) + (1 + 3i/4)] = (1 + 3i/8).$$

Usually the initial payment is made in instalments as the work proceeds and an allowance needs to be made for the interest which accrues. For example, if interim payments of equal amounts of the initial costs, including fees, were to be spread over monthly intervals for two years, the adjustment would need to be as follows:

$$1/24 \,[1 + (1 + i/12) + (1 + 2i/12) + \ldots + (1 + 11i/12)$$
$$+ (1 + i) \,[[1 + (1 + i/12) + (1 + 2i/12) + \ldots + (1 + 11i/12)]]$$
$$= 1/24 \,[12 + i/12.11/2 \,(1 + 11)] \,[1 + (1 + i)]$$
$$= 1/48 \,(48 + 46i + 11i^2)$$

Thus at 5 per cent the interest element would be just over 11 per cent. Hence if the initial cost of the building was £100 000 and it was payable monthly over two years, its worth at the date of take over would be over £110 000.

Whether or not it is worth while introducing such refinements depends on the relative relationships between initial and running costs for the various designs being compared. Absolute costs are usually of less importance than relative costs in such comparisons. Moreover, of course, the errors in the estimates may have as large or larger effects than the effect of refinements in calculating the interest.

THE USE OF COMPOUND INTEREST FUNCTIONS

The four tables given in this appendix provide all the interest functions required to calculate the present worths or annual equivalents likely to be needed. Some further examples will demonstrate their use over the main part of the range of circumstances likely to be met. The range of interest rates provided should be adequate for most circumstances. Values at other rates of interest can be obtained from standard collections of interest rates.

Example A.5. Find the present worth of the maintenance costs of a building with a life of fifty years given that the annual cleaning costs are £200, the annual decoration costs are £100, the costs of internal and external painting are £1000 every five years and that a new roof covering will be required every thirty years at a cost of £10 000. Take interest to be 5 per cent. The present worth is:

$$
\begin{array}{lll}
& a_{50} & \text{£} \\
\text{£}200\,(18{\cdot}256) & = 3\,651{\cdot}2 & \text{(Table A.2)} \\[4pt]
& a_{50} - v^{50} & \\
\text{£}100\,(18{\cdot}1687) & = 1\,816{\cdot}9 & \text{(Table A.3)} \\[4pt]
& v^5 + v^{10} + \ldots + v^{45} & \\
\text{£}1000\,(3{\cdot}2167) & = 3\,216{\cdot}7 & \text{(Table A.3)} \\[4pt]
& v^{30} & \\
\text{£}10\,000\,(0{\cdot}2314) & = \underline{2\,314{\cdot}0} & \text{(Table A.1)} \\[4pt]
\text{Total} & \,\underline{10\,998{\cdot}8} &
\end{array}
$$

It will be noticed that the annual cleaning costs are incurred each year for fifty years because cleaning is spread throughout the year and is still necessary whether or not the building is shortly to be demolished. The annual redecoration costs, which probably consist largely of cleaning and touching up paintwork, are taken to be incurred at the end of the year and are not, therefore, incurred at the end of the fiftieth year.

Example A.6. Find the annual equivalent cost over the life of a building with an initial cost of £100 000, annual costs of £3000 for regular cleaning, quinquennial repairs of £10 000 and replacement costs every twenty years of £20 000. The life of the building can be taken as sixty years and interest at 5 per cent. The annual equivalent is:

$$
\begin{array}{lll}
 1/a_{60} & \text{£} & \\
100\,000\,(0{\cdot}05283) & = 5\,283{\cdot}0 & \text{(Table A.4)} \\
3\,000\,(1{\cdot}0) & = 3\,000{\cdot}0 & \\[4pt]
v^5 + v^{10} + \ldots + v^{55} & & \\
10\,000\,(3{\cdot}3722) = 33\,722 & & \text{(Table A.3)} \\[4pt]
 v^{20} + v^{40} & & \\
20\,000\,(0{\cdot}5189) = \underline{10\,378} & & \text{(Table A.3)} \\[4pt]
 1/a_{60} & & \\
44\,100\,(0{\cdot}05283) = 2\,329{\cdot}8 & & \text{(Table A.4)} \\[4pt]
& \underline{10\,612{\cdot}8} &
\end{array}
$$

Example A.7. Find the annual equivalent value for a building with a life of sixty years of a component which costs £1000 to install, lasts thirty years and then needs to be replaced at a cost of £1200, and which in the meantime costs £100 a year for an annual overhaul and an extra £500 every five years. Interest can be taken as 5 per cent. The first step is to summarize the stream of payments to be met. These are:

Initial cost £1000.
Annual payment £100 from year 1 to year 59.
Quinquennial payments £500 from year 5 to year 55.
Single payment £1200 − (£500 + £100) i.e. £600 after 30 years.

The next step is to calculate the present worth, this is:

$$
\begin{aligned}
&& £ && \\
1000\,(1) &= 1\,000 \cdot 0 && \\
\frac{a_{60} - v^{60}}{} && && \\
100\,(18 \cdot 8757) &= 1\,887 \cdot 6 && \text{(Table A.3)} \\
v^5 + v^{10} \ldots + v^{55} && && \\
500\,(3 \cdot 3722) &= 1\,686 \cdot 1 && \text{(Table A.3)} \\
v^{30} && && \\
600\,(0 \cdot 2314) &= 138 \cdot 8 && \text{(Table A.1)} \\
&\,\overline{4\,712 \cdot 5} && \\
&&& 1/a_{60}
\end{aligned}
$$

The annual equivalent can now be calculated, viz. 4 712.5 (0·05283)

$$= £249 \qquad \text{(Table A.4)}$$

APPENDIX B
Cost and Price Data

COSTS AND PRICES

There is some confusion over the use of the terms costs and prices. Strictly, costs relate to factors of production and prices to sales but sales to the first producer are factors of production to a subsequent producer. Generally, in construction, costs are incurred by the producer and contractor, and prices by the purchaser of the finished product. Perhaps more important is the distinction between costs to the contractor, tender prices for building works and the final price of building works. Costs to the contractor depend on the prices of labour, materials, plant and management, together with the level of productivity achieved. In preparing a tender price, these costs and levels of productivity have to be estimated. The contractor, in fixing the tender price, takes account of the expected costs and the market factors. These include both the state of competition and the nature of the contract. In the short term, when overheads to the contractor are fixed, it is worthwhile to take on work as long as the prime costs are covered and there is some contribution to fixed overheads. Consequently, when work is short tender prices may barely more than cover prime costs. When work is plentiful a substantial contribution to long-term profits will be sought. Hence, over time, tender price levels may fluctuate much more violently than cost levels. Contractors will also take account of their expectations of contract variations. They may price relatively keenly overall, but price work expected to be omitted at relatively low unit prices and work expected to be increased at relatively high unit yields.

CHANGES IN PRICE LEVELS

Prices of materials and labour change in step only up to a point. Some fluctuate around the general level of price increase because of short-term changes in world prices of the raw material or because of changes of bargining conditions. Others have a different relative price trend because of the effects of technological change and increasing market demands which allow economies of scale (Figures 6.1–6.3).

Whereas price indices for building materials and components are usually based on price changes of a fixed specified group of materials and components, price indices of building work generally, in effect, are based on a variable set of components of building work. This is because building work changes in its specification over time as forms of structures and their components change. For example, the nature of housing being constructed varies over time in form, size, types of materials and standards. Indices intended to measure changes in prices of a fixed bundle of building work are generally either based on weighted movements in the prices of materials and labour (there should be an allowance for productivity changes and market factors) or weighted movements in the prices of measured work. If no allowance is made for market factors, the index measures building costs rather than prices. Indices based on tender prices measure changes in prices at which building is contracted. Indices based on final prices measure the prices the purchaser finally pays. Both may reflect changes in the specification of the building work. In the short term, the indices can differ substantially according to their method of construction and it is important to choose the appropriate index when comparing prices fixed at different dates. In the long run, especially when inflationary forces are strong, the method of construction of the index has relatively less effect and can often be ignored, but it is still necessary to compare like with like.

Some idea of the way in which price indices can vary in the short run is given below (Table B.1).

TABLE B.1 COST AND PRICE INDICES (1970 = 100)

Year	Costs of new construction	DQSS tender prices	LA housing tenders	Price index of LA housing (E and W ex London)	Index of prices of new dwellings mortgaged to building societies
1973	147	197	181	189	206
1974	185	230	213	218	219
1975	223	228	235	238	239
1976	257	241	248	254	259
1977	301	271	279	283	285

Source: *Housing and Construction Statistics No. 24 4th Quarter 1977 − HMSO*

The long run prices have risen at an increasing rate with general inflation. Over the decade 1950−60, prices rose at less than 5 per cent a year; over the next decade the average annual increase was 6 per cent and over the last seven years, 25 per cent a year (Table B.2). Hence, to compare 1970 building prices with those for 1977, it is necessary to multiply by 2·74, while to compare 1950 prices with those for 1977 the multiplier would be 6·23.

TABLE B.2 BUILDING PRICE INDICES (1970 = 100)

Year	Index	Year	Index	Year	Index
1950	44	1960	63	1970	100
1951	50	1961	67	1971	109
1952	56	1962	69	1972	119
1953	55	1963	71	1973	140
1954	56	1964	74	1974	166
1955	58	1965	76	1975	205
1956	61	1966	78	1976	241
1957	62	1967	85	1977	274
1958	63	1968	90		
1959	62	1969	91		

Source: *Combination of price movements from a number of price indices.*

REGIONAL PRICE INDICES

Construction prices vary with the locality of the work. Systematic differences have been found in the prices of public authority dwellings and with other buildings. The regional differences are most marked in the case of one- and two-storey dwellings; they are less marked for large buildings for which national contractors usually compete. The regional differences are likely to reflect the types and forms of construction as well as differences in building costs. All the indices point to London as the most expensive area. Scotland also tends to have a high relative cost level (Table B.3). It is probable that there are also cost differences between city, town and country; these are probably reflected in the regional figures. The Department of the Environment recognizes the regional price differences in its cost yardstick (Table B.3).

PRICES OF BUILDINGS AND WORKS

Building prices for complete buildings are usually quoted per square metre based on a floor area measured between external walls and without any deduction for internal walls. Average prices are usually quoted without the inclusion of special equipment and excluding external works, other than those adjacent to the building. Prices per square metre reflect buildings of

TABLE B.3 REGIONAL PRICE DIFFERENCES

Region	Dwellings		Non-residential	Public Authority housing, Yardstick costs (variation price contracts)
	1 and 2 storey	8 storey and over		
Scotland	120	107	91	–
North	91	97	106	105
North West	104	101	97	100
Yorks and Humberside	95	98	102	100
Eastern	95	98	110	100
Wales and West Midlands	100	100	100	100
South West	105	102	109	100
South East (ex/London)	105	102	102	100
London Metropolitan area	–	–	–	112·5
Greater London	130	110	124	120 (Outer) 135 (Inner)

Sources: *Urban Development in Britain*, P.A. Stone, CUP (1970)
Architects' and Builders' Price Book, Spon, 1979.

average size, standard and form of construction. Hence actual prices can vary markedly from such average prices, reflecting differences in such factors, as location, marketing conditions and so on. For some types of building; for example, shops, the price of such variable items as shop fronts and fittings are frequently excluded. Despite the variations in the prices of particular types of buildings, variations in prices between building types are much greater.

Average unit prices of buildings are valuable for a number of purposes, for example, for obtaining a first approximation of likely prices and hence some idea of the types of building which the client can afford, for checking a price estimate built-up on details and for costing urban development.

Average price levels are given in builders' price books, such as Spon and by the Building Cost Information Service of the Royal Institution of Chartered Surveyors. Extensive analysis of price data has indicated that Spon average prices are representative, although the variations around the average are considerable. A much more detailed set of average prices is provided by the Building Cost Information Service. Sets are issued to subscribers several

TABLE B.4 AVERAGE PRICES OF BUILDING TYPES PER SQUARE METRE: £'s (AS AT END 1978)

Type of building	Price per square metre
Industrial buildings and warehouses	110–150
Workshops	185
General offices	260–300
Offices (air conditioned), banks etc.	320–350
Schools	200–230
Universities	200–290
Low cost housing—houses	135–160
Low cost flats	165–185
Residential institutions	165–230
Hotels	230–265
Hospitals and nursing homes	300–340
Health centres, clinics etc	220–240
Libraries	230–270
Service stations	210–250
Retail trade	150–200
Catering establishments	230–300
Concert halls, theatres, cinemas	280–380
Public halls, community centres etc.	180–200
Sports centres	200–300
Churches	250–300

Source: *RICS, Building Costs Information Service*
Architects' and Builders' Price Book, Spon

times a year. They quote averages and indications of variations.

Information on the price of external works is less widely available. Generally it is only given in books concerned with the costs of urban development, such as in the books of the author listed in the Bibliography.

Some idea of the range of building prices per square foot is given above (Table B.4).

BUILDING DESIGN PRICE RELATIVES

The relation between prices and design parameters has been examined for a number of building types, for example, for floor, area, number of storeys, shape and form, for housing, factory buildings, hospitals, university and school buildings. Some of these results have been published, while others can be inferred from cost yardsticks.

Economics of scale have been estimated for a number of types of buildings. In the case of public authority houses, the rate at which the prices per unit area change with changes in floor area is given approximately by the following formula:

$$Y_a = Y_o \left[(1 \cdot 5 - (\tfrac{1}{2} \cdot X_a)/X_a)/X_o)\right]$$

where Y_a is the price per square metre for the required area 'a'
Y_o is the price per square metre for given area 'o'
X_a is the required area 'a'
X_o is the given area 'o'

This formula is based on local authority price data and would not apply outside the range of floor areas of such dwellings, about 50 to 120 square metres. For example, if a dwelling of 100 square metres cost £150 a square metre, one of 80 square metres would cost approximately:

£150 $(1 \cdot 5 - \tfrac{1}{2} \cdot 80/100)$ = £165 a square metre.

Corresponding price relatives are given for factory buildings (see *Economics of Factory Buildings*). Similar size—cost relatives for various public buildings such as hospital and local authority buildings can be inferred from cost yardsticks (see *Architects' and Builders' Price Book*).

Price relatives for dwellings in relation to the number of storeys are given in the author's *Urban Development in Britain* and for factory buildings in his *Economics of Factory Buildings*. The latter also provides information of price relatives in relation to shape. The price relatives for various designs of houses are given in publications of the Building Research Establishment (see Bibliography).

PRICES OF BUILDING ELEMENTS

Costing alternative designs for building elements can be approached through detailed costing of drawings and specifications using prices for measured work. These are given in builders price books such as Spon and in trade journals such as the Architect Journal and in The Building Cost File prepared by The Building Cost Information Service. Since the aim is to produce comparative cost estimates, it is only necessary that the prices should be reasonably up-to-date and representative. Often costing can be based on comparative prices or approximate estimates, again available in Spon.

Elemental costs can be checked by comparing the results against cost elements summarised from tender prices. These are prepared and published by the Building Cost Information Service, Spon and Architect's Journal.

MAINTENANCE COSTS

Maintenance can be divided between repairs and renewals on the one hand and decoration on the other. A distinction must be made between maintenance and improvements and adaptions. The costs of repairs and renewals at constant prices tends to increase with age, while decoration costs tend to average out at a constant amount in real terms.

It would be expected that maintenance prices per unit of work would rise more rapidly than the unit prices for new work. The evidence that this happens is not very strong and it is probable that the price indices given for new work (Table B.2) broadly apply to maintenance costs. The regional price differences (Table B.3) are probably also broadly applicable.

HOUSING MAINTENANCE COSTS

Studies of housing maintenance costs suggest that for local authorities costs for renewals increase directly with age, while those for repairs and decoration remain constant. Adjusting for price rises, the figures (Clapp, 1963 see Bibliography) suggest annual costs for an average house of about £50 for decorations, £17 for repairs and £1·35 for each year of age for renewals; for a 40-year-old house the renewals cost would be about £54. Other studies would suggest that the maintenance costs for two- to four-storey flats would be about 13 per cent higher and those for high blocks 39 per cent higher.

MAINTENANCE AND OTHER RUNNING COSTS

While studies have been made of maintenance costs of particular types of building (see Bibliography) routine data is collected by the Building Maintenance Cost Information Service. This covers all types of occupancy costs. Data is collected for the following items:

Improvements and adaptations.
Decoration — external, internal.
Fabric maintenance — External walls, roofs, other structural items, fittings and fixture.
Fabric maintenance — internal finishes.
Services — plumbing and internal drainage, heating and ventilating, lifts and escalators.

Services — electric power and lighting, other services
Cleaning — windows, external services, internal.
Utilities — gas, electricity, fuel oil, solid fuel, water rates, effluents and drainage.
Administrative — service attendants, laundry, porterage, security, rubbish disposal, property management.
Overheads — property insurance and rates.
External works — repairs and decoration, external services, cleaning and gardening.

These data are collected from participating members of the cost service each year for each building with which they are concerned, together with data on the size, and specification of each building. The costs are expressed in terms of 100 square metres of floor area.

Some idea of the average costs of the elements for a number of building types is given below (Table B.5). These figures have been adjusted to end 1978 price levels. These elements do not, of course, correspond to those generally used in costs-in-use calculations. The best method is to cost on the basis of planned maintenance, staff requirements and calculated energy consumption. The results can then be compared with actual running cost expenditure to check the level and if necessary adjust.

TABLE B.5 AVERAGE SAMPLE RUNNING COSTS £'s PER 100 SQUARE METRES

Type of building	Industrial	Office	Old people homes	Schools	Universities	Laboratories
Decoration	96	68	62	27	57	67
Fabric maintenance	58	71	42	51	41	134
Services maintenance	87	148	18	24	77	652
Cleaning	216	323	*	*	267	331
Utilities	850	412	451	254	424	847
Administrative costs	168	603	1128	333	337	443
Overheads	426	844	380	369	305	491
Total	1901	2469	2081	1058	1508	2965

* Included with Administrative Costs

Source: *Building Maintenance Cost Service Limited.*

APPENDIX C
Statistical Treatment of Durability and Maintenance Data

DATA FOR MEASURING DURABILITY

Because of the difficulty of defining failures and because only a few people maintain adequate records of failures, it is difficult to obtain adequate data for measuring durability. Buildings tend to become economically obsolete long before they fail physically; their physical life is more or less infinite. Design cost evaluations are based on the economic life and it is of value to establish the life expectations of the various classes of buildings. During the course of the life of a building many of its parts are renewed. Similarly in the course of the life of a building component its parts are gradually renewed. Statements about life expectancy therefore relate to the identity of a building or a component, the renewal of minor parts being treated as maintenance.

Little information of value can be obtained from individual statements about incomplete lives or even from statements about the age when an identity was completely replaced. Similar buildings and components will behave differently, partly because of random differences in themselves and partly because of random differences in their use. Reliable indications of durability can only be obtained from random samples of experience. The basis for such data are registers of buildings. These need contain no more than the date of construction and the dates at which each component is replaced. If in addition they contain an account of the repairs carried out and their costs, they will also provide a basis for estimating maintenance costs.

MEASURING DURABILITY

If the only information available is the ages of the building or components still in use, it is only possible to assume that the life will exceed the current age of the oldest. The proportions of components in each age group provide no additional information unless there is some information relating to the number which originally entered each group and what has happened to them. Similarly, estimates about life cannot be made from information about the ages of death without a knowledge of the proportion whose life ended at that age.

In order to determine life expectations it is necessary to know both the number at risk at each year of age and the number which were demolished or scrapped. The probabilities of life ending at each age can then be calculated. These can be applied to a stationary population to determine the way in which their number will be reduced and the average period of durability.

THE LIFE TABLE METHOD

It will be supposed that data of the type described above has been obtained for a sample of buildings, or components of a particular type and used in a particular set of conditions. The sample might, for instance, relate to electric cookers or to gas water heaters fitted in domestic premises. For each member of the sample it would be necessary to know its age at the beginning of the year, whether it was still there at the end of the year and whether it had been removed and scapped because of failure, or in order to part exchange it for a more modern type. If a component in the latter class is still in use at the end of the year it can be counted but if there is no knowledge of it, it needs to be eliminated both from the number at risk and from the number scrapped. It will be noticed that it is not necessary to be able to study complete lives. In fact, the method described produces results which are more representative of current experience than would be obtained from the study of complete lives. The data can be arranged in the following way (Table C.1).

It will be seen that no firm conclusions can be drawn from the number in each age group. The rapid rate at which the number declines with age is just as likely to reflect the rate at which the stock was built up as the rate at which it has been scrapped. It is possible that not many of the type of component observed were sold until about seven years ago and that sales increased rapidly in the last year. On the other hand, it could be argued that there are many failures in the first year of life and that the rate is then fairly steady until the seventh year, after which it rapidly increases with age. A study of the number scrapped is again inconclusive. It might be thought that the fifth to eighth years is the period when the chance of failure is the greatest and that those surviving then have a good chance of several more years' life. This would indicate two groups of components, a result perhaps of differences in type, condition of use or situation associated with differences in durability. It may be noticed that by coincidence both the average of the stock at risk and the average age of those scrapped is six years.

In order to obtain a true picture of the probabilities of scrapping it is necessary to compare the number scrapped against the number of that age which were at risk. These observed probabilities are given in Column 4, Table C.1. It will be seen that the probabilities increase with age but in a rather

TABLE C.1 OBSERVED AND FITTED PROBABILITIES OF SCRAPPING

Age	No. at risk	No. scrapped	Observed probability of scrapping	Fitted probability of scrapping
0–1	52	1	0.02	0.03
1–2	20	1	0.05	0.04
2–3	20	1	0.05	0.06
3–4	20	2	0.10	0.09
4–5	18	2	0.11	0.13
5–6	15	3	0.20	0.18
6–7	15	4	0.27	0.25
7–8	10	4	0.40	0.34
8–9	4	2	0.50	0.45
9–10	2	1	0.50	0.59
10–11	3	2	0.67	0.77
11–12	1	1	1.00	1.00

The number at risk is the number at the beginning of the year.

erratic manner. The erratic increases merely reflect the smallness of the sample. It is usually correct to assume that the true probabilities in the population of all components (see Appendix D) increase with age in a regular way. The true probabilities are estimated by fitting a mathematical curve to the observed probabilities. This can be carried out in a variety of ways. The easiest is to plot the observed probabilities and to draw a smooth curve through them so as to obtain the closest possible fit. Other methods are to fit the curve statistically or to difference the observed probabilities and build up a fitted curve on the basis of regular changes in one of the higher order of differences. (A book on curve fitting should be consulted if further details are required.) The fitted values can be obtained from the fitted curve (Figure C.1). It will be noticed that the probability of being scrapped does not reach 50 per cent until the ninth year.

In order to obtain a measure of the average age reached by the component before it is likely to be scrapped, it is necessary to apply the probabilities of scrapping to a given stock of components and calculate the rate at which the stock will be reduced to zero.

Suppose, for example, the stock was taken as 1000. During the first year 1000 (0.03) = 30 would be scrapped, leaving 970 at the beginning of the second year. During that year 970 (0.04) = 38.8 would be scrapped, leaving 931 to the nearest unit at the beginning of the third year. In this way a life

208 *Building design evaluation*

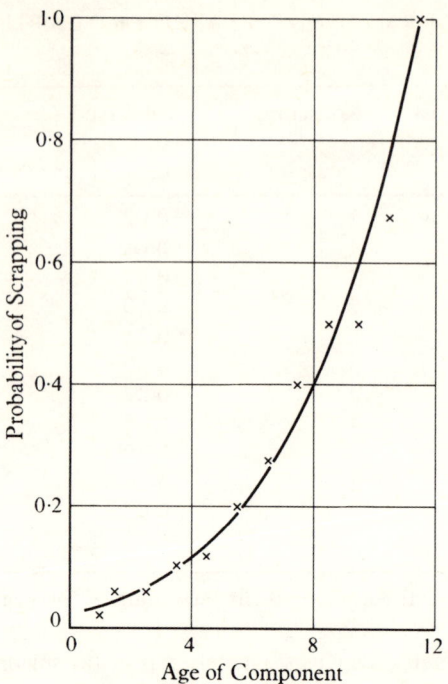

Figure C.1 Observed and fitted probabilities of scrapping

table can be constructed to show the way in which a given stock would gradually be reduced by scrapping until it was exhausted (Table C.2). The opening stock in the Table C.2 has been taken as unity only for convenience. Any other value could have been taken.

Estimating costs from average lives

In order to find the average expectation of life it is first necessary to calculate the average number existing in the middle of the year (Table C.2). This is half the sum of the number existing at the beginning of the year and the end of the year and is denoted by L_z.

$$L_x = 1/2\,(l_x + l_{x+1}).$$

L_x represents the total years of the life enjoyed by components aged x during that year of life. The total number of years of life of all the components is obtained by summing the L_x's. The total years of life is denoted by T_x.

TABLE C.2 LIFE TABLE OF A COMPONENT WITH A STOCK OF UNITY

Age	Probability of scrapping	Stock at beginning of year	No. scrapped	No. surviving	Average No. a middle of year	Total No. of years
x	p_x	l_x	d_x	l_{x+1}	L_x	T_x
0	0.03	1.0000	0.0300	0.9700	0.9850	6.3558
1	0.04	0.9700	0.0388	0.9312	0.9506	5.3708
2	0.06	0.9312	0.0559	0.8753	0.9033	4.4202
3	0.09	0.8753	0.0788	0.7965	0.8359	3.5169
4	0.13	0.7965	0.1035	0.6930	0.7448	2.6810
5	0.18	0.6930	0.1247	0.5683	0.6307	1.9362
6	0.25	0.5683	0.1421	0.4262	0.4973	1.3055
7	0.34	0.4262	0.1449	0.2813	0.3538	0.8082
8	0.45	0.2813	0.1266	0.1547	0.2180	0.4544
9	0.59	0.1547	0.0913	0.0634	0.1901	0.2364
10	0.77	0.0634	0.0488	0.0146	0.0390	0.0463
11	1.00	0.0146	0.0146	0.0000	0.0073	0.0073

210 *Building design evaluation*

$$T_x = L_x + T_{x+1}.$$

The expectation of life, e_0, can be obtained by dividing the total number of years of life of the component by the total number of components originally in the group. To obtain the complete expectation, $\overset{\circ}{e}_0$, a half must be added to adjust for the fact that scrapping will occur throughout the year and not only in the middle of the year.

$$\overset{\circ}{e}_0 = 1/2 + T_0/L_0.$$

The general formula for the expectation of life is $\overset{\circ}{e}_x$, where

$$\overset{\circ}{e}_x = 1/2 + T_x/l_x.$$

This gives the expectation of life for a component of age x. Thus the expectation of life for the component whose life table is given (Table C.2) is

$$\overset{\circ}{e}_0 = 1/2 + 6 \cdot 3558/1$$
$$= 6 \cdot 86 \text{ years}.$$

A component of, say, three years of age would have a future expectation of life of

$$\overset{\circ}{e}_3 = 1/2 + 3 \cdot 5169/0 \cdot 8753$$
$$= 4 \cdot 52 \text{ years}.$$

Obviously the total expectation of life rises with the age of the component since the expectation of the younger components includes the expectation of those which will be scrapped early in their potential lives.

The capitalized value of the replacements can then be calculated by discounting the costs of replacement expected to arise every $\overset{\circ}{e}_0$ years. The life of the component discussed might be taken as seven years. The discounted value of the replacement costs would then be:

$$v^7 + v^{14} + v^{21} + v^{28} + \ldots$$

the series terminating during the life of the building in which the component is used. The discounted values are, of course, multiplied by the cost of the component.

The actuarial method of estimating costs

It will be appreciated that the pattern of replacements is indicated more accurately by the expected proportions of scrapped components, the d_x's, than by the average expected life. The d_x's are, of course, the rates of scrapping for a given population of components. The replacement for a scrapped component forms part of a new population. Thus an attempt to trace the scrapping and replacement of a population of components fixed in a group of buildings would be very complex, since different series of populations would be superimposed one upon another, each of which would give rise to its own distribution of scrapped components and hence replacements, thus starting a fresh series of populations. These difficulties do not arise if the annual cost of replacing the original population is related to the components in existence during each year and upon which charges can be raised. The concept is that over the lives of a population of components a charge must be levied sufficient to cover their capital cost with interest and this is collected through equal annual charges levied on those items actually in existence each year. A charge calculated in this way is equally applicable to the replacements, whenever they occur, as to the original population.

The capitalized cost of replacing the components in the initial population is the discounted value of the expected proportions of scrapping:

$$d_0 v^{1/2} + d_1 v^{3/2} + d_2 v^{5/2} + \ldots$$

What is required is the equivalent annual cost of replacement to be levied on the components surviving. In the first year there will be l_0 components upon which the charge can be levied, in the second year l_1 and so on. The capitalized value of charges of unity levied on each surviving component will be:

$$l_0 v^0 + l_1 v^1 + l_2 v^2 + \ldots$$

It will be noticed that it has been assumed that whereas the scrappings are spread throughout the year and occur on average in the middle of the year, the charges are levied on components existing in the beginning of the year. This is normal practice. The equivalent annual cost is:

$$1/(1+i)^{1/2} \cdot \frac{\sum_{x=0}^{\infty} v^x d_x}{\sum_{x=0}^{\infty} v^x l_x}.$$

This equivalent annual cost is applicable to each component of that type which is fitted. It is an average cost of replacement which allows for the rate at which components are scrapped and for replacement charges to be levied only on components from the population which remains. Each replacement component in its turn carries a similar charge. The capitalized value can be found in the usual way. The capitalized value is, of course, not affected by the assumption as to when the charge is levied.

The equivalent capitalized value is:

$$a_n/(1+i)^{3/2} \cdot \frac{\sum_{x=0}^{\infty} v^x d_x}{\sum_{x=0}^{\infty} v^x l_x} \cdot$$

times the value of the component.

DATA FOR MEASURING MAINTENANCE COSTS

It is only rarely that data are specially compiled for measuring maintenance costs. Usually the records from which data are obtained have been compiled for some other purpose, e.g. controlling the labour force and maintenance expenditure. The information varies considerably in detail; sometimes it can be related to individual components, sometimes only to groups of components or types of work. However, the data generally have some value for determining the general level of expenditure. When information relating to a particular type of component is not available, the costs can only be built up by costing a programme of preventive maintenance and checking the level of the sum of a number of such costings against recorded expenditure.

Mainteance costs are related to the size of the component to be maintained. Size is approximately measured by initial cost and it is often convenient to convert the maintenance costs to percentages of the initial costs. This enables different sized of the same type of component to be treated as homogeneous, thus increasing the number of observations in the group and hence the reliability of the resulting statistics. Since costs change over time as a result of inflationary price rises, they must be deflated before being compared with the initial prices. The maintenance cost percentage is thus:

Mainteance cost percentage for the xth year of life

$$= \frac{100 \cdot (\text{maintenance cost for } x\text{th year})(\text{price index, Year o})}{(\text{initial cost at Year o})(\text{price index Year } x)}$$

Example C.1. The maintenance cost for a given component for year 1960 was £15; the component cost £90 in 1950, when the price index for that type of component was 120; the corresponding price index in 1960 was 180. The maintenance cost as a percentage of its initial cost is:

$$\frac{100.\ 15.120}{90.180} = \frac{100}{9} = 11 \cdot 1 \text{ per cent.}$$

Usually the maintenance cost percentages will vary with age — generally only decoration and servicing costs are unaffected by age and even decoration is often cyclical. The maintenance cost percentages are therefore plotted against age to determine if there is any relationship and what it is. For housing maintenance a linear relationship with age has been established. For individual components maintenance costs often form a curve convex to the x-axis. The maintenance costs rise with age and decline again as the component reaches the end of its life and it ceases to be worth to replace worn out

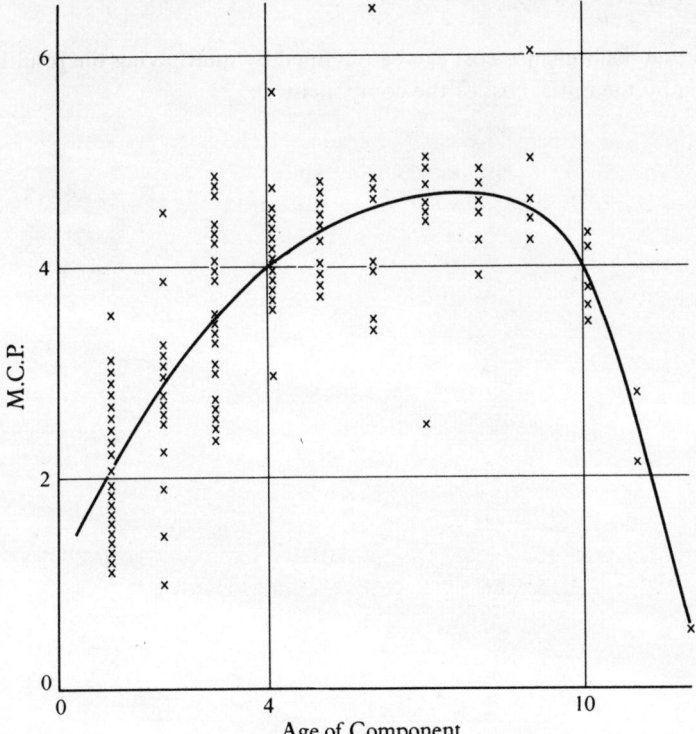

Figure C.2 Observed and fitted M.C.P.'s

parts. The relationship with age can be found by fitting a mathematical curve, by smoothing the averages for each year, or by drawing a freehand curve through the observations (Figure C.2). The cost at each year of age can then be read from the fitted curve.

Strictly, the maintenance cost should be related to the probability of the component being in existence at each year of age and hence requiring maintenance. The annual maintenance costs associated with each year of age should therefore be weighted by the L's (Table C.2).

The capitalized value is therefore:

$$v^{1/2} (MCP)_0 . L_0 + v^{3/2} (MCP)_1 . L_1 + \ldots = \frac{1}{(1+i)^{1/2}} \sum_{x=0}^{\infty} v_x (MCP)_x . L_x$$

where $(MCP)_x$ is the maintenance cost percentage for components aged x.

The average annual cost can be obtained as before by dividing the above expression by $\sum_{x=0}^{\infty} v^x . l_0$.

The actual maintenance cost can be obtained by multiplying the resulting expression by the initial cost of the component.

APPENDIX D
Sampling and errors

SAMPLING

The object of this Appendix is to provide readers who have little knowledge of statistics with an understanding of the first principles of sampling and the propagation of errors. The treatment is deliberately simplified and is not intended to be rigorous. Any reader who wishes to pursue the matter should refer to one of the texts on this subject.

Usually the data available represent only a sample of the items to be measured. The need is usually to draw inferences about a population while the only data available relate to a sample. For example, there might be a need to establish the price per square metre of 255 m/m brickwork. Clearly, it would not be practicable to measure the cost of every metre constructed, even over a short period of time, and the price can only be measured on the basis of a sample. It is important that the sample should be representative of the whole population. Extensive studies have indicated that it is more or less impossible for an observer to choose a truly representative sample. Representative samples can only be obtained by selecting each item at random by a method which ensures that each member of the population has an equal chance of selection. For example, a sample of brickwork prices should be selected so that each price which has been quoted has an equal chance of selection. This might be achieved by first listing all the firms handling this type of work and drawing a random sample of them weighted in proportion to their volume of work of the required type and then drawing a random sample from the prices obtained by each of the firms selected in the first stage. A random sample is one drawn by chance, such as the winning numbers in a sweepstake.

Normally, however closely a job is defined, all the measurements relating to it vary. The amount of materials, the labour expenditure and the overheads all vary from one job to another. Similarly the means of a number of separate samples would vary, although the larger the samples the less the means would tend to vary. Consequently in making inferences about a population value from a sample value, it is necessary to be able to estimate how far the population mean is likely to vary from the sample mean. This can be estimated from the variation of the values in the sample about the sample mean.

216 *Building design evaluation*

Suppose it is required to estimate the price per square metre of some type of work such as 255 m/m brickwork. A random sample is drawn from the population of prices and there is available a sample of n prices which can be represented by

$$x_1\ x_2\ x_3\ x_4\ \ldots x_{n-1}\ x_n.$$

The mean value $\bar{x}$ is the sum of all the values divided by their number.

$$\bar{x} = \frac{1}{n}\sum_{i=1}^{i=n} x_i$$

It can be shown that the most efficient measure of the way the values vary is obtained by summing the squares of the differences between each individual value and the mean. The sum of squares naturally tends to be larger the larger the number of items in the sample. The measure of variation is therefore standardized by dividing the sum of squares by their number less 1; this is called the Variance.

$$\text{Variance} = \frac{1}{n-1}\sum_{i=1}^{i=n}(x_i - \bar{x})^2. \text{ This is denoted by } s^2.$$

The square root of this quantity s is called the standard deviation and can be used to provide a measure of the standard error of the mean. This equals

$$s_z = s/\sqrt{n}.$$

It has also been found that most types of observations have values which are distributed in a certain way, in accordance with what is known as the normal curve. The normal curve is a symmetric curve which conforms to a given shape whatever the scale of the values. Among other things is provides the basis of a measure of the chance of a population mean lying within given increments (expressed in terms of the standard error of the mean) of the sample mean. The population mean lies between

$$\bar{x} + ts/\sqrt{n} \text{ and } \bar{x} - ts/\sqrt{n}$$

The values of t have been calculated and depend on n, the size of the sample and p the probability of being certain of the correctness of the inference. Naturally t increases in size as the degree of certainty is increased and falls as the size of the sample is increased (Table D.1).

TABLE D.1 VALUES OF t

Size of sample = n	$p = 0.05$	$p = 0.01$
2	12.7	63.7
5	2.8	4.6
10	2.3	3.2
20	2.1	2.9
∞	2.0	2.6

A value of $p = 0.05$ gives 95 per cent certainty of the correctness of the inference and $p = 0.01$ gives 99 per cent certainty.

An example will indicate how these principles are applied.

Example D.1. Suppose that the prices given by a sample of a given type of work are:

$$29, 21, 25, 30, 19, 32, 23, 23, 22, 26$$

their sum would be 250 and their mean value 25, viz:

$$\bar{x} = \frac{1}{n} \sum_{i=1}^{i=n} x_i = \frac{1}{10}(29 + 21 + 25 + \ldots + 26) = \frac{250}{10} = 25.$$

The differences from the mean are:

$$+4 - 4 + 0 + 5 \ldots + 1$$

and the sum of their squares is:

$$16 + 16 + 0 + 25 + \ldots + 1$$

and their sum is 160.

$$\text{Variance } s^2 = \frac{1}{n-1} \sum_{i=1}^{i=n} (x_i - \bar{x})^2$$

$$= 160/9 = 17.7.$$
$$s = 4.2 \text{ (say)}.$$

The standard error of the mean $s_{\bar{x}} = s/\sqrt{n}$
$$= 4.2 \sqrt{10} = 1.33 \text{ (say)}.$$

The population mean lies between $\bar{x} \pm t \cdot s/\sqrt{n}$.

If the probability of being correct is to be 0·95, $t = 2\cdot3$ and the population means lies between

$$25 \pm 2\cdot3\,(1\cdot33)$$

i.e. between 21·96 and 28·06.

Thus the means of 95 per cent of the samples would be expected to be between 22 and 28. This is more or less equivalent to saying that there is a 95 per cent probability that the population mean lies within these limits. The limits could be reduced by taking a larger sample or by accepting a lower level of probability.

STATISTICAL ERRORS

Thus it will be seen that the estimate derived from the process of sampling is a range, not a single value. A range can also result from inaccuracies of measurement. Measurements to the nearest millimetre are only correct to plus or minus half a millimetre. Other estimates are also often only correct within given limits. For example, the life of a material can never be known to an exact number of years. All values from which costs-in-use are built up are subject to error in this way. It is, therefore, necessary to know how errors combine.

PROPAGATION OF ERRORS

Errors combine according to the ordinary laws of algebra. Taking x_1 and e_1 to represent a value and its error and x_2 and e_2 to represent the value and error of another item to be combined with it, one obtains:

Error of a sum

$$(x_1 + e_1) + (x_2 + e_2) = (x_1 + x_2) + (e_1 + e_2).$$

Error of a difference

$$(x_1 + e_1) - (x_2 + e_2) = (x_1 - x_2) + (e_1 - e_2).$$

Error of a product

$$(x_1 + e_1)(x_2 + e_2) = x_1 x_2\,(1 + e_1/x_1)(1 + e_2/x_2).$$

Error of a quotient

$$(x_1 + e_1)/(x_2 + e_2) = x_1/x_2 \; (1 + e_1/x_1)/(1 + e_2/x_2).$$

If the brackets in the case of the errors of a product and a quotient are multiplied out it will be seen that the expressions can be simplified because subsequent terms after the first few will normally be very small.
Thus the error of a product becomes:

$$x_1 x_2 \; (1 + e_1 x_1 + e_2/x_2 + e_1 e_2/x_1 x_2)$$

while the error of a quotient becomes:

$$x_1/x_2 \; (1 + e_1/x_1 - e_2/x_2 - e_1 e_2/x_1 x_2 + (e_2/x_2)^2 \text{ and higher powers}).$$

Generally, however, positive and negative errors will be equally likely and the errors of the estimates will combine in unfavourable as well as in favourable ways. However, relative errors are likely to be less than unity and will generally be small and hence their products and squares will normally be very small and can be ignored.

In the most unfavourable circumstances the errors will combine in the following ways:

Error of a sum

$$(x_1 \pm e_1) + (x_2 \pm e_2) = (x_1 + x_2) \pm (e_1 + e_2).$$

Error of a difference

$$(x_1 \pm e_1) - (x_2 \pm e_2) = (x_1 - x_2) \pm (e_1 + e_2).$$

Error of a product

$$(x_1 \pm e_1)(x_2 \pm e_2) = x_1 x_2 \; (1 \pm (e_1/x_1 + e_2/x_2)) \; \text{(approx.)}$$

Some examples will clarify the use of these formulae.

Example D.2

Sum

$$(20 \pm 2) + (15 \pm 3) = 35 \pm 5.$$

Difference

$$(20 \pm 2) - (15 \pm 3) = 5 \pm 5.$$

Product

$$(20 \pm 2)(15 \pm 3) = 300\,(1 \pm (2/20 + 3/15)) = 300\,(1 \pm 3/10). \text{ (approx.)}$$

Quotient

$$(20 \pm 2)/(15 \pm 3) = 20/15\,(1 \pm (2/20 + 3/15)) = 4/3\,(1 \pm 3/10). \text{ (approx.)}$$

Frequently the number of items will be large and their errors will compensate each other. In such cases the best estimate for the errors of sums or differences will be:

$$\pm \sqrt{(e_1^2 + e_2^2 + e_3^2 + \ldots + e_n^2)}$$

Example D.3. Find the sum of 15, 20, 6, 4, 30 and 25 where the errors are plus or minus 1, 2, 1, 1, 2 and 5 respectively but the errors are expected to be compensating.

$$\text{The sum} = 100 \pm \sqrt{(1^2 + 2^2 + 1^2 + 1^2 + 2^2 + 5^2)}$$
$$= 100 \pm \sqrt{(36)} = 100 \pm 6.$$

Often samples are designed to give the same relative errors for each item, say p per cent. Then in the most unfavourable circumstances the error in a sum or a difference is:

$$\pm p/100 \text{ (sum or difference).}$$

Where the errors are compensating the error becomes

$$\pm p/100 \sqrt{(x_1^2 + x_2^2 + \ldots + x_n^2)}$$

Example D.4. Find the error in the sum of 6, 8, 3, 5, 3, 1 where each figure is correct to ± 10 per cent.
In the most unfavourable circumstances the error is:

$$\pm 10/100\,(26) = \pm 2 \cdot 6.$$

Where the errors compensate the error in the sum is

$$\pm 10/100 \sqrt{(6^2 + 8^2 + 3^2 + 5^2 + 3^2 + 1^2)} = \pm 1 \cdot 2.$$

Bibliography

CHAPTER 1

Building Economics. P.A. STONE (Land Ownership and Resources, Dept. of Estate Management, University of Cambridge, 1958)
Building Economy. P. A. STONE 2nd Edition (Pergamon, 1976)
Cost Repetition Maintenance. (Economic Commission for Europe, U.N., 1963)

CHAPTER 2

A Short Collection of Actuarial Tables. (Cambridge University Press, latest edition)
Building Economy. P.A. STONE 2nd Edition (Pergamon, 1976)
Building Standards and Costs. P.A. STONE *(Royal Institute of British* Architects: Annual Conference, 1966)
The Relationships of Capital, Maintenance and Running Costs. Ministry of Public Building and Works (H.M.S.O., 1970)

CHAPTER 3

'Design Economics — Building Today and Tomorrow'. P.A. STONE (*J. Roy. Inst. Surveyors,* **92** (7), 1960)
'Design Evaluation for a Hospital Building'. P.A. STONE (*Architects' Journal,* **140** (10), 1964)
Factory Buildings, Evaluation and Decisions — Better Factories. (Institute of Directors, 1963)
Local Authority Offices. (Department of Environment, 1971)
The Economics of Factory Buildings. (Factory Building Studies No. 12, H.M.S.O., 1962)

CHAPTER 4

The Design of Roofs for Single-Storey General-Purpose Factories. P. MANNING (University of Liverpool, 1962).

The Economics of Building Design P.A. STONE (J. Roy. Statist. Soc., A123 (3), 1960).
The Economics of Factory Buildings (Factory Building Studies No. 12, HMSO, 1962)
Functional Life as a Basis for Design. J.C. HAMILTON (*Industrialization Forum* **6**, No. 3 and 4 U.S.A., 1975)

CHAPTER 5

An Introduction to Cost Planning. (*R.I.C.S.*, 1971)
Estimating and Cost Control. J. NISBET – Batsford 1961
'Examples from Bills of Quantity (Operational Format)'. E.R. SKOYLES (*Quantity Surveyor* **25** No. 6, May/June 1969)
Local Authority Offices (Department of Environment – 1971)
The Economics of Factory Building (Factory Building Studies No. 12, H.M.S.O., 1962)
'The Economics of Multi-storey Buildings'. F. WOOLARD (*Architectural Science,* University of Sydney, 1956)
'The Functions and Uses of Bills of Quantities', (*Chartered Surveyor* **95** (8))
'The Wilderness Cost of Building Study Group'. (*R.I.C.S.* 1964)
Ultimate Cost of Building Walls. C.T. GRIMM and J.C. GROSS (Structural Clay Products Institute, Washington, 1958)

CHAPTER 6

Building Economics. I.H. SEELEY (Macmillan, 1977)
An Introduction to Civil Engineering Economics. (Institution of Civil Engineers, latest edition)
Cost Repetition Maintenance. (Economic Commission for Europe, U.N., 1963)
'The Economics of Building Design'. P.A. STONE (*J. Roy. Statist. Soc.,* **A123** (3), 1960)

CHAPTER 7

'Administration and the Costs of Hospital Maintenance'. P.A. STONE (*The Hospital,* **60** (7 and 8), 1964)
'Analysis of a Questionnaire on Attitudes to Risks'. S.J. MELINCK, S.K.D. WOOLLEY and R. BALDWING (J.F.R.O. Fire Research Note 962).
Architects' and Builders' Price Book. DAVIES, BELFIELD and EVEREST (Spon [annually])
'Cost Comparisons in Housing Maintenance'. M.A. CLAPP (*Local Government Finance,* **67** (Oct), 1963)

Cost Repetition Maintenance. (Economic Commission for Europe, U.N., 1963)
'Decision Techniques for Town Development'. P.A. STONE (*Operational Research Quarterly*, **15**, 185–205, 1964)
'Double Glazing and Double Windows'. (*Building Research Station Digest* 1409 H.M.S.O).
'Energy Consumption and Cost in Two Large Air-Conditioned Buildings'. (*Building Research Station Current Papers* 40/68)
Estimating for Buildings and Public Works. B. DAVIES (Price Building Estimator Publications)
'Factors Affecting the Relative Costs of Multistorey Housing'. COST RESEARCH PANEL (*J. Roy. Inst. Surveyors*, **90** (9), 1958)
Factory Building Studies:
    Nos. 2. *The Lighting of Factories*
         3. *Floor Finishes for Factories*
         7. *Structural Frameworks for Single-storey Factories*
        10. *Electricity Supply and Distribution*
        11. *Thermal Insulation in Factory Buildings*
        12. *The Economics of Factory Buildings*
           (H.M.S.O., 1961/2)
Flats and Houses 1958. (Ministry of Housing and Local Government, H.M.S.O., 1958)
Guide to Current Practice. (Institution of Heating and Ventilating Engineers, London
'Heat Losses Through Ground Floors' (*Building Research Station Digest* 145, H.M.S.O.)
Homes for Today and Tomorrow. (Ministry of Housing and Local Government, H.M.S.O., 1961)
Hospital Costing Returns. Department of Health and Social Security (H.M.S.O.) (annual)
Housing, Town Development, Land and Costs. P.A. STONE (The Estates Gazette Ltd, 1963)
'Investigation of Maintenance and Energy Costs for Services in Office Buildings'. N.O. WILLBANK, J.P. DOWALL and A. SLATER. (*Building Research Station Current Paper* 38/71)
Laxton's Building Price Book. P.J. WALTERS (Kelly's Directories Ltd (annually))
'Maintenance Standards and Costs'. R.F. STEVENS (*Building Research Establishments Current Paper* 55/74)
'Occupancy Costs of Offices'. H.J. PARKINS, R.F.C. HOW., J. HOOPER and M.T. Poole, (*Building Research Establishments Current Paper* 44/77, 1977)
Recommended Practice for the Lighting of Buildings (Illuminating Engineering Society, London)

'Refuse Collection from Houses and Flats by Pipeline'. R.G. COURTNEY and D.E. SEXTON (Building Research Establishement Current Pages 4/73)
Techniques for Valuing Social Assets. P.A. STONE. *New Horizons in Land and Property Values* (Roy. Inst. Surveyors, 1966)
Thermal Insulation of Buildings. G.D. NASH, J. COMRIE and H.F. BROUGHTON (H.M.S.O., 1955)
The Maintenance of Buildings: Conference Report 1965. (Ministry of Public Buildings and Works, 1965)
'Standardised U-Values'. (*Building Research Station Digest* 108, H.M.S.O.)
'The Maintenance and Running Costs of School Buildings'. M.A. CLAPP and B.D. CULLEN (*Building Research Station Current Paper* 72/68, 1968)
Thermal Insulation of Building. C.C. HANDISYDE and D.J. MELLUISH (H.M.S.O., 1971)
'The Tender Prices of Local Authority Flats'. W.J. REINERS (*J. Roy. Inst. Surveyors*, **91** (2), 1958)
Traffic in Towns (H.M.S.O., 1963)
Weekly and Monthly Journals:
  Architects' and Builders' News
  Architects' Journal
  Building
  Chartered Surveyor
  Civil Engineering and Public Works Review
  Municipal Journal
  Surveyor and Municipal and County Engineer

CHAPTER 8

The Economics of Building Designs. P.A. STONE (*J. Roy. Statist. Soc.*, **A123** (3), 1960)
The Economics of Factory Buildings. (Factory Building Studies No. 12, H.M.S.O., 1962)
'Hospital Planning and Decision Techniques', P.A. STONE (*The Hospital*, **58** (11), 1962)

CHAPTER 9

'Cost Predition: A guide to Design Decisions'. P.A. STONE (*Architects' Journal*, **133**, 3437, 1961)
Statistics in Theory and Practice. L.R. CONNOR (Pitman, latest edition)
'The Economics of Building Designs'. P.A. STONE (*J. Roy. Statist. Soc.*, **A123** (3), 1960)

CHAPTER 10

'Cost Benefit Analysis in Town Planning'. N. LICHFIELD (*Urban Studies*, **33** (3), 1966)

'Decision Techniques for Town Development', P.A. STONE (*Operational Quarterly*, **15**, 185–205, 1964)

Economics of Planned Development. N. LICHFIELD (The Estates Gazette Ltd, 1956)

Housing, Town Development, Land and Costs. P.A. STONE (The Estates Gazette Ltd, 1963)

'Urban Development and Cost Prediction'. P.A. STONE (*Town Planning Review*, **30** (3 and 4), 1959/60)

CHAPTER 11

' A Cost Study of Concrete and Steel Framework'. D.V. MASKELL (J.F.R.O., *Fire Research Note 905*, 1972)

'Attic Housing'. S.A. COVINGTON (*Building Research Establishment – Current Paper* 49/78)

'Basements in Housing: A Feasibility Study'. S.A. COVINGTON (*Building Research Establishment – Current Paper* 4/78)

'Clear Spanning First Floors in Housing'. S.A. COVINGTON (*Building Research Establishment – Current Paper* 22/78)

'Conserving Energy in Buildings'. P. BURBERRY, L. ALDRIGE and B. DAY (*Architects' Journal*, November 11th, 1974)

'Construction Technology'. W. VILLARS (*Architects' Journal*, January, 3 1979)

'Design Evaluation for a Hospital Building'. P.A. STONE (*The Architects' Journal*, **140** (10), 1964)

'Economics of Structural Fire Protection'. R. BALDWIN (*Building Research Establishment – Current Paper* 45/75)

'Energy Conservation'. (*Building Research Establishment – Current Paper* 56/75)

Factory Buildings, Evaluation and Decisions – Better Factories. (Institute of Directors, 1963)

Heating Installations. (M. of P.B. & W. – 1967)

'Life–Cycle Costing in the Hotel Industry'. J.J. CLARK and R.H. PEUNER (*Industrialization Forum* **6** No. 3–4 U.S.A., 1975)

'Maintenance and Operating Costs of Modern Boilers'. R.N. MILNER and R.C. WORDSWORTH (*Building Research Establishment – Current Paper* 59/78, 1978)

'Occupancy Costs of Offices'. H.J. PURKIS, R.F.C. HOW., N.J. HOOPER and

M.T. POOLE (*Building Research Establishment – Current Paper* 44/77)
'Office Building Design for Low Energy Costs'. M. EDGE, R. WINCH and W. BURT (*Estates Gazette,* Dec 30th, 1978)
'Passive and Active Fire Protection – The Optimum Combination'. R. BALDWIN and P.H. THOMAS (J.F.R.O. *Fire Research Note* 963)
'Permanent Supplementary Artificial Lighting of Deep Hospital Wards'. A.H. COAKRAM, J.B. COLLINS and N.O. MILBANK (*Building Research Station – Current Paper* 30/70)
'Potential Water Economy Measures in Dwellings'. M.E. RUMP (*Building Research Establishment – Current Paper* 65–78)
'The Design of Economic Dwelling Forms', G.G. TRICKEY (*Architects' Journal,* July 23, 1975)
The Economics of Factory Buildings. (Factory Building Studies No. 12, H.M.S.O., 1962)
The Economics of Safety – Explosions'. S.K.D. COWARD (J.F.R.O. *Fire Research Note* 982)
Thermal environment – some economic considerations'. P.A. STONE (Thermal environment in modern buildings – IHVE/BRS Symposium 1968)
'The Structure, Size and Costs of Urban Settlements'. P.A. STONE (Cambridge University Press, 1973)
'Urban Development in Britain'. P.A. STONE (Cambridge University Press, 1970)

CHAPTER 12

' Cost Benefit Analysis in Town Planning.' N. LICHFIELD (Cambridge C.C., 1966)
Economics, Town Planning and Traffic. D.J. REYNOLDS (Inst. Econ. Affairs, 1966)
'Estimating the Social Benefit of Constructing an Underground Railway in London'. C.D. FOSTER and M.E. BEESLEY (*J. Roy. Statist. Soc.,* **A126** (46–78), 1963)
Housing, Town Development, Land and Costs. P.A. STONE (The Estates Gazette Ltd., 1963)
The Assessment of Priority for Road Improvements. D. J. REYNOLDS (Road Research Technical Paper No. 48, H.M.S.O., 1960)
'The Structure, Size and Costs of Urban Settlements'. P.A. STONE (Cambridge University Press, 1973)
'Value for Money in Town Planning'. N. LICHFIELD (*J. Roy. Inst. Surveyors,* 1959)

'Urban Development in Britain'. P.A. STONE (Cambridge University Press, 1970)
'Urban Development and Cost Prediction'. P.A. STONE (*Town Planning Review,* **30** (3 and 4), 1959/60)

CHAPTER 13

Factory Buildings, Evaluation and Decisions. P.A. STONE. *Better Factories.* (The Institute of Directors, 1963)
'Hospital Planning and Decision Techniques'. P.A. STONE (*The Hospital,* **58** (11), 1962)
'The Economics of Building Design'. P.A. STONE (*J. Roy. Statist. Soc.,* **A123** (3), 1960)
The Economics of Factory Buildings. (Factory Building Studies No. 12, H.M.S.O., 1962)

CHAPTER 14

'A Cost Benefit Analysis Applied to Foamed Plastic Ceilings'. I.C. APPLETON (*Building Research Establishment – Current Paper* 50/77)
'An Integrated Life-Cycle Costing and Energy Model'. G. MECKLER (*Industrialization Forum* **16** No. 3–4, U.S.A., 1975)
A Survey of Quality and Value in Building. M.E. BURT (*Building Research Establishment,* 1978)
Cost Benefit Analysis – A Survey. A.R. PREST and R. TURVEY. (*The Economic Journal,* Vol. **75** (300), 1965)
'Cost Benefit Analysis and Public Expenditure'. G.H. PETERS (Eaton Paper 8 IEA 1966)
'Design Decisions for Town Development'. P.A. STONE (*Operational Research Quarterly* **15**, 185–205, 1964)
Economics of a New Factory. P.D. REYNOLDS (*Better Factories, The Institute of Directors,* 1963)
'Efficiency in Government Through Systems Analysis'. R.N. MCKEAN (John Wiley, New York, 1958)
Terotechnology Handbook. Department of Industry (H.M.S.O., 1978)
The Finance and Analysis of Capital Projects. A.J. MERRITT and A. SYKES (Longmans, 1963)
'The Structure, Size and Costs of Urban Settlements'. P.A. STONE (Cambridge University Press, 1973)
Threshold Analysis. J. KOZLOWSKI and J.H. HUGHES with R. BROWN (Architectural Press, 1972)
Water Resource Development. O. ECKSTEIN (Harvard University Press, 1958)

Index

Accumulation of a fixed sum, 177–178
Acturial method, 211–212
Adaptation, 16, 21, 23, 38, 60, 81–15, 107, 113, 116, 154, 157–158
Adjustment for annual time pattern, 192–193
Ages, 59–62, 205–212
Air-conditioning, 19, 129–131
Allowances for inflation, 11, 52–59, 196–198, 212
Alterations, 81–85, 107, 157–162
Amenity, 24, 72–74, 143, 149–153, 171–176
Amortizing capital, 11, 177–195
Annual allowance, 62–65
Annual costs (*see* Running costs)
Annual equivalent costs, 10–14, 35–36, 154–163, 190–195
Annual equivalent worth, 190–195
Annual expenses, 100
Annual revenue, 100
Appearance, 1, 3, 10, 18, 22–23, 28, 30, 72–74, 100–101
Area (*see* Space)
Artificial environment (*see* Lighting Heating, *and* Ventilation)
Asbestos cement cavity deck, 44–45
Asbestos cement goods, 26–30, 44–48
Asbestos cement sheets, 46–48
Assumptions (*see* Prediction Errors)
Average age, 207

Average prices, 200

Balance sheets, 45–46
Beams, 116
Benefits, 10, 16, 72–75, 137, 147–149, 171–176
Bespoke building, 16
Bills of Quantities, 66–69
Bill rates, 41
Blocks, 43–46
Blocks of flats (*see* Housing)
Boarded roof, 44–45
Boundaries of project, 171
Break-even chart (*see* Decision diagrams)
Breakdowns, 163, 165–167
Break-even points, 14–15, 76–81, 165–166
Brick, 22, 43–44, 120
Brick walling, 46–47
Building addition space, 109
Building components, 26, 40–42, 69, 154, 196–197
Building Cost Information Service, 199
Building elements, 22, 37, 40–44, 47, 89–90, 201
Building forms, 112
Building operations, 41–42
Building prices, 198
Building price indices, 197, 198
Building shapes, (*see* Shapes)
Building sites, 17–18, 30, 105, 109–112
Building use, 36–40, 107, 196–197

Index

Building valuation, 6
Building work, 66
Built environment (see Town Planning)
Built-up walling, 46
Business expenses (see Taxation)
Business sector, 57–58, 170
Bygones, 154

Capital, 11, 170
Capital costs (see First costs)
Capitalized costs of roofs, 47
Capitalized costs of walling, 46
Capitalized value, 13, 210
Carpets, 136
Cast iron goods, 28–30
Cavity deck, 44, 45
Ceiling prices, 104
Central government, 62–65, 102–103
Change of premises, 107
Changing cost ratios, 77
Charities, 62, 99, 101
City centre, 19, 129–131
Cleaning, 22–23, 72, 119, 131–132, 202–203
Client, 5–6, 8, 9, 19, 99–105
Climate, 19
Codes of practices, 168
Columns, 116–120
Comfort, 1, 3, 5, 9, 24–25, 72, 101, 131–135
Common elements, 37, 47, 89–90
Common errors, 91
Commercial building, 6–9, 161–162
Commercial client, 6–9
Commercial development, 148
Commercial potential, 17
Commercial services, 137
Communications, 17–18, 109–111
Community, 99, 103–105, 137–138, 148
Community costs, 9, 52, 58, 143–147, 150–153

Community values, 72–74, 150–153
Comparability, 160
Comparative errors, 89
Comparative life assessment, 61–62
Comparing effect of errors, 87–97
Comparisons of existing buildings, 16
Comparison of locations, 111–113
Comparisons of new and traditional solutions, 77–81
Comparison of office sites, 112–113
Compensating errors, 88, 220
Competitive price of new material, 164–165
Complete lives, 208, 210
Complex of ends, 174
Complex of projects, 175
Components (see Building components)
Compound interest, 11, 177–195
Concrete, 22, 115–121
Conditions for cost equality, 78–81
Consequences of traffic, 74, 148–153
Construction costs, 3, 10–11, 14, 66–69
Consumers, 5, 101–104, 136
Consumption, 5, 9–10, 101–104
Contingency costs, 81–85
Continuous heating, 123–131
Convenience, 1, 3, 9, 101–104
Conversion costs, 61–62, 157–162
Costs (see also Community costs)
Cost benefit, 72–75, 171–176
Cost data, 196, 197
Cost effective analysis, 170
Cost equivalence (see Equivalent costs)
Cost of failures, 165–168
Cost indices, 197
Cost of operations, 15, 18–21
Costs of traffic (see Consequences of traffic)
Cost ratios, 15, 76–81
Critical heating time, 123–126

Curtain walling, 115–120
Curve fitting, 206–208, 212–214

Daylighting, 2, 18–19, 121–126
Decoration, 15, 162–164, 212
Deep building, 18–21, 114–115
Deep rooms, 114–115
Delight, 9
Demountable partitions, 23
Decision diagrams, 79–85, 157–160
Design development, 45–51
Design parameter, 48–49
Developer, 5–6, 99, 100, 105, 149–153
Developer's balance sheet, 7–8
Developer's profit, 7–8
Development costs, 99–104, 137–143
Development for sale, 6
Dimensions of space, 21
Discount (*see* Interest)
Discounted cash flow, 170
Discounted values, 26, 64–65, 170, 178–189, 210
Disturbance costs, 16, 66, 69–70, 163
Domestic refuse handling, 35–36
Double glazing, 19, 24, 121–126
Drawing inferences, 97–98
Ducted cables, 33
Durability, 22, 26–30, 59–62, 171–177, 205–208

Economic conditions, 52
Economic life, 11, 12–14, 205
Economy of scale, 114
Electrical heating, 30–33
Electricity, 76, 128, 132
Elemental analysis, 40–43
Elements (*see* Building elements)
Elevation, 20
Embedded cables, 30–33
Ends, 169, 171–175
Entrepreneur, 99, 170–171

Equipment, 140, 154–157, 166
Equivalent costs, 6, 10, 13–15, 18, 35, 154–162, 189–192, 211–212
Equivalent worths, 26, 177–195
Errors (*see* Prediction errors)
Errors of differences, 218–220
Errors of quotients, 218–220
Errors of products, 218–220
Errors of sums, 218–220
Estate services, 145
Evaluating flows of payments 182–192
Evaluating human death and injury, 166–167
Evaluating maintenance costs, 182–191
Evaluating streams of payments, 26–39, 182–192
Evaluating uncertainty, 76–85
Exchequer payments, 104–105, 139–143
Existing building, 16, 108, 111, 157–162
Exposed area, 23
External elements, 40–43

Fabric heat losses, 70–71, 128–131
Factor costs, 104
Factors of prediction, 52–65
Factors of production, 8, 101, 107–109, 170–171
Factory building, 49–51
Failure rates, 39–62, 165–168, 205–212
Failing running costs, 76–81
Fenestration (*see* Lighting)
Final consumer, 136
Final prices, 196
Financial costs, 10
Finishes, 162
Fire risks, 166
Fire resistance, 23
First costs, 3, 14, 15, 17, 19–20, 31, 46, 62–65, 91–7, 177–195

Index

Fitted curves, 208, 214
Fixing costs, 26
Flat roofs, 126–120, 123–126
Flats (*see* Housing)
Flexibility (*see* Adaptability)
Floor finishes, 134, 166
Floor loads, 20, 49
Flows of payments, 26–39, 177–195
Fluorescent lighting, 131–134
Form, 114–115
Fork lift truck, 37–39
Foundations, 40–43, 46, 49–51
Frames, 40–43, 47–51, 115–120
Fuel, 15, 70–72, 121–134
Functional group, 40–45
Furniture, 135–136
Future costs, 36, 52–53
Future generations, 171
Future prices (*see* Future costs)

Gantry crane, 37–39
Geographical location, 111–113, 139–143
Glazing, 18–20, 23–24, 114–115, 117–119, 121–126
Government agencies, 100, 102–105
Government departments, 62
Grading attributes, 75
Grants, 99, 103–105, 144
Group replacement, 164

Handling equipment, 37–39, 157
Harmonizing conflicting interests, 152–153
Hazards, 165–167
Heat balance, 70–71, 126–131
Heat gains, 70
Heat loss, 24
Heating, 2, 19, 23–24, 30–33, 43–49, 70–72, 98, 116–131, 155–156
Heating costs (*see* Heating)
Heating installation, (*see* Heating)

Heating and ventilating systems, 128–131
Hospital, 15, 163–164
Hotel, 62
Hours of use, 24, 126
Householders' labour, 34–36
Housing, 15, 137–149, 160–161
Housing costs and prices, 197, 199
Housing maintenance, 202

Imponderables, 74–75, 150–153, 171–176
Improvement, 69, 157–162
Imputed rents, 70
Incidence of risk, 165–168
Incidence of taxation (*see* Taxation)
Independent errors, 88, 218–220
Indirect costs, 72–74
Industrial buildings, 20, 62–65
Industrial clients, 9
Industrial development, 149
Industrial sites, 110
Inference from sample, 86, 215–218
Inflation, 11–12, 36, 52–57, 196–198
Initial costs (*see* First costs)
Innovations, 164–165
Insulation, 22–23, 41–45
Insurance, 167–168
Interest (*see also* Rate of interest), 11, 13–14, 57–59, 177–195
Internal communications, 21
Internal element, 40–43
Internal environment (*see also* Heating and Lighting) 18, 70–75, 114
Interpretation (*see also* Errors), 26–39, 173
Investment, 7–8, 76–85
Investment allowance, 62–65
Investment comparison, 170–171
Investor, 6, 101

Labour prices, 52–57, 196–197
Land (*see* Building sites)
Land costs, 17–18, 110–114, 137–147
Land use, 7–8 (*see* Land lists)
Layout, 18–21, 107–114
Least predictable parameter, 76
Level of illumination, 131–134
Life, 2, 11, 13–14, 26–29, 31–32, 52, 59–62, 205–212
Life cycle costs, 170
Life expectation, 205–212
Life table method, 205–212
Lifts, 20, 135–136
Lift operator, 135–136
Lighting, 2, 9–10, 19, 21, 23–25, 71, 117–126, 131–134, 203–204
Linear maintenance cost relationship, 200–201
Lintels, 46–47
Load bearing walls, 116
Local authorities, 35, 36, 62, 105, 140–153
Local authority housing price formula, 201
Local authority services, 140–153
Location, 17, 110–114

Maintenance, 15, 21–28, 50, 61, 69, 131–134, 154–167, 202–204, 212–214
Mark allocations, 75
Market, 6, 99, 171–175, 196
Masonry, 22
Material prices, 53–57, 196–197
Maximum prices, 105
Measuring durability, 205–208
Measured work, 66–69, 197
Mechanical ventilation, 128–131
Metal deck, 44–45
Method of operation, 20–21
Modernization, 81–85, 107–111, 157–162

Mortgage debts, 12
Movement costs, 112–113, 148–153
Movement of prices, 53–57, 196–198
Multi-storey buildings, 20, 137–151, 198–199

National accounts, 104, 175–176
National economy, 175–176
National project comparisons, 175–176
National resources, 106, 175–176
Natural light (*see also* Lighting), 19, 120–126
Neighbours, 74–75, 102–104, 136–137
New building, 16, 107–111
New material, 62, 164–165
No action test, 17, 62, 81–85, 162
Noise, 19, 23, 74, 121, 129
Non-framed buildings, 43–44
Normal curve, 216
Number at risk, 205–208
Number of storeys, 51, 114–115, 137–151, 198–199

Observations, 205–208, 212–214
Observed probabilities, 205–208
Obsolescence, 59–62, 155–156
Occupier, 101–104, 106
Office buildings, 15–19, 20, 112–114
Office sites, 112
One way/two way post-tensioned plate, 115–120
Open space, 150
Operating costs, 3, 34–39, 70–72, 121–126, 128–131, 148, 162–165
Operating labour (*see* Operating costs)
Optimum design, 99

Index

Optimum number of storeys, 49–51
Optimum shape, 114–115
Optimum solution, 9, 46–51
Overspill, 148–153

Painting, 28–30, 162–164
Partitions, 22
Period of discount, 177–195
Period of use, 121
Performance standard, 168
Permanent surfaces, 163
Planned maintenance, 164, 165–167
Planning (*see* Town planning)
Planning regulation, 19, 151–153
Plantings, 136
Points system of evaluation, 144
Population, 215
Population mean, 216
Posterity, 171
Prediction errors, 29–32, 35–39, 76–98, 157, 159–160, 162, 165–168
Prefabrication, 43
Preliminaries, 67
Present worth, 15, 26–34, 177–195
Preventive maintenance, 212
Prestige, 5, 8, 73, 115
Prices, 3, 12, 20, 29, 52–57, 66–69
Prices of building elements, 201–202
Price data, 196–202
Price indices, 197–199
Price levels, 196–199
Price limits, 105
Price of land, 6–9, 105, 112–113, 137–143
Price relatives, 200
Priorities, 174
Private client, 99–103
Private developers, 6–9, 99–103, 137–143
Private housing, 137–143
Private occupiers, 101–102
Probabilities, 76–85, 206, 212, 215–218

Probability level, 215–218
Probabilities of scrapping, 206–208
Producers, 5
Production resources, 105
Production costs, 69–70, 156
Production losses, 69–70
Production sector, 100–103
Productivity, 53–57, 196–197
Propagation of errors, 87–91, 218–220
Protection, 165–168
Public bodies, 9, 58, 102–105, 140–153
Public clients, 102, 140–153
Public developers, 140–153
Public housing, 140–153
Public occupiers, 102–105
Public utility services, 143
Purchasing power, 52–53

Quality, 115, 131–132
Quantifying benefits, 169–170, 171–176

Random selection, 215
Rainwater goods, 26–30
Rate of discount/interest, 11, 13, 57–59, 170–171, 177–195
Rate of return, 160, 170–171
Real costs, 12–13, 52–59
Rebuilding, 16, 107–111, 101–102
Recorded expenditure, 212
Recreation facilities, 175
Redevelopment, 107–111, 140–143
Refuse ducts, 35–36
Regional prices, 68, 198–199
Regional price indices, 198, 199
Register of buildings, 205–206
Relative price changes, 53–57
Remedial maintenance, 164
Renewals, 26–30, 61–62, 68–69, 154–161, 202–204, 212–214
Rent, 11, 13, 140–143
Rent control 139–140

Reorganization, 108–111
Reorganization of building uses, 81–85, 108–111, 157–164
Repairs (*see* Maintenance)
Replacements, 68–69, 154–161, 202–204
Representative samples, 215–218
Resale value, 60–61
Residual value, 57, 60–61
Resource costs, 9, 52, 174–175
Responsibility of clients, 101–103
Returns, 5–6, 8
Revenue, 7, 171–175
Reusing existing sites, 110–111
Risks, 165–167
Rounding off errors, 218–220
Road development, 150–153, 175–176
Roof comparisons, 23–42, 44–45, 47–49, 96–99, 115–120
Roof glazing, 20, 117–120, 123–126
Roofing felt, 47–48
Running costs, 2–3, 9, 14, 18–21, 28–32, 35–39, 70–74, 109–136, 140–143, 154–168, 202–204, 212–214

Sampling, 86–87, 215–218
Satisfaction, 3, 9, 144–145
Scarce factors, 36, 174
Scrapped units, 206–208
Schools, 15
Sector interests, 99–104
Sensitivity of comparisons, 91–98
Services, 18, 21, 103–104
Service cost, 34–36, 70–72, 140–143
Service personnel, 135–136
Shape, 18–21, 49–51, 114–115
Short-term advantages, 171–172
Shutdown period, 166

Significant differences, 86–87
Simple interest, 177
Single-storey building, 20, 114
Sites (*see* Building sites)
Site access, 17–18
Site costs, 7–8, 112–114
Site potential, 17–18
Site prices, 7–8, 105, 112–114
Site values, 60, 143–145
Size of sample, 215–217
Social costs and benefits, 72–75, 103–104, 136–137, 147–148, 151–153, 171–176
Social projects, 151–153, 171–176
Social rate of interest, 172
Social sector, 159–160, 147–148, 171–176
Solid fuel heating, 30–32
Space, 16, 18–21, 49–51, 113–114, 157–158
Space frames, 115–120
Space heating (*see* Heating)
Spans, 115–120
Specialized work, 67
Staff morale, 5, 72–74
Standards, 168
Standard deviation, 216–217
Standby equipment, 167
Standards of maintenance, 69
Statistical errors, 69, 215–218
Statistical inference, 86–87
Statistical treatment of data, 205–214
Statutory life, 62–64
Statutory standards, 168
Steel frame, 40–49, 116–117
Storage building, 37–39
Storeys, 20–1, 49–51, 112–113, 140–143
Subsidies, 9, 62, 103–105, 137–143
Substructure, 40–43
Suboptimization, 5
Surtax, 62–64

Index

Surveyor Collaborative, 68
System building, 43

Taxation, 9, 13, 37, 53, 58, 62−65, 103−105, 168
Temporary buildings, 115
Technical obsolescence, 155−156
Tenants' costs, 140−143
Tenants' satisfactions, 144−145
Tenants' valuations, 35−36, 147−148
Tender prices, 196
Terotechnology, 170
Testing innovations, 76−81, 96−98, 164−165
Therms, 46
Thermal insulation, 23−24, 41−48, 116−120
Threshold analysis, 175
Timber, 23
Time, 26−34, 177−195
Town planning, 72−75, 111−114, 136−153
Trading services, 100−103
Traffic (see Consequences of traffic)
Transfer costs, 69−70, 143−153
Transfer payments, 62−64, 104−105, 143−153, 171−175
Transport costs and benefits, 17−18, 110−113, 140−143, 173
Tungsten lighting, 132−134
Type of client, 99−106
Type of costs, 66−75
Type of structure, 115−120

Ultimate Costs, 170
Uncertainty, 2, 76−85, 157−160, 169−176, 215−220
Under-the floor electric heating, 30−33

Unencumbered floor area, 115−116
Unit prices, 66−69, 198, 200
Urban planning (see Town planning)
Use of glass (see Glazing)
Useful floor space, 18−21
Users' costs, 10, 99−105
U-Values, 44−45, 116−123

Value, 5−6, 10, 16, 35−39, 99−100, 103−104, 136−153, 169−176
Value for money, 1−5, 10, 45−46, 99−100, 137−140, 169−176
Value of convenience, 35−36
Value of imponderables, 74−75
Value of money, 12
Value of satisfaction, 66
Value of 't', 216−218
Value housing, 137−153
Variability, 87, 215−218
Variance, 216−218
Variation analysis, 91−98
Ventilation, 19−20, 70−72, 114−116, 128−131
Vertical access, 49, 135−136
Vitreous enamel ware, 26−30

Wall claddings, 43−47, 120−124
Wall design, 22−23, 43−44, 46−47, 120
Wall glazing, 121−123
Washing, 162−164
Water-borne refuse disposal, 35−36
Weights for indices, 197
Weighting value of resources, 175−176
Windows, 18−21, 121−126
Working capital, 11